EDENS
Lost & Found

EDENS
Lost & Found

How Ordinary Citizens
Are Restoring Our Great Cities

Harry Wiland and Dale Bell

WITH JOSEPH D'AGNESE

CHELSEA GREEN PUBLISHING COMPANY
WHITE RIVER JUNCTION, VERMONT

Photographs by Wiland-Bell Productions unless otherwise noted.

Managing Editor: Marcy Brant
Editor: Mary Bahr
Copy Editor: Collette Leonard
Proofreader: Nancy Ringer
Indexer: Daniel E. Brannen Jr.
Designer: Peter Holm,
Sterling Hill Productions

Printed in the United States
First printing, April 2006
10 9 8 7 6 5 4 3 2 1

Library of Congress Cataloging-in-Publication Data
Edens lost & found : how ordinary citizens are restoring our great American
cities : PBS series companion book / Harry Wiland ... [et al.].
        p. cm.
Includes index.
ISBN-10: 1-931498-89-X (cloth)
ISBN-13: 978-1-931498-89-0 (cloth)
ISBN-10: 1-933392-26-6 (paper)
ISBN-13: 978-1-93392-26-4 (paper)
1. Urban beautification--United States--Citizen participation--Case
studies. 2. Community development, Urban--United States--Case studies. 3.
Reclamation of land--United States--Citizen participation--Case studies. 4.
Urban ecology--United States. 5. Sustainable development--United States.
I. Wiland, Harry. II. Edens lost & found (Television program)
HT175.E34 2005
307.1'416'0973--dc22
                                                        2005015843

Chelsea Green Publishing Company
Post Office Box 428
White River Junction, VT 05001
(800) 639-4099
www.chelseagreen.com

Chelsea Green sees publishing as a tool for cultural change and ecological stewardship. We strive to align our book manufacturing practices with our editorial mission, and to reduce the impact of our business enterprise on the environment. We print our books and catalogs on chlorine-free recycled paper, using soy-based inks, whenever possible. Chelsea Green is a member of the Green Press Initiative (www.greenpressinitiative.org), a nonprofit coalition of publishers, manufacturers, and authors working to protect the world's endangered forests and conserve natural resources. *Edens Lost & Found* was printed on New Life Opaque, a 30 percent post-consumer-waste recycled paper supplied by Cascade.

For Holly, Winona, and Julia, who make it all worthwhile.
—H.W.

For Nature's first lessons learned at Camp Timanous and
for Thor Heyerdahl, one of our first environmentalists.
—D.B.

CONTENTS

Y ou will not find in this book a single reference to a president, nor a parliament, nor a pope. Nor will you find any discussion of federal legislation or litigation. Nor will you discover any long lists of agency acronyms.

The revolution that this volume describes is simply too humble, too authentic, and—in the end—too powerful to need or desire any reference to the ordinary seats and sources of authority.

On the surface, *Edens Lost & Found* chronicles the brave efforts of ordinary Americans doing their best to bring hope and beauty to our cities. These are simple and heartwarming stories about neighbors caring enough to imagine a different future for their neighborhood. And sometimes their actions directly impact only a single city block.

But make no mistake about it: the true implications of their efforts are not just local. They are global.

That's because, over the next several decades, human activity in the world's cities will either sink the planet—or save it.

For the first time in human history, the majority of the world's people live in cities. And though cities cover only 2 percent of Earth's surface, they already consume 75

percent of the planet's natural resources. As more people continue crowding into cities, that figure will climb even higher, which means that urban areas have become the main driver in the ecological crisis.

At the same time, many cities are sinkholes of human suffering, especially for a marginalized population of low-income earners and people of color. Especially in the United States, the word *urban* has become synonymous with the word *problem*. Many urban neighborhoods are plagued by economic desperation, violence, pollution, and crumbling infrastructure.

And, all too often, top-down policy choices make bad matters worse. For instance, California now spends more money on prison cells than it does on college classrooms, supposedly in response to an epidemic of violence and drug trafficking in our cities. And yet defunding hope and opportunity for underprivileged youth only fuels despair and desperation—actually undermining community safety in the name of protecting it.

Bottom line: as our cities now function, they harm both the people within them and the ecosystems that surround them. Current city planning exacerbates the two crises that will define the new century: sweeping environmental destruction and radical social inequality. Unless we make a dramatic U-turn in urban policy, we will further imperil both our society and our planetary life-support systems.

Thankfully, a better and wiser path is beginning to emerge from within urban America itself. That path is beautifully chronicled in these pages and in the accompanying PBS documentary series.

This book is one of the first major attempts to chronicle the beginnings of a new American movement—a quiet countercurrent that has the potential to both heal the earth and flood our inner cities with renewed hope and opportunity.

And while this book chronicles many private and volunteer efforts, the spirit they embody is already beginning to spill out into the marketplace. The ecological crisis is pushing up demand for technologies, products, and services that truly honor the earth. By meeting that demand, new eco-entrepreneurs could create a massive boom in new technology, wealth creation, and job creation. And those new jobs could create a ladder up and out of poverty for jobless urban residents.

In other words, the answer to our ecological crisis also answers our social crisis. The surest path to safe streets and peaceful communities is not more police and prisons but ecologically sound economic development. Such an approach can lead us to a new, green economy—one with the power to lift people out of poverty while respecting and repairing the environment.

Because of massive urbanization on a global scale, our species will survive only by creating cities that work for people and with nature. In the modest and hopeful efforts to recreate Eden, we may be seeing the seedlings of a new urban politics and economics that can transform our civilization.

Imagine eco-industrial parks sited on land once blighted by brownfields and prisons. Imagine nonprofit Solution Centers, training young urban workers in new technologies and ancient wisdom. Imagine urban youth creating zero-pollution products to sell. Imagine formerly incarcerated people moving from jail cells to solar cells—helping to harvest the sun and heal the land.

Imagine cities like Oakland, Watts, Detroit, and Newark blossoming as Silicon Valleys of green capital. Imagine global cooperation to give Africa and other struggling regions the means to grow economically, while preserving their natural environments. Imagine China and India powering up with clean energy and leading the world in sustainable enterprise.

With their garden hoes and paintbrushes, the local heroes and she-roes highlighted here may be carving the only viable path away from ecological and social catastrophe.

And in so doing, they may be quietly teaching a great lesson in leadership to those in power. May we all learn from their great examples.

VAN JONES
August 2005

"People are coming back to cities to live and raise their families with a new appreciation for their environment."

—RICHARD M. DALEY, MAYOR OF CHICAGO
(AT THE OPENING OF MILLENNIUM PARK)

This book and our four-part PBS mini-series *Edens Lost & Found* tell the story of how four great American cities—Chicago, Philadelphia, Los Angeles, and Seattle—are meeting the challenges of urban renewal. We chose these four cities because they are each successfully dealing with challenges that collectively represent the spectrum of issues most urban areas can no longer ignore. Both the book and the film were born on the sunny streets of Venice, California, at about 5:30 AM some years ago. It was way too early for the in-line skaters, bodybuilders, and sidewalk musicians, but it was not too early for revolutionary ideas. One of us, Harry, was accustomed to walking his dog at that early hour. From time to time, he'd bump into another Venice resident, Andy Lipkis, who used the early morning hours to walk his pooch and clear his head. The two guys got to talking.

Though only in his early fifties, Andy has been working as an activist in California for nearly thirty-five years. His cause, which first captivated him when he was fifteen years old, is trees. Originally, he set about simply replacing diseased, dead, and dying trees that had been strangled by the urban smog gnawing at the California hills. But these days he has bigger goals. Now, he wants to use trees to save people and their cities.

For the first time in history 80 percent of Americans are living either in cities or in their rapidly growing suburbs. Every year we gripe that our taxes are rising, but we hardly think about the high costs of having so many people living in a single place: the cost of building and repairing roads, the cost of guaranteeing that clean water is there when we turn on the tap, the cost of managing floodwaters, the cost of heating and cooling our homes and businesses.

Gradually, citizens and community leaders are waking up to the fact that we cannot depend on "big government" anymore to solve our problems. If cities are going to survive—let alone thrive—we have to come up with cheaper, cleaner, smarter ways to deal with these environmental hurdles. Much of the cash our cities spend each year on these issues might be better used to enrich schools, museums, parks, community centers, senior programs, public health programs, and the lives of all residents many times over. But before we can reallocate those funds, we have to beat back the monster of consumption and an unwitting legacy of poor planning.

On those early neighborhood walks, Andy rattled off some of his crazy ideas: that trees are excellent, inexpensive tools for improving cities because they clean air, shade buildings and people, capture and store water, block winter winds, and reduce the need to crank up the old air conditioner during warm weather. He was not alone, he said, in thinking this way. There were other people in cities across the country who were putting together their thoughts on these issues. People like Debra Shore of Chicago Wilderness, Joan Reilly and Blaine Bonham of Philadelphia Green, and Miranda Maupin, senior planner at Seattle Public Utilities, who is the lead designer of a large, new, eco-friendly development in Seattle.

The more Andy talked, the more exciting the walks became. Both of us, Harry and Dale, were amazed to learn that Andy's organization, TreePeople, had created a software program that projects the economic and health benefits to the Los Angeles area if various trees were planted in strategic places. We asked whether all of this stuff—the software, Andy's ideas, like-minded people in other cities working to solve long-standing environmental problems—represented a new movement, and if so, what it was called. Andy said it was all about sustainability.

Those first few conversations and trips to TreePeople were the beginning of a marvelous education for the two of us and our production company, Wiland-Bell Productions. Throughout our work in public television we had long been interested in environmental issues. The moment we heard the word *sustainability*, we felt as if we'd seen the crest of the new wave. We became committed to telling the story of how tree planting and other simple strategies build neighborhoods and restore the lost art of community. We felt that this story would be best told through the extraordinary "ordinary" people leading the charge.

Over the past three years we have met farmers who are growing fresh, nutritious food in the shadow of skyscrapers. We met daring architects and builders who are using cutting-edge technology to build energy-efficient "green" buildings. We met urban planners, public utility managers, and some visionary politicians who are taking steps to wean their cities off increasingly scarce federal funds. We peeked over the shoulders of engineers who are building the mass transit systems of tomorrow. We filmed philanthropists who are envisioning grand public parks, and plunking down many millions to attract top artists and landscapers to build them. We stumbled across cab drivers who moved mountains with a single petition, schoolchildren itching to clean up local waterways to save the salmon population and the teachers inspiring them, young parents standing up to drug dealers and reclaiming city streets for their kids and their vegetable plots, and elderly activists who have barely the strength to move but the courage to speak. Some of these people are the poorest of the poor, but they taught us that intelligent city planning leads to civic engagement and community building. They have also taught us to feel a sense of community and to reevaluate and prioritize what is important in our lives.

We hope that the profiles of these people will inspire you to action in your own neighborhood. In our first chapter, we'll outline some of the principles at work in the "New American City." In the next four chapters, you'll hear the voices, arguments, and concerns of the people themselves. And in our epilogue, we'll share some great strategies for building community groups, enlisting help from your neighbors and politicians, getting the media to take notice, and learning how to speak up.

We're not saying you have to read this book and start stumping for the latest cause. Sometimes it helps simply to be informed, to understand the buzzwords and concepts shaping the America we now live in. Our cities are made up of vibrant and beautiful communities, filled with green spaces and inspiring neighbors. We hope this book moves you to get to know yours, wherever you may be, and possibly even make things better.

HARRY WILAND AND DALE BELL
Santa Monica, California

"There are those who look at things the way they are, and ask *why*? I dream of things that never were, and ask *why not*?"
—ROBERT F. KENNEDY, AFTER G. B. SHAW

The Path to Sustainability

If you wander in the woods in the spring-time, you will catch the forest at its most magical time. The long period of winter dormancy is over, and the green shoots of leaves are sprouting everywhere. The smallest plants leaf out first, taking advantage of the abundant sunshine. As the weeks pass, taller trees and plants yawn to life. Finally, the tall giants awaken and shelter the forest with a dense, green canopy. All summer long, the sun shines and temperatures can soar. It makes no difference to the woods. Shielded by vast, leafy umbrellas, the forest floor remains cool and shady.

When the leaves fall in autumn, they drop to the ground and break down into soft, black earth. Dead plants and trees also become soil. This rich, new mulch fertilizes everything it falls upon, and not a molecule of the old organism goes unused. When it rains, this soft layer of earth acts like a giant sponge, sucking up rainwater and storing it for later use. Deep underground, a complex network of tree roots also sucks up rain, so much that a mature oak tree can capture fifty-seven thousand gallons of water.

Perhaps more than anything else, the forest demonstrates nature's conservation of resources and simple sustainability. By that we mean that the forest ecosystem wastes nothing, and that the needs of the present generation of trees, animals, and other organisms are met without depleting the resources needed for future generations. Everything that goes into the system remains in the system, in some form or another. Each dead tree feeds another, every raindrop is harvested, and as long as average weather conditions persist, this cycle can go on forever, without ever running out.

While most humans enjoy the woods, let's face it: we don't live there. In fact, the majority of Americans, 80 percent of us, live in "urban ecosystems," that is, large cities and nearby suburbs. Designed for commerce and human habitation, these built environments have often grown quickly, without sustainability in mind. When it rains, all that precious rain—drinkable, fresh water that cannot be absorbed by metal, concrete, and pavement—is funneled out to rivers and seas instead of being captured for human use.

Apartment buildings, offices, and skyscrapers are giant heat magnets, soaking up sunlight and relying upon expensive fossil fuels to keep them cool and habitable. To get around, most people are obliged to drive, thus expending even more fossil fuels that degrade the air they breathe and harm their health.

We've strayed a long way from the perfection of the woods. Many facets of metropolitan life are unsustainable. Because one city has squandered its water, it must buy water from another. Because oil is a finite resource, every drop used literally means one drop less for future generations. Because most vehicles don't burn cleanly, excess residue fills the atmosphere in the form of planet-warming carbon dioxide (CO_2), harmful smog, and soot. In continuing these wasteful practices we harm ourselves, and, increasingly, we must spend more and more money to maintain our lifestyles.

Amidst the seeming onslaught of bad news for the environment and community, the successes can be overlooked or understood only as isolated events. *Edens Lost & Found,* though, documents and celebrates the countless small yet powerful initiatives that people are taking all across the country—something so widespread as to amount to a new movement. Ordinary citizens, government officials, environmentalists, architects, urban planners, and others are banding together to conceive new ways to reverse the trend toward destructive city life.

The *Edens Lost & Found* project took three years and numerous visits to four different cities—Chicago, Philadelphia, Los Angeles, and Seattle—to collect impressions, interviews, and ideas about this movement. This book describes some of these strategies, but our primary goal is to inspire you through the voices of people whose determination, vision, and courage are ensuring a better future. You may not live in one of the four cities we profiled, but the issues that confront them collectively represent most of our urban challenges. We hope your eyes will be opened when you see how people have effected real and lasting changes in their towns, in their neighborhoods, on their streets, and on their very blocks.

As they did, so could you.

The problems can seem so overwhelming and so large in scale that it is easy to feel that there's little you can do to help the planet or that what you *could* do involves too much sacrifice.

But, as the saying goes, the longest journey begins with a small step. There are many steps you can take right this minute. Every day we make dozens of routine choices that either add to the toll we exact on the environment or relieve it slightly— from what we eat, to the containers we use, to what we throw away, to how we use water, to how we get around. This book, drawing on the lessons learned from the production of *Edens Lost & Found,* is intended to encourage us all to understand the significance of our choices and the power we each have to advance the goals of urban sustainability.

WHAT'S A SUSTAINABLE CITY?

It's easy to see how the word *sustainable* applies to the woods. But what does the word mean when applied to the scale of a city? In 1987, the World Commission on Environment and Development, in its report to the United Nations, developed a definition of sustainability that has been widely adopted:

> Sustainable development is development that meets the needs of the present without compromising the ability of future generations to meet their own needs.

Early in this project, we had an interesting talk with Paul Brown, a top executive at CDM, a major engineering firm. His company builds roads, bridges, massive drinking-water facilities, storm drains, and solid waste treatment projects for city governments all over the world, including all four cities in this book. We asked him if it was hard to get city officials, residents, and politicians behind the notion of sustainability. After all, the principles of the environmental movement have been contested, resented, and dismissed by people with opposing agendas or viewpoints, and the two sides have often been at odds. His answer surprised us.

"There's far less conflict in my world than there would have been twenty years ago," Paul said cheerfully. "People are more interested in learning how they can plan a city more efficiently, without wasting resources like precious drinking water. All this comes down to money. In this country the EPA is getting tougher on what can and cannot be dumped into waterways. Years ago, you could get away with a lot more. Now, it costs you a lot, and it's recognized as wasteful. For years, we designed cities and suburbs in this country in order to get rid of water. Now we're thinking, 'Well, maybe you don't want it to go away.' If you can use the water that rains on you, you don't have to go somewhere else to get it. You're more independent. You save money. Everyone I meet these days is thinking this way. So, I'm very hopeful."

Indeed, as the degradation of our urban environment becomes untenable, costly, and even catastrophic, people from all backgrounds, professions, and political orientations have begun to cooperate in unprecedented ways and with great results. We view this trend as part of what Andy Lipkis referred to as the drive toward sustainability.

Time for Change

A city is the ultimate consumer of resources, the ultimate producer of air and water pollution, and the ultimate contributor to climate change. City life can damage human health. Steel and concrete displace the natural environment, destroying plant and animal life. Urban environments rob resources from other regions, even other nations.

Let's look at one of the cities in this book.

Los Angeles is a vibrant city in a beautiful environment. But its early builders had little understanding of or appreciation for the power and function of nature and its cycles. The environmental damage wrought by the development of Los Angeles as an urban setting takes a heavy toll on all of us and threatens the viability of the city for future generations.

In the woods, trees and shrubs catch rainfall and release it slowly into the ground. This cycle produces nutrients, fresh water, and clean air. Even in a semiarid landscape like in Los Angeles, the ecosystem once provided everything that native people, plants, and animals needed to thrive.

But in building Los Angeles, we interfered with the natural cycles of energy and water by sealing the soil with thousands of acres of concrete and asphalt, doing much more damage than anyone would have imagined.

Wasted Energy

With well over 60 percent of Los Angeles's surface covered with pavement, very little of the sun's energy is absorbed by vegetation. Instead, it heats up the pavement, and thus the air, needlessly overtaxing air conditioners that combat this excess heat at huge costs— huge in terms of dollars, fuel expenditure, and pollution. Power plants as far away as Utah, New Mexico, and Colorado pollute the pristine high desert environment to generate electricity used to run air conditioners in Los Angeles. Crazy, right? Electricity is often considered "clean energy," and it *is* in the sense that it does not pollute the immediate area where it is used, as a car does

when it spews exhaust. But many electric plants burn coal in order to generate those kilowatts, which does pollute the atmosphere around those plants. And strip mining for coal destroys the landscape in yet another location. Is there some way to break this chain of wastefulness and pollution?

Wasted Water, Filthy Water

In Los Angeles, vast quantities of water are imported from distant regions, while fresh water that would normally flow into Mexico or the sea is little more than a saline solution by the time Los Angeles is finished using it to water lawns and wash cars. The fifteen inches of rain that falls on Los Angeles every year could, if captured, meet more than half of that city's annual needs. But because rainwater has historically been regard as a "problem" rather than a "resource," very little of it is saved and used to refresh the soil under the City of Angels and replenish its groundwater.

In Los Angeles, rainfall is channeled to roadways, where it sluices together with oil, pesticides, animal waste, grocery bags, Styrofoam, and other trash. Now a toxic soup, the water gurgles down the city's storm drains directly out to the beaches, into the bay, and on to cities and counties downstream. Los Angelenos know this all too well. They can hardly fail to notice the dregs of this effluent washed up on the sand and in the creeks and rivers after a heavy rain.

Wasted Dollars

In the last half of the twentieth century, billions of dollars were spent on massive (and in hindsight, misguided) flood control projects that accommodated Los Angeles's poor approach toward rainfall. Likewise, Los Angeles built even larger landfills at increasingly distant locations (vastly increasing the fuel needed to transport waste there), because it failed to implement simple steps to reduce the amount of trash the city and county generated.

By ignoring the integrated character of nature and its cycles, Los Angeles—a land of dreams for millions of Americans and people worldwide—has become something of a nightmare because unsustainable levels of energy and water must be consumed to meet the needs of so many people living in one place. Unknowingly, or not, Los Angeles designed its technologies and infrastructure as if there were no social, economic, or environmental costs. This great metropolitan area failed to recognize the human cost in terms of mental, physical, and emotional health. Now, because of this poor design, Los Angeles must spend outrageous amounts on water and energy and infrastructure, leaving few extra funds for things like schools and job creation.

By the way, we don't mean to pick on Los Angeles here. (It's our city, after all.) All the cities in this book are grappling with similar problems, and we are indebted to them for letting us air their laundry in this project. For example, both Chicago and Philadelphia experienced oppressive heat waves in the

After poor early planning, Los Angeles must overhaul its infrastructure if it is to provide clean air and adequate water for its growing population. Photo by Ricardo Aguero

1990s that might have been less deadly if the cities had been designed more sustainably. Sometimes the challenges facing a city are regional in nature. Seattle, a model "green" city, is employing natural drainage techniques to reduce toxic rainwater from flowing unchecked into its waterways and harming its wild salmon population.

RETOOLING AMERICA'S CITIES

Americans have had a love–hate relationship with their cities. When immigrants began flocking in great numbers to the United States in the 1880s, cash-strapped cities couldn't keep up with the basic sanitary services necessary to support their burgeoning populations. Cities became known for their noisy, crowded, unhealthful conditions, a perception that lingers to this day. After

World War II, Americans scampered to the suburbs in search of safety, security, and a healthier way of life. Corporations and businesses soon followed their far-flung workforces, gobbling up farmland and wild spaces outside cities to build office parks. The 1970s were desperate days for American cities. Deprived of tax revenues, many governments deferred maintenance of their parks, mass transit systems, and public spaces. The filthy, neglected, crime-ridden city became a self-fulfilling prophecy.

Not all cities declined in this manner, and every city has its bright spots. Cities have an allure. Suburbanites are drawn here to earn paychecks, take in a show, eat a fine meal, and do some high-end shopping. In fact, now a new generation is taking a second look at cities, as places not only to visit but to live in as well. "We spent all this time and money trying to make a home for our kids in the suburbs," a Los Angeles architect tells us, "but all they want to do is spend time downtown. To them, suburbs are boring."

This classic argument could fill another book. We don't want to be misinterpreted as slamming suburbs. After all, they are an intrinsic part of the metropolitan ecosystem. In fact, at this point in our history, some American suburbs are more than fifty years old and have their own culture, vitality, and traditions. We know well that millions of Americans enjoy living in a suburb. But plenty of other Americans would side with the architect's kids. Either they chose to stay in the cities where they were born, or they

are moving to cities from somewhere else, seeking excitement, a shorter commute, or an older home with character. This reverse migration to cities depends on a number of factors: how comfortable, healthy, safe, and friendly neighborhoods and the city as a whole can be.

Part of what makes cities so magical is their permanence. You can take your child to see the Statue of Liberty, the Liberty Bell, or the Space Needle this year, and someday they will have the privilege of visiting those same iconic sites with their kids, grandkids, and great-grandkids. Cities are larger-than-life places that have stood the test of time. Once something's set in stone in New York, Chicago, or Los Angeles, it's usually there to stay. Yet, ironically, to preserve our great cities we must figure out how to make them as permeable and ever changing as that forest we visited earlier.

Before we begin, however, we must realize that cities and the suburbs they spawned are joined together at the hip. To the bird flying overhead, there isn't much difference between the two. Everything that goes on within the vast metropolitan area is the responsibility of all its inhabitants.

Today urban planners promote an "integrated resource" approach to solving the problems of urban metropolitan ecosystems. From all our talk about trees, you may have gotten the impression that we're advocating planting more trees in America's cities. Indeed we are, but doing that alone would not be enough. Forests are more than just

William Penn called Philadelphia his Green Countrie Towne. The restoration of Logan Square, like that of many other public spaces throughout the city, honors Penn's original vision.

the trees in them, and cities need more than trees to march healthily into the twenty-first century. A truly integrated approach uses most or all of the following tools.

Open Space and Public Parks

Biologically speaking, cities can't breathe because hard surfaces, such as concrete and asphalt, encase so much of their ground. As we've already seen, impermeable surfaces are unforgiving. Parks and open spaces ventilate cities with their trees and permeable surfaces, such as grass, gravel, mulched landscaping, and even leaf-covered soil. They also absorb rain, which reduces the likelihood of floods and polluted waterways and builds up precious drinking water reserves. Open spaces

Something as simple as planting trees in urban neighborhoods can raise property values, reduce crime, and improve community health.
Photo by Tom Iraci, U.S. Forest Service

and parks offer numerous benefits to humans too, but we'll get to that in a bit.

Urban Forestry

The phrase *urban forestry* often refers to the idea of *strategically* planting trees to serve a greater social good. Tree roots capture water, thousands of gallons at a time. The more trees a city can plant, the more water it will ultimately have in underground reserves. Leaves happily absorb sunlight and give us shade, which makes city streets more hospitable for pedestrians. These are just some of the reasons all the cities in this book practice large-scale tree planting.

Watershed Management

The word *watershed*, which you'll see throughout this book, refers to any geographic area that collects rainwater. The layers of soil and stone under the watershed area behave like one of those water filter pitchers so many people keep in their refrigerators. You pour in the water, and it trickles down through layers of charcoal pellets or sand, which filter out impurities. The earth works the same way. Historically, urban watersheds were notoriously neglected as demand for new construction trumped concern for their protection. Thankfully, a growing movement enlists citizens' help to protect watersheds and employs natural drainage technologies, such as porous parking surfaces, gravel- or sand-filled trenches called swales, and landscaping designed to slow water down and let it seep into the earth.

Environmentally Conscious
Waste Disposal and Recycling

Every city grapples with garbage and recycling issues. The challenge will never go away. As long as there are humans, we will produce trash that must be disposed of in some way. New city planning initiatives stress reusing solid green waste—such as mulching leaves or composting vegetable matter—so it doesn't need to be carted to dumps and landfills at community expense. Later, in our Los Angeles chapter, we'll look at an exciting proposal to chop up all of Los Angeles's green waste and use it as yard mulch. Think of the time and money that will save on hauling tons of this stuff to a landfill!

Green Building

There's not a homeowner alive who doesn't know that good insulation can save her thousands of dollars over the life of her home. Green building, a new movement in construction techniques and architecture, emphasizes the use of state-of-the-art materials and smart design to build more energy-efficient homes and commercial structures. But green building goes well beyond high-tech foam insulation and compact fluorescent lighting. Conscientious green builders harvest and reuse old materials such as bricks and lumber, take precautions to prevent damaging the natural environment of a work site, and seek to use earth-friendly fuels to power their large machines. Engineering and construction firms, large

and small, that utilize green building practices are becoming more and more common all across the United States.

Mass Transit

No city can survive long without the use of mass transit. If people are not given a good, reliable way to reach their destinations, they'll resort to using their cars. That's a choice we cannot afford as a nation since single-occupant vehicles spew tons of CO_2 into the atmosphere, hastening the buildup of smog and poor air quality. In the battle between your car, your home, and your office place, your car is the most inefficient consumer of fuels. Thankfully, nearly all the cities you'll read about have some innovative transit system in the works.

The Integrated Approach

These six tools create livable, self-sustaining cities. While some overlap between them exists, each has a distinct goal. Open spaces, parks, and urban forestry all have something to do with trees, but a park achieves something quite different from a sidewalk strategically planted with trees. The goals of the green architecture movement are distinct from those of mass transit and waste disposal systems, but people who live in green-built communities will need the first, and certainly generate the second.

All of these elements have one thing in common: they try to mimic functions that occur all day long in the woods by minimizing waste, cooling down surroundings,

Philadelphia Green, a thirty-year-old project of the Philadelphia Horticultural Society, has been transforming the city by creating beautiful gardens in formerly vacant lots.

capturing and retaining water, reducing pollution, and reusing or recycling everything they can. A city that tries to become sustainable by emphasizing only one of these components is certainly on the right track, but its efforts will always be ineffective without the others. We've had a century of mass transit in some cities, and it hasn't made them significantly more sustainable. American cities have a grand tradition of parks, too, but parks alone do not make a city sustainable. Only a concerted effort to integrate all the city's processes does.

And there lies the rub. Integration on the scale we're proposing is a superhuman task. We said before that cities are durable, that once a city block is built, it may remain unchanged, or minimally changed, for the better part of a century. Inserting open space, building parks, or even finding space on sidewalks to plant trees can be exceedingly difficult and expensive when the matrix of a city is already in place.

If you think concrete is unyielding, you haven't tried budging or expanding the roles of municipal agencies. In the cities we visited, the better part of sustainability could not proceed unless citizens were talking to city agencies and those agencies were talking to each other. In the most fascinating example, Los Angeles had one agency whose mission was to buy, procure, and convey water to the county and yet another agency whose mission was to protect Los Angeles County from massive water events such as floods and storms. One agency spent billions bringing water to town. The other spent billions getting rid of it. Not until citizen activists challenged this wasteful arrangement did the two agencies realize that they were really in the watershed management business.

No doubt about it, integrating resources is a tall order for any city. It can't be done overnight. It requires hard work, intelligent planning, and patience. Citizens who want to be involved in the process have to be prepared for the long haul and take comfort in the small successes. For many of the people you'll meet, cleaning a vacant lot and planting a garden was a joyful and appropriate use of their talents. For their cities as a whole, it was a right step on the path toward sustainability.

IN PRAISE OF URBAN FORM

After all this, you may well think that cities are beyond hope, but that's not true. In fact, cities do a great deal that is right, and they impart lessons that are serving us well in new communities. The shape of cities—the often gridlike arrangement of streets, how homes and buildings are designed and structured, where development is located, what types of developments are allowed, what areas are protected, how various parts of a city are linked to others, and a host of other attributes—is what people refer to when they use the term *urban form*. We think cities can also illustrate the idea of sustainability when they exhibit the following characteristics.

Cities are dense

When you travel to big cities, you are first bewildered and then delighted by all the activity going on around you. In a rural setting, one acre of land might contain a house and a few outbuildings. In the suburbs, an acre could hold four to eight houses, sometimes more. In a city, that single acre can hold an enormous apartment building that is home to hundreds, possibly thousands, of people. It is not unusual in big cities to have structures that "stack functions." A predominantly residential building could, for example, rent ground-floor space to a couple of merchants. Underground, the same building might house a subway station or walkway to other buildings in the neighborhood, not to mention infrastructure for municipal utilities, such as gas, power, and phone lines. At first, this all seems too complicated, too much activity for one little plot of land. But many experts argue that this complexity is easier on the planet because it radically conserves real estate and the need for development outside the city, it conserves energy, and it promotes community. From a cultural standpoint, density adds richness to city life because there are so many more opportunities—for work, living, entertainment, dining, creativity—than anywhere else.

Cities are pedestrian-friendly

Cities vary greatly in their walkability, but density usually means that the average person will find more to do within walking distance than in the suburbs. In fact, suburban shopping malls mimic this attribute of great cities: a densely populated mall allows you to visit fifty shops on foot. Today, urban planning seeks to boost the density of cities, and then increase the number of essential services, such as supermarkets, dry cleaners, banks, post offices, and so on, so that people can tend to their most important errands in a short walk, without relying on cars or even mass transit. This goal isn't appropriate for all cities, but neighborhoods become more attractive to renters and buyers when they are more than purely residential. If you can walk to the park, grab a burrito on the way, and drop off a letter at the post office, you yourself have stacked functions too, while expending merely muscle and calories. Experience shows neighborhoods like this are increasingly desirable.

Cities can mediate climate, build community, and encourage self-policing

Cities are built of heat-retentive materials, but if designed properly, a city block will shade itself during some of the hottest times of the day. One reason we find historic European cities so charming is that the streets are often human-scale, too narrow for cars but perfect for strolling. Even in the heat of an Italian summer, one can wander down the cobblestoned backways of Venice and feel relatively cool, because the buildings cast shadows along the walkway. Granted, in big cities it is impossible or unwise to replace bigger streets with smaller streets, but trees can shade both sidewalks and the cars parked on them.

Recently, architects and city planners have begun introducing positive attributes of urban form into new housing developments as part of a movement called New Urbanism. In some developments, they have laid out streets that are impassable by cars but ideal for pedestrians, bikers, and people walking dogs or pushing baby strollers. One example is Celebration, Florida, a town where Victorian-style homes graced with porches face the street.

In early American homes, porches served as outdoor living rooms, halfway points between the intimacy of a family's house and the outside world. Porches allowed people to survey everything that occurred in the vicinity. In the city, the same function was served by front stoop. The cheek-by-jowl construction of city row houses means that families grow up within feet of each other. They can develop close ties and look out for each other. Every action happening on the block—good or bad—can be observed by neighbors hanging out on their stoops in warm weather, or out of their front windows in cold seasons. Call it what you like—snooping, curiosity, neighborliness—this friendly surveillance can act like a kind of built-in security system for the entire neighborhood.

But what can happen doesn't always happen. In some of the neighborhoods we visited, criminal activity had run rampant for so long that neighbors had become inured to it. Instead of speaking up, they turned a blind eye to the goings-on. What happened in these places? Clearly, a critical ingredient is necessary to evoke that watchdog response. Architecture, design, and urban form are not enough. What is that special ingredient?

This is the chief engine of city life: community.

PUTTING PEOPLE BACK INTO THE CITY

Economists will tell you that cities exist because of commerce, and certainly this factor provides a strong economic reason for cities to be where they are. All the cities in this book were founded along waterways to facilitate trade, but what gives cities their vibrancy is the people who live in them—the action of so many human beings living and working in the same place. Without people, the city dies.

In the course of this project, we met numerous people who are working to help the dream of sustainability come alive. Some of them, to be honest, didn't even know the word *sustainability*. They were following their instincts and common sense. They did what they felt was necessary to make their city neighborhoods better places to live. They thought gardens would be nice, so they worked to build them. They were appalled at the state of their local waterways, so they dedicated themselves to cleaning them up.

Something wonderful happened when they did this. Their projects obliged them to cross paths with other people. It allowed them to explain themselves and what they were doing. Little by little, others were intrigued and joined them. Before you knew it, a powerful feeling of community had taken root, and the people felt more connected to their city than ever before.

In metropolitan Chicago, ordinary citizens lent their hands to restoring and preserving thousands of acres of prairie lands. In Philadelphia, crime-ridden neighborhoods were transformed into urban paradises because citizens decided to stop looking the other way. They spoke up. They got involved. They reported drug dealers and pimps to the police. At the same time, they picked up trash and began planting trees. In our visits to Philadelphia, we learned that planting trees had an unexpected benefit: it raised property values by 15 percent. A relatively inexpensive item—a $15 tree plucked from a local

The JFK Boulevard gateway in Center City is one of Philadelphia's many
public green spaces. Courtesy of the Pennsylvania Horticulture Society

nursery's lot—generated greater economic value because it elevated the perception of neighborhood. An excellent example of urban forestry made by a community.

Earlier, we explained how important parks are to the biological health of cities, but parks benefit our social health as well. All humans have a need to connect with nature and the outdoors. In the suburbs, your backyard might meet that need, but when you want to run errands, you hop in your car and are enveloped in a kind of personal cocoon all the way to your destination. In the city, the act of walking to the park becomes a communal activity. You pass shops along the way, say hello to neighbors, run into a few tradespeople who've done work for you in the past. You are engaged. You are drawn out of yourself (sometimes whether you want to be or not). In a city park, you run into still more people, some of whom are not from your neighborhood. Again, you are lifted out of your smaller world and exposed to different people from different backgrounds and cultures.

Humans are quirky, funny creatures. We might not strike up a conversation with a stranger the first time we meet, but habitual encounters embolden us. We don't like to be the first ones to take action, but as soon as someone else does, we are happy to pitch in. Sooner or later, the strangers in the park or on the stoop across the way become part of our everyday community. These friendships knit a city together. We connect and belong. Someday, when we are invited to a block party or asked to participate in a fund-raiser or local event, we are happy, even touched, to join in. We belong.

From the air looking down, parks and community gardens are patches of crucial greenness set against the black-and-gray milieu of the city. They are tools that perform vital scientific functions: they cool, drink in water, sanitize air, and make oxygen. But from the ground, these places are so much more than that. They are hubs of human activity. Like those apartment buildings with delis and record shops on the ground floor, parks and gardens perform multiple tasks. They're stacking functions.

Human community is probably the most important tool in the integrated resource planning of any great sustainability movement. Without people, the trees will not get planted, the trains will never run, the parks will fall silent, and the open spaces will never come to be.

WHERE DO YOU FIT IN?

Each tree that grows in the forest is an independent entity. Each day it harvests food, sunlight, and water from its environment to make a living for itself. Yet planted alone in the middle of a barren field, the tree won't live long. There are no taller trees to shade it, no dead leaves to feed it, no grass or smaller plants to slow down and capture the water it needs to drink. The tree may be independent, but it thrives best when it lives with others of its kind to create a stable, nurturing, habitable community.

Each of us is that tree. This is the stirring metaphor behind the sustainability movement. Nature not only serves as a biological model for bringing balance to our lives, but offers a very real spiritual guide as well.

This book is about learning to live in *relationship* to the earth and each other. For some of us, that may mean spending our spare time planting trees and tending our compost bin. For others, it will mean turning our energies to community activism, alerting others to the benefits of creating a sustainable urban ecosystem, forming grassroots and neighborhood groups to support policies that are environmentally beneficial, and letting elected leaders know what the public wants.

One person's action can be monumental, and together individual acts can truly change the world. When we plant and care for trees, alone or together, we begin to build an internal place of peace, beauty, safety, joy, simplicity, caring, and satisfaction. The results encourage us to take on larger challenges.

Planting a tree is an unequivocal good. It also separates gesture and sentiment from true commitment. It gently but ruthlessly extracts commitment from the mere gesture. Trees demand care—our continued involvement, interest, and nurturing. Without it, they die. Planting has the ability to transform our own behavior and that of our culture.

The words *community* and *commons* are from the same root. Traditionally, the commons in England were used to graze cows—common land, respected and maintained by all, for the good of all. Our modern-day commons are around us still—the streets, parks, air, beaches, ocean, rivers, streams, and forests—but for some reason we don't feel personally responsible for them. What happened?

Humans moved out of villages and into cities. There, it was easy to sink into anonymity. It still is. Losing touch with your neighbors and your community takes no effort. You can simply nod and head up to your apartment without stopping to chat. You can draw the blinds and watch TV. You can drive past the guy mowing his lawn, give him a half-hearted smile and wave, and never learn his name.

By moving to big metro areas, we gave up many of our responsibilities to governments and institutions. The larger cities grew, the less in touch with our neighbors and the natural environment we became. We forgot that we are obligated to each other and our surroundings. We assumed we had no control over our environment and, therefore, no role to play in preserving or enhancing it.

Yet the synergy of people working together can create the magic that produces sustainable communities. From tree planting to sharing rich compost and having monthly cookouts and block-club activities, we learn to interact with our neighbors. Instead of being drained by strenuous work, we're revitalized. Instead of feeling alienated, we create family. Instead of feeling helpless, we are empowered. Instead of wondering who we are, we *know*.

CITIES AT THE CROSSROADS

Today our country is at a crossroads. Our populations are growing, our city budgets are constantly strained, and some segments of the populace are always in need. If large cities are going to be part of the solution, if they are going to live up to their promise as centers of culture and ideas, they must sculpt themselves into models of sustainability. This is the next big step in the great American experiment. We have an obligation as the world's wealthiest nation and its biggest consumer to show that harmony with one's natural surroundings is not only attainable, but also profitable and desirable. But how do we get there from here?

While you can liken it to turning a massive ship on a dime, it *is* possible to change the way we manage our cities. In 1997, Paul Hawken, businessman, environmentalist, and author, addressed an audience of engineers, landscape architects, building architects, and urban foresters who gathered in Los Angeles to begin the work of creating plans for a sustainable city. He finished his speech about "what it will take" with the following vision:

Imagine a world where the resources are not scarce, but sufficient to all. Imagine a world where there are more jobs than people, a planet where forests are increasing, topsoil is being formed, wetlands are thriving, coral reefs are growing, fisheries are healthy and the atmosphere is not affected by our activities below.

Imagine a city with tree-lined rivers, promenades and restaurants alongside, and bays that are as pure as oceans anywhere. Imagine a city that is so covered with trees, it looks like a forest from an airplane. Imagine, for a moment, a city that has become whisper-quiet. Hydrogen-powered hybrid-electric cars exhaust only water vapor. Open space corridors have replaced unneeded freeways. Houses pay part of their mortgage costs by the excess energy they produce.

Imagine a city where there are no active landfills. Imagine worldwide forest cover is increasing; atmospheric CO_2 levels decreasing for the first time in two hundred years; effluent water leaving factories cleaner than the water coming into them. Imagine industrialized countries reducing resource use by 80 percent while improving the quality of life; dams being dismantled; environmental regulations regarded . . . as unneeded, quaint and anachronistic; living standards doubling worldwide; and a vibrant business sector depending upon and promoting these developments.

Is this the vision of a utopia? A Panglossian fantasy? In fact, the scenario is neither. The changes described could occur within as short a period as fifty years, as the product of economic and technological trends that you can implement and put in place.

Notice that much of what Hawken envisioned is already possible. We don't need to wait for a *Star Wars* breakthrough in science. There's no special technology required to plant an urban forest or drive a fuel-efficient car. (The hydrogen-powered economy is a few decades off, but a handful of automakers are already selling hybrid-electric cars that get twice the mileage of the car you're currently driving.) We have a marvelous future ahead!

Edens Lost & Found is dedicated to the promise of positive change. After all the time we've spent on this project, we would argue that city dwellers are happier and the city richer, finer, and more harmoniously balanced when two important ingredients are in place: sustainability and community. We've seen it with our own eyes. We've walked the greener streets, and come away inspired. Sustainability. Community. On these two pillars rests all else.

Well-designed green space in urban areas not only contributes immeasurably to quality of life but also helps cities with heat and water management. Photo by Chris McGuire, courtesy of the City of Chicago

CHICAGO

City of the Big Shoulders

Like many great cities, Chicago was born *because* of its advantageous natural attributes. Early fur traders wanted an easy way to transport their beaver pelts and other goods from the Great Lakes to the Mississippi and all the burgeoning territories along the way. Whoever controlled those waterways had a pipeline that stretched all the way to the Gulf of Mexico. During his 1673 expedition with Jacques Marquette, the French explorer Louis Joliet became convinced that the site would someday be "the gate of empire, the seat of commerce." Time proved him right. But as the tiny trading post turned into a massive city, growth threatened to destroy the very qualities that gave it life.

By the nineteenth century, Chicago was a sprawling, filth- and crime-infested city. A city of steel mills and slaughterhouses and train yards. A city of corrupt politicians and fearsome gangs. A city of tense neighborhood wards where ethnic groups regarded each succeeding wave of immigrants with suspicion. Through it all ran a river befouled with the refuse of meatpacking plants and teeming factories. From a safe distance wealthy industrialists ruled this heap of humanity like feudal lords.

But some of those more fortunate citizens had consciences, and following the devastating fire of 1871 they did what they could

Chicago has a long history of civic improvement. Above left, the rail yards outside Ward's office. Above right, how it looks today thanks to the work of Ward and others. Below, opening day of the Field Museum in 1921.

to transform, reform, and rebuild the city. Aaron Montgomery Ward, the entrepreneur who built a far-reaching mail-order catalog empire, determined to restore the lakefront as a public space. This was no easy feat. In his day, the area east of Michigan Avenue had been deemed "public ground," but a succession of city councils had done little to make the area palatable to the public at large. When Ward looked out from his office window each morning, he saw an eyesore littered with railroad tracks and commercial debris. Neighborhood gangs congregated here for impromptu prizefights, prostitutes trolled for clients, and squatters lived in squalid shacks. Ward, who had been influ-

enced by the work of the social crusader Jane Addams, founder of Hull House, fought the city for years for the right to turn this vast space into a park. One would think his wealth and influence would have made it easy. It wasn't. He ended up fighting all the way to the Illinois Supreme Court, spending seven years and $50,000 (equivalent to roughly $1 million today) in court fees. Later he remarked:

Had I known in 1890 how long it would take me to preserve a park for the people against their will, I doubt if I would have undertaken it. I think there is not another man in Chicago who would have spent

the money I have spent in this fight with the certainty that even gratitude would be denied as interest. I fought for the poor people of Chicago, not the millionaires. . . . Perhaps I may yet see the public appreciate my efforts.

The Field family, owner of Marshall Field's department store, sponsored a different project. They donated funds to build a massive natural history museum, first known as the Columbian Museum of Chicago—in honor of the "Columbian Exposition," as the 1893 World's Fair in Chicago was known—on the shores of Lake Michigan. And wealthy patrons of the arts contributed funds to construct the Chicago Art Institute. (Ironically, Montgomery Ward fought these projects, because they occupied valuable space that he thought should be devoted wholly to public grounds.) When crowds flocked to the fair in 1893, they beheld a city well on its way to becoming the architectural jewel of the United States.

The man who planned that exposition, architect Daniel Burnham, later created the Plan of Chicago, regarded as one of the nation's first attempts at city planning. Burnham saw Chicago as a "Paris on the Prairie," and he dreamed of building the kind of fabulous public monuments one saw throughout Europe, particularly France. He envisioned wide boulevards, public fountains, and a glorious central city hall with a dome. The cornerstone of the "Burnham Plan," as it was called, was a ring of forest

preserves encircling the city and green space along the city's lakefront. Visitors and native Chicagoans can thank Burnham every time they sally up beautiful Lakeshore Drive.

The view from that street—not to mention the view from Mr. Ward's old office window—has changed greatly over the years. Chicago owes much of its splendor to buildings designed by Burnham and other great architects such as Frank Lloyd Wright (who designed more than one hundred buildings in the greater metropolitan area), William LeBaron Jenney, Louis Sullivan, Dankmar Adler, and John Root. The "Chicago School" of architecture created the first tall buildings using steel skeletons overlaid by rich decorative ornamentation. Sullivan, who coined the phrase "form follows function," wanted buildings to "read" like office buildings at a glance. You can still sense the underlying three-dimensional steel bones of such great Chicago buildings as the Manhattan, the Chicago, the Marquette, the Guaranty, and the Brooks buildings.

Today, visitors to the Windy City witness a city remaking and rebuilding itself again, this time with the help of concerned Chicagoans of every stripe. The city is taking a hard look at the remnants of its industrial past and is slowly reshaping its landscape with new goals in mind. Unsightly railroad tracks and parking lots that once occupied prime real estate downtown have been tucked underground, leaving room for a glorious public space above: Millennium Park. Legions of weekend volunteers have cleaned

Long neglected, Calumet River and nearby Calumet Lake have recently benefited from the dedication and stewardship of local citizens of all ages.

up the 156-mile waterway that first enchanted Marquette and Joliet—so much so that beavers have returned to the Chicago River in droves. Around the shores of Lake Calumet, on the city's southeast side, where cooling slag from steel mills once tainted the night sky red, old prairie lands teem again with songbirds and wild strawberries, and ecotourism is on the rise. Even in the most urban of neighborhoods, parks, trees, and grassland are flourishing. Indeed, from the air one observes how many of Chicago's hardest edges have been softened with a fringe of green. Outside the city, in the greater metro area that is home to the majority of the region's population, exist more than two hundred thousand acres of rare ecosystems that are being preserved through the help of voters and their county boards.

In the city, much of the newfound commitment to nature and civic life owes itself to Mayor Richard M. Daley, who has openly championed the principles of sustainability and urged the development of natural habitat and green public recreation areas. Since Daley took office in 1989, flower gardens have been planted in road medians, wrought iron streetlights have been erected and festooned with hanging flower baskets, and nearly three hundred thousand new trees have been planted throughout the city. Chicago's City Hall now boasts a lush garden on its roof, which captures rainwater and cools the surrounding neighborhood during heat waves. Still, the administration has its work cut out for it. Thorny problems remain. How, for example, will the city tempt environmentally sensitive businesses to its old steelmaking quarter to fulfill the urgent need for more jobs in that region?

Daley's initiatives would not have prospered without thousands of grassroots activists demonstrating daily that a revitalized Chicago is their kind of town. In this chapter, you'll learn about some of these projects and how eager citizens helped shape their shimmering city in a garden.

WHY A GARDEN?

Edens Lost & Found focuses on plans to encourage green space and gardens in our nation's cities—a widespread and growing phenomenon. Why so much emphasis on greenery when the ills of a city seem considerably more complex? Green space offers something that the grittiness, excitement, and bustle of cities often cannot. Most human beings thrive in nature. In terms of quality of life, the ability to duck into a park, sit on a bench, and disappear into a book while a breeze rustles leaves or birds sing in the trees cannot be underestimated. Under a tree we can hear ourselves think. Sitting on a patch of grass, our eyes take in shapes, colors, and textures we don't take time to appreciate in everyday life.

While it is hard to put a price on parks and nature in urban environments, it has become possible to measure their economic and social benefit. Green space is not just a nice thing to have around. Parks improve property values and help reduce crime by strengthening neighborhood ties. And on a deeper, biological level, plants, wetlands, and gardens perform a crucial function in urban settings: they keep us healthy—and can save us millions of dollars to boot. In fact, it's increasingly clear that preservation of nature is critical to the survival of cities.

To understand why, we need only consider two huge public health issues facing cities today: the management of heat and water.

Gaze across the top of the urban landscape and you see black, asphalt-topped roofs soaking up sunlight, getting hotter and

Mayor Daley of Chicago is largely credited for spearheading the effort to transform what was once an unattractive transportation hub on Michigan Avenue in downtown Chicago into a prime recreation destination.

View of North Lawndale in Chicago's west side.

hotter on a summer's day. Underneath, air conditioners are laboring away to cool off interior spaces that could easily climb past 100°F if they weren't artificially cooled. In neighborhoods where air conditioning is scarce, heat kills. In July 1995, when the mercury climbed into the upper 90s and low 100s for a week, 739 Chicagoans died.

Part of the problem is Chicago's design: cities just aren't built to keep cool in the heat of summer. Tightly packed buildings made of brick and stone and steel and asphalt—materials that absorb heat—radiate heat back into the neighborhood. Sidewalks and asphalt streets do the same—even street signs soak up heat! As a result, temperatures are typically warmer in cities than in nearby suburbs and rural areas. Climatologists call this the "urban heat island effect." As the reality of global warming sinks in, city planners worldwide have been looking for ways to reduce the heat island effect.

At the same time, most cities need to better manage their water resources. Every time it rains, precious drinkable water hits the hard, paved surfaces of our streets and runs away. Often, rainwater comes down so fast and in such quantities that it cannot be readily used. Sometimes whole city blocks become flooded. Sidewalks, curbs, storm drains, and sewer systems in modern cities are designed to funnel excess water out to the nearest river or sea.

If storm runoff reaches those places unchecked, it will be filled with the contaminants of modern life: pesticides and herbicides, auto fluids and soot, rotting food residues, trash, bits of rubber and metal that have abraded off vehicle tires and brake pads, and much, much more. The EPA now insists that municipalities clean up excess storm water before they release it into the waterways, a critically important requirement but one that costs huge sums of money.

Meanwhile, some of these same cities experience regular periods of drought. The solution is simple. If water can be allowed to soak into the earth, valuable reserves of groundwater accrue—exactly what happens in natural settings. When rainwater seeps into the soil, some of it is sucked up by plant roots, and the rest ultimately replenishes underground layers of stone and earth called aquifers. This slow and steady capture of water also happens to be the best method ever designed to purify water. As water trickles down past the layers of earth, contaminants are filtered out and purer water remains. Later, if and when we need it, we can pump that water out of the ground and send it to water treatment plants to be cleaned further for drinking.

The wasteful cycle of treating and getting rid of excess water, along with having to manage drought, is forcing cities to search for a more sustainable solution. Luckily, the dilemmas of heat and water can both be solved by nature, and local governments are taking notice. The more you can replace hard city surfaces with soft permeable soil and vegetation, the cooler temperatures will be and the more water you'll save. This, then, is the logic behind the multitude of gardens in this book. The four cities we profile are encouraging more green space with three goals in mind: hang onto the water, cool down the city, and create environmentally friendly places for people to live. Chicago, in particular, has made great strides toward this goal.

SOMETHING'S GROWING AT CITY HALL

On a summer day the view from the roof of Chicago's City Hall is something to behold. The Windy City is spread out before you, filtered through a haze of colorful plants native to American soil: columbine, coreopsis, yarrow, bellflowers, wild indigo, and twenty thousand more in hundreds of different varieties. A bee zips across buffalo grass to alight on a purple aster. If you could fly like

that bee, you'd see the garden in all its glory, massive plantings of vegetation growing in the shape of sunbursts across the top of this one-hundred-year-old municipal building.

In the year 2000, Chicago's City Hall embarked on a creative plan to cool off the roof of its building, reduce the heavy flow of rainwater and heavy flooding, and create a beautiful habitat for birds and other creatures. The Daley administration called in a team of architects, landscapers, and engineers to design and build what is known as a "green roof." Gardens like these have been used with great success in Europe, and Chicago wanted to both learn and demonstrate what was possible with this technology.

We say "technology" because building a green roof is not simply a matter of hauling a bunch of clay pots and containers to a roof and planting everything that catches your eye at a local nursery. Green roofs are slightly more complex: the plantings themselves are incorporated into the structure of the roof. If done correctly, a green roof will actually weigh less than a conventional roof garden and impart much-needed shade and insulation to the building below.

To build the garden the team left the old layers of insulation on the roof and added a fresh layer of waterproofing and a root barrier. They spread four to eighteen inches of a special lightweight soil mixture developed in Germany on the roof. Rooftops tend to be windy and dry, so designers chose shrubs, herbs, and wildflowers, such as purple coneflower *(Echinacea)*, that once grew wild on

Chicago's City Hall leads by example in a city increasingly populated by rooftop gardens, which provide insulation and mitigate
runoff from heavy rains.

green roof's keepers have noticed a reduction in the amount of water running off the roof to sewers below. The plants also do a better job of managing heat than a typical black tar roof. On hot days, they reflect heat, shade City Hall, and cool off the air by slowly releasing moisture through the pores in their leaves. They purify air too, transforming excess carbon dioxide into precious oxygen.

It's magical, really, what a simple thing like a garden on a roof can do. Some people don't believe it until they see the numbers, so Chicago proudly trumpets the nitty-gritty details: The green roof saves taxpayers $4,000 to $5,000 a year in heating and cooling costs. On a hot day, the air is actually about fifteen degrees cooler in the garden than it is on nearby rooftops. When surfaces in the garden are a toasty 86°F, the temperature of an average blacktop roof is a too-hot-to-touch 168°F! What's more, Chicago may be the only city in the United States whose city hall makes and sells its own honey. City Hall's plants are pollinated by a swarm of bees that live in the rooftop apiary.

Mayor Daley wants to see more green roofs sprouting on the Chicago skyline. One day, as he walked around the roof, he stopped to take in the view. "If you look across the buildings you can see how many acres we can recover with green technology," he said, gesturing toward the sea of blacktop roofs. "It doesn't have to be like this. You look over and you see the beautiful architecture and you could see green roofs too. It would be beautiful!"

the American prairie and are adapted to these conditions. Everything is held in place by the roots of thousands of native plants, carefully selected for Chicago's climate.

As hoped, when it rains, the plants and soil soak up the rain like a sponge. Already the

Things to Keep in Mind about Green Roofs

Installation of a green roof tends to cost about 50 percent more than a conventional roof. But green roofs last about 50 percent longer because the plants and soil shield the roof's surface from the destructive effects of the sun and elements.

A green roof should be professionally installed. Be sure to check building codes in your area before getting started. Most likely, officials will require blueprints drawn up by a licensed structural engineer or architect.

You might consider skipping the green roof and planting a conventional rooftop garden using terra-cotta pots and containers instead. That's fine. This is the time-honored way of adding greenery to roofscapes. But bear in mind that water, snow, soil, and plants all add extra weight to any structure. If your project starts to get complicated—incorporating decking, irrigation systems, trees, et cetera—you should consult a professional who can calculate how much weight your existing roof can handle.

Live in the suburbs and don't have a flat roof suitable for a garden? That's easy: move back to the city!

What's under the Green Roof?

Like a patch of land you'd find in the woods, a green roof is made up of several layers that mimic natural processes. Here's what's going on under the sod:

PLANTS: usually drought-tolerant native plants

SOIL: usually a lightweight mix that gives nutrients and drains well

FILTER MAT: lets water soak through but keeps tiny grains of soil from blowing or washing away

DRAINAGE LAYER: made of lightweight gravel, clay, or plastic, it wicks away excess water to a drainage system or stores it long-term

INSULATION LAYER: helps moderate the flow of heat into and out of the building

ROOT BARRIER: strong enough to withstand punctures by strong roots

WATERPROOF MEMBRANE: protects building from leaks

ROOF: the "hard" surface that everything's sitting on

Illustration by MSR Design, Inc. /American Wick Drain

THE GREAT PUBLIC SPACE

For decades, Chicago wrestled with major issues: How can we add more public space when space is already too tight downtown? How do we get rid of ugly parking garages and train tracks without banning cars and trains entirely? How can we encourage people to start riding their bikes to town instead? For Chicago, the answer lay in a single project: twenty-five-acre Millennium Park.

One of the city's biggest eyesores used to sit smack in the middle of downtown, on Michigan Avenue just north of the Art Institute. Here, in a twenty-foot-deep canyon, commuter trains and an eight-hundred-car parking lot occupied ground that had once been a heavily polluted industrial site. The real estate was among the choicest in town, the perfect place for a beautification project. But how to do it? As a major transportation hub, the site was too necessary to eliminate— yet too unattractive and clangorous to be tolerated indefinitely.

City officials had talked about the problem since the 1970s, but little got done until Mayor Daley arrived on the scene. The task of turning the site into something practical, functional, and beautiful was assumed to be too expensive an undertaking. "The genius of the mayor," says John Bryan, the chief fund-raiser of the project, "was realizing that he could build an underground parking garage first and start earning some revenue. Trains also would be tucked belowground. He called in the architects and had them build a 4,500-space garage, and pretty soon he had enough money to float municipal bonds. The bonds brought in $175 million."

Nonetheless, the city needed more money to develop the site aboveground. One day, out of the blue, John Bryan—then CEO of Sara Lee—got a call from the mayor at his office downtown.

"Think you can raise some money for me?" asked the mayor.

Bryan had done his fair share of fund-raising over the years, and now that he was getting set to retire, he thought he'd have plenty of time on his hands to devote to the cause. "How much money are we talking about?" he asked.

Daley didn't flinch: "Oh, $30 million."

"No problem," replied Bryan, and off he went.

"Of course," he confides now, four years later, "at first we were just talking about building a nice little outdoor pavilion. We had no idea—not the mayor and not me— how much we would actually bring in, and how much we would be able to do with it."

Bryan got to work phoning major corporations in town and some of the better-known philanthropic Chicago families. People were interested, but they wanted to know what their money would buy. The plans got more and more ambitious as the pledges trickled in. Donors got increasingly excited when they saw that top-notch artists and architects, such as Frank Gehry, had been tapped. "No one wanted to give their money for something dull and uninteresting," says Bryan.

Frank Gehry's plans for Millennium Park tranformed an unsightly 800-space parking garage into a 4,500-space underground garage with the world's largest green roof. Photo by Chris McGuire, courtesy of the City of Chicago

The Great Lawn and Jay Pritzker Pavilion in Chicago's Millennium Park.

"The selling point was being able to say we would bring in the world's best designers and give Chicago to the world. The best of this generation will stand in this park forever."

The $30 million dollar goal grew—to $210 million!

As construction went forward, Daley opted to enlarge the vision, adding eight additional acres to the park and upping the price tag considerably. The press hounded him when one of the earlier parking garages had to be torn down and reconstructed. "They went after the mayor on those overruns," recalls Bryan. "But they left me alone. It was as if no one was interested in what the private sector was doing to contribute to this park."

Building a twenty-five-acre park was bound to be expensive. But scaling back on the dream would have meant, in a way, that the golden age of urban parks was dead. Instead, they went to work rounding up the money, and their effort became a marvelous example of public and private sectors working together to achieve a dream. In the end, the final tab topped $475 million, with everything aboveground—the trees, the grass, the structures and sculptures—made possible by contributions from private donors or corporations like BP, Exelon, SBC, Wrigley, and Chase.

Builders rushed to get the job done in time for the millennium, while the local media continued to predict a financial fiasco. Some thought it ridiculous to spend so much on a park when teachers were threatening strikes, or when so much of the economy seemed at a standstill. Finally, the park opened in 2004 and the populace was overwhelmed. The result was a harmonious complex that gives back to the earth almost as much as it gives to the people of Chicago. What is Millennium Park? Well, depending upon your interests, it's a band shell; a home to perennial gardens, fountains, restaurants, sculptures, and monuments; an indoor theater; an ice rink; four parking garages; a commuter train platform; and a world-class three-hundred-bicycle station where you can park your wheels, rent a locker, take a shower, and head off to work.

Millennium Park is arguably the world's largest green roof, with the bulk of the planting spread atop four garages. Air and water issues are mitigated by more than nine hundred elm, maple, hawthorn, pear, crabapple, white fir, and red bud trees, which help the park function as a mini-watershed. Because trees shade buildings and cool the air, they reduce the demand for air conditioning. And, a mature urban tree reduces the amount

Construction of Millennium Park was completed in 2004 to tremendous public response.

of carbon dioxide (CO_2) in the air by about 115 pounds per year. It does this in two ways: by using CO_2 to make food for itself, a process called photosynthesis, and by lowering the amount of CO_2 pumped into the atmosphere by power plants. The California Energy Commission has actually calculated that the CO_2 reduction achieved by a single tree has a dollar value of $920 per ton per year. Shade trees cost only a few dollars to plant. "They absorb pollution, add oxygen to the air, and temper the heat gain that the city gets every summer," says Ed Uhlir, the park's chief engineer, "but they're also important emotionally to people, for them to come recreate safely in the outdoors."

Ed Uhlir, Millennium Park's chief engineer.

Crown Fountain was designed by Spanish sculptor Jaume Plensa.

People not only recreate, they appropriate. Take Crown Fountain, for instance. The monumental fountain, designed by the Spanish sculptor Jaume Plensa, was conceived as a giant work of art. Every five minutes, the two towers flash an image on their fifty-foot-high screens, while torrents of water cascade over them. Students from Chicago's School of the Art Institute photographed one thousand portraits of Chicago residents, which the fountain's computer occasionally selects from its database. But the first summer the fountain debuted, local kids moved in and used the fountain another way. Decked out in swim trunks, they love huddling at the base of the fountain, counting down the seconds until the floodgates open and torrents of water crash down on them. Beats a yard sprinkler any day.

Small or large, parks build community. A city is enriched when its citizens have more places to hang out, visit with friends, and meet new people. Chance encounters in a park can lead to lifelong friendships. Such spaces are even more necessary today than they were decades ago, since more and more Americans are starved for unscripted interaction with their neighbors.

"In a sprawling area we just have to spend more time in metal boxes taking us from one area to another so we use up a lot more time," says David Putnam, a Harvard professor of public policy and author of *Bowling Alone: The Collapse and Revival of American Community.* "Our lives are lived

The built environment within Millennium Park echoes the shapes and forms of the natural world. Photo by Chris McGuire, courtesy of the City of Chicago

Declining Social Interaction:
Trends over the last 25 years

Attending club meetings	down 58 percent
Family dinners	down 33 percent
Having friends over	down 45 percent

Surprising Facts:
"Joining one group cuts in half your odds of dying next year. Ten minutes of commuting reduces social interaction by 10 percent."
—from *Bowling Alone*

David Putnam, a Harvard professor of public policy and author of *Bowling Alone: The Collapse and Revival of American Community.*

in large triangles, one point being where we sleep, one point being where we work, one point being where we shop. When we used to live in villages, the distance between those three corners used to be measured in feet or hundreds of yards, but now in Los Angeles or any really large sprawling area, the distance between those points for anyone might be thirty or forty or fifty miles. And [in] that kind of world it's not clear where home is, it's not clear where you should be basing your community."

An orchestral performance in the theater at Millennium Park.

Detractors who wondered whether Millennium Park would be worth the expense appear to have gone mute. But parks and greenery are just one reason for the burgeoning pride in Chicago. The city has become more livable, and its once-beleaguered infrastructure is functioning well. Within the first six months of the park's opening, more than five million people visited—a record for any public space in the city. "Statistics are difficult to come by with precision," says Bryan. "What we have is mostly anecdotal. Every place I go, people are telling me that they've gone, they took the relatives who have come from out of town. 'I went, I saw, I loved it' is the reaction. It's amazing how good art and architecture moves people."

If you build it, they will come. If you build it beautifully, they'll *keep* coming.

TOWARD A WIRELESS CHICAGO

A hallmark of a healthy community is the democratic distribution of information and opportunity. Some might think it a stretch to regard information and access to education as natural resources, but we think they are. No one questions that everyone should be able to enjoy clean air, clean water, open spaces, and a healthy environment to grow up in. These are all considered part of a concept called "environmental justice." We submit that, these days, justice has to include access to Internet technology. Used correctly, the Web can be a powerful tool for environmental improvement. Think about it: You can use the Web to find ways to moderate

The Wondrous World of Frank Gehry

The architect chosen to breathe life into Millennium Park is Frank Gehry, the pioneering designer whose structures have been dubbed the most "profound and brilliant works of architecture of our time" by the *New York Times*. Born in Canada in 1929, Gehry is now based in Santa Monica, California. He is recognized as the architect of the innovative Guggenheim Museum complex in Bilbao, Spain, the Music Center in Los Angeles, and the Marin County, California, Civic Center. Sensuous curving forms characterize many of his structures. Gehry repeats a similar motif in Millennium Park: once in the park's bandstand, the Jay Pritzker Pavilion, and again in the adjacent BP Bridge that spans Columbus Drive and connects the park to Daley Bicentennial Plaza. Both structures use shimmering stainless-steel panels for a sculptural effect. The bridge is the first Gehry has ever designed.

use of gas and electricity. The Web allows people to telecommute, thus reducing destruction of natural resources that would be consumed in the daily commute. When you pay your bills online, another letter doesn't have to be delivered by trucks that use fossil fuel.

While the Internet might allow people to connect with a geographically broad community of people who share specific interests, we think it's more useful as a knowledge bank. Rich or poor, you can research health information and educational opportunities and interact with local government. In this sense, access to the Web has become an important tool for social change, and an entrée to what's going on near you.

Yet many Americans do not have Web access. Millions of young people cannot visit online libraries, read free books, explore colleges they might like to attend, research loans to help them pay for their education, or learn more about the leadership of their cities, or even how to lodge a complaint to the right government office. While it's certainly possible to do these things offline, if you are unplugged you are arguably missing out on opportunities.

Opportunities are what Chicago's Center for Neighborhood Technology (CNT) is all about. The nonprofit organization has devoted itself to coaxing the social and economic value out of cities. Many of its projects are a wonderful blend of green

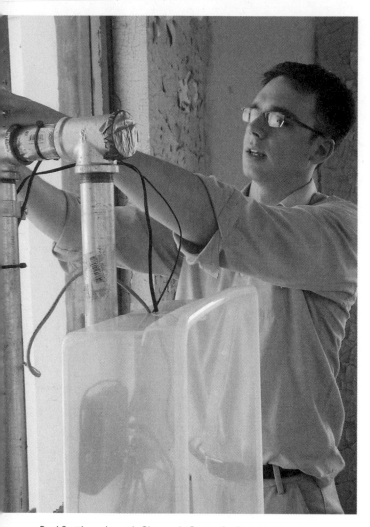

Paul Smith works with Chicago's Center for Neighborhood Technology to bring high-speed Internet service to underserved areas of the city.

The secret weapon in their plan is WiFi, the technology that allows one high-speed connection to be shared by multiple wireless users. CNT received a grant that allowed it to bring WiFi to as many as 250 people in each of four different neighborhoods: Pilsen, a largely Mexican-American community in Chicago's Lower West Side; North Lawndale, a primarily African-American community in Chicago's west side; Elgin, a working-class community about forty miles northwest of Chicago that is becoming increasingly Latin-American; and West Frankfort, a remote former coal mining community in downstate Illinois.

Residents who don't own and cannot afford a computer can receive a refurbished system, most of which are donated by area colleges and local governments. CNT also solicits donations through its Web site and written proposals for donations from companies and foundations. It recently received another grant from the National Cristina Foundation, which pairs nonprofit organizations with computer donations. And in another example of cross-community partnerships, CNT bought a dozen low-cost computers from Wayside Cross Ministries, a religious group, that were refurbished by a youth technology program run by Korean-American Community Services. Kids learn how to fix up the computers, and others down the line get to use them. A win-win system all the way around. CNT expects to place about five hundred computers over the course of the project.

grassroots thinking and cutting-edge technology. Recently, one of Chicago's major Internet providers announced it would not seek to penetrate lower-income neighborhoods because the company didn't see much of a market there. But CNT's project leaders already had a project in the works to bring free Internet services to four of these neighborhoods.

To get the best bang for its buck, the organization has given some computers to the Homan Square Community Center in North Lawndale, which reports residents are delighted to have this link to the community. One young woman used the Web to apply to Loyola University online, and she now uses the Web regularly to do coursework. Another woman had been sharing a dial-up connection at home with her mother and sister. Since all of them were taking college classes, it was virtually impossible to get anything done, since the phone line was always tied up and the computer connection was notoriously slow. With the neighborhood's new high-speed connection, all three women can surf the Web without tying up the phone, and online coursework has become a breeze thanks to the higher speeds.

"Internet access has been shown to be one of the most important determiners of economic success and education success," says Bill Comisky, a CNT technical advisor, "so it's important that residents in the Homan Square area have that kind of access. . . . The whole digital divide issue used to be between people who have computers and Internet access and people who don't have computers and Internet access. Now it's between people who have high-speed, always-on Internet access and people who don't. That's what we're addressing here with the wireless community network."

What Is WiFi?

WiFi, or wireless fidelity, bypasses the labor-intensive process of wiring a neighborhood for high-speed Internet. The technology works the way walkie-talkies do: high-frequency radio signals radiate from a central transmitter in concentric circles and are picked up by computers equipped with a computer card that receives and broadcasts back its own signal. The farther the signal travels from the original transmitter, the weaker the signal gets. But if extra transmitters, called repeater nodes, are mounted on houses or outside apartments in a neighborhood, the signal will bounce from node to node, growing stronger as it repeats. CNT had no trouble finding volunteers to let them mount nodes on their houses. How fast can people be up and running? Fast! In the summer of 2005 CNT held an old-fashioned "barn raising." They erected one hundred nodes in a single weekend with help from community residents.

Pictured below are Nicole Friedman, Bill Comisky, and Paul Smith of Chicago's Center for Neighborhood Technology, a nonprofit organization working to bring high-speed internet connection to Chicago's low-income neighborhoods. The project has expanded opportunities for citizens in these neighborhoods.

RESTORING THE PRAIRIE

To make a prairie it takes a clover and
one bee,—
One clover, and a bee,
And revery.
The revery alone will do
If bees are few.

—EMILY DICKINSON

Illinois calls itself the Prairie State, though
many of its citizens have never seen a prairie
and do not know what one looks like.
Prairies are open fields populated by special,
resilient grasses, wildflowers, and other
plants—but no trees. Many common garden
perennials got their start in the American
prairie. Because a prairie is treeless, there's
no shade, and the grasses are constantly
exposed to the harsh rays of the sun. They
have adapted to their environment, growing
rapidly even in the hottest summers, sucking
up tons of CO_2 to feed their fertile structures. If struck by lightning, a prairie will
burst aflame, and fire will whip through the
dry grasses, turning the fragile-looking stalks
and flowers to cinder. A scorched prairie is a
terrible sight, but it doesn't last long. Shaped
by evolution over thousands of years, prairie
plants quickly regenerate themselves when
burned, better than most dense forests do.

From the windows of Chicago's Sears
Tower, you can see vast urban landscape,
punctuated by factories, cut by waterways,
and obscured at times by billowing steam
and smoke. Where in this landscape is the
seemingly indestructible prairie, and how far
would you have to go to find it?

That's the question a young man named
Steve Packard asked himself nearly thirty
years ago. Steve grew up in Massachusetts,
where he spent a lot of time outdoors, but he
never thought he would make the stewardship of land his life's work. A young man
during the 1960s, he devoted himself to
antiwar causes. While he spent most of his
time as a peace activist, he paid the bills
doing lots of different side jobs. He taught in
preschools. Built air conditioners. Pulled
steel in steel mills. Unloaded fruit on the
docks in New York. In the late 1960s, he
came to Chicago to work for a film company, editing documentaries. This job lasted
longer than most. He hooked up with some
people who were shooting a documentary on
the peace movement and civil rights.

In 1974 President Nixon, besieged by
Watergate, resigned from office. For many
who had opposed the Vietnam War, the resig-
nation felt like the end of an era. Steve sensed
that his own days as a political activist were
drawing to a close. "What am I going to do
now?" he wondered. "I have no skills. No
real talent. I need something to do."

Inspired by a 1972 book called *Prairie:
Swell & Swale*, which depicted images of
prairie lands along Lake Michigan taken by
Swedish photographer Torkel Korling, Steve
bought a bike and spent time riding around
Chicago, in search of its wild places. For a
while he was convinced that Illinois's nickname was a misnomer. "I'd ask people what

Steve Packard has worked for the past thirty years to restore indigenous species to the prairies near Chicago.

the words 'the Prairie State' meant and no one could tell me. I thought that was funny. Maybe it was a myth if no one knew what it was."

Eventually he found remnants of prairie in the region. One afternoon he wandered down a preserve path, using Korling's book as a guide, trying to identify the wildflowers he found. By then he'd done enough reading to learn that the American prairie was becoming endangered. Humans were illegally dumping waste on the grasslands. Precious swaths of land were being lost to development. Poachers illegally hunted birds and other creatures. And woody species were

gaining a toehold on turf where they didn't belong.

This last was a little complicated. By nature, the American prairie had evolved a perfect way of restoring equilibrium every time woody species grew too rampant. During lightning storms, the grasses would catch fire. Species that had not adapted to fire died off, and tough prairie grasses grew back abundantly. Native Americans—who appreciated the deer, elk, and bison of the prairies and oak savannas—helped this process along as soon as they realized what

Why Connect with Your Community?

"A society contains a built-in blueprint for failure if the elite insulates itself from the consequences of its actions. . . . Could this happen in the United States? It's a thought that often occurs to me here in Los Angeles, when I drive by gated communities, guarded by private security patrols, and filled with people who drink bottled water, depend on private pensions, and send their children to private schools. By doing these things, they lose the motivation to support the police force, the municipal water supply, Social Security, and public schools."

—JARED DIAMOND, author of
*Collapse: How Societies
Choose or Fail to Succeed*

nature did to protect itself. They staged burns to give prairie grasses the edge.

"In our culture there's a strange alienation that tells us that humans bring corruption to everything that is natural," says Steve. "But that's just not true. Humans have been involved in the prairie as far back as twelve thousand years ago, when the glaciers first receded. We played a role in how the prairie looked. We're the reason it was the way it was."

Controlled burns, so necessary to American Indian culture, disappeared as Europeans moved into the prairie states. The early colonists saw fires as unnatural and disastrous and stamped them out wherever they could. Today, people are surprised to find that the Chicago metropolis area still has prairies, wet-

lands, and oak land of global significance. Much of the land was plowed by early settlers for corn and soy—the roots of old native plants created rich soil for crops. In fact, the Midwest used to be called "the empire of locked roots" because those native plants were so strong. Settlers had to invent a steel plow to break up the sod. They didn't do all that work to see their crops go up in smoke. Fire suppression and agriculture as a priority dominated America's attitude toward nature for centuries, and as a result the prairie was dying out.

Sitting in these diminishing fields, Steve Packard wondered whether he could apply to nature the same energy and skills he'd applied to the antiwar movement. He believed that if humans intervened, they could save the prairie just as Native Americans had. Steve had done some reading on the subject. He knew that some scientists had been experimenting along these lines. They burned entire fields, then sowed native seed and watched as long dormant or rare species rebounded.

Steve Packard knew he was contemplating a huge, Johnny Appleseed–like undertaking: there were thousands of acres in Illinois alone.

"I remember sitting there and telling myself, 'This is dangerous! This could take the rest of your life! Look away! Think twice! If you commit to this, it's going to take a long, long time. It's not something you can work on a little while and walk away from. It's closer to adopting a child.

If you commit to that child, you have to be there forever.'"

And Steve wondered: Why do it at all? Who cares about grass, really? Why does it matter if one species of grass lives or dies? Soon enough, he answered his own question.

"That's like saying who needs museums?" Steve says. "Comic books and newspapers have pictures, don't they? Well, the prairie is an ancient ecosystem. It's a snapshot of what this part of the world looked like thousands of years ago. What's left is one one-hundredth of one percent of what was once here. The tropical rain forest has a better chance of survival than the prairie! If the prairie goes, we lose ancient, beautiful, precious things like butterflies and birds and snakes and frogs that used to live here. No one has even counted all the fungi and nematodes that would be lost. Now, true, the world won't come to an end if they're gone, but we have to live with the fact that more ancient things have been destroyed."

Steve's passion contains a good measure of pragmatism. He also describes, in practical terms, what happens when prairies disappear. "The species that take root are things like buckthorn, which is a shrub that grows tall and shades out the grass," he says. "What's left is nothing but dirt. Without that dense network of roots to hold it in place, the soil erodes dramatically. Ravines get bigger and bigger. The fertility of soil degrades. Our waterways fill up with that runoff dirt, which means that when it rains, we get more severe flooding."

The major prairie grasses are designed by evolution to be warm-season plants. That means that they do most of their growing when the weather's hot, absorbing the maximum amount of CO_2 out of the air when we need it most. Many exotic species such as buckthorn are cold-season plants; they thrive and grow in cooler months, preferring to lie dormant during hazy, hot, and humid seasons.

And so we return to the two issues we first mentioned at the beginning of this chapter: heat and water. Now it's easy to see why restoring the prairie is so important to Chicago's overall goal of sustainability. If you want to build a cooler city, a city with cleaner air, a city that is less vulnerable to dangerous floods, you must save the prairie. On a purely selfish level, the prairie can save your life.

Shortly after that revelation in the fields, Steve took steps to achieve his goal. He read what little there was to read, and during summers he would head into the fields and began his real education. He was among the earliest group of volunteers who helped restore Chicago's prairie spaces. He and other volunteers spent weekends chopping down and burning piles of nonnative plants and trees, then reseeding the land with plants that make a healthy prairie. It was exhausting work that required expertise. You needed to know exactly which plant was which. You needed to collect the native seeds intelligently. Someone had to test the seeds to learn how they grew and pass that knowledge along to the volunteers.

The cover of *Chicago Wilderness*, the eponymous publication of an organization dedicated to preserving habitat in the Chicago area. Photo by Jim Nachel

The work progressed at a glacial speed. Nights he returned home with aching bones, his shins and hands scraped and cut. The fields looked worse: the ground looked bare where they had cut away the brush. Steve learned to be patient. "We'd work in only an acre or a half-acre at a time," says Steve, "so you could see what you were doing. And over time, little by little, you could see the results over the years. Every year, the prairie looked better and better."

Steve eventually became a leader in his field. He organized Chicago Wilderness, a coalition—a "group of groups"—comprising more than 175 different organizations devoted to preserving Chicago's wild places. Today those lands are a model for the rest of the nation. Nearly 11 percent of Cook County, the county that contains Chicago, consists of preserved places.

On a recent walk, Steve, now sixty-one, showed a visitor the result of his work. "What I'm walking through here is a restored savanna. We started working on this site twenty-five years ago," he says, referring to a type of grassland with scattered oak trees. "This is a kind of natural community that was thought to be extinct. These plants wouldn't be here without the work that's been done. The birds that are singing, they wouldn't be living here, raising their babies here, if the habitat hadn't been restored."

He stops and bends to the earth.

"This one here is prairie dropseed grass, the grass of grasses, very typical grass of the high quality of savannas. This one here is Indian grass. All the grass was planted. Some of the wild orchids are thriving here, a number of them endangered species, because people did the work here to put them back."

"I compare restoration to building a cathedral," he continues. "There are so many types of expertise involved, and it takes generations. The pace of restoration of nature in the Chicago metropolitan area is picking up by orders of magnitude. We used to tackle areas that were an acre or two and it was a challenge to know how to do it," he recalls. "Pretty soon we could get ten-acre or one-hundred-acre pieces. Now we're working on a thousand and making plans for ten-thousand-acre pieces. So it's been an inspiration in my lifetime and other people's lifetime to see something that was incomprehensible become something that people can take care of."

Some would call his single-mindedness an obsession. Steve says it's more like dedication. "Chicago Wilderness was formed because there was a bigger challenge than volunteers could handle," he says. "Initially this was all volunteers doing this, but there are three hundred thousand acres of beautiful nature that are very much appreciated by the people, worth tens of billions of dollars, and we realized it would take millions of dollars to do the work to keep it healthy, so the Chicago Wilderness collaboration began looking for federal money, state money, and local money, and more importantly reaching out to more partners. Now there are so many, it's hard to keep track. Educational groups, community groups, service groups, public agencies from all levels, and not-for-profit agencies that are working together to make this a model for nature as a part of life in a developed culture."

People volunteer, Steve says, for a reason that is more rational than emotional. "It's the same thinking that inspires people to become scientists or painters or to be kind to children. They want to do something good and do something beautiful. The acres we saved were like foundlings left on our doorstep, needy but showing great promise."

Steve's Tips on Volunteering

"The volunteer community has a place for everyone. Some people like to work with others. Some don't. Some like numbers." If you pitch in and help, you'll find out what you're good at soon enough.

Advertise that you need help everywhere you go. "I remember one winter we were working in a field and saw some cross-country skiers. We put up a sign that said, 'When it doesn't snow, come get a workout with us.' Sure enough, after they finished skiing, a bunch of people came over to ask us how to get involved!"

It's best to start by volunteering for an established group. They'll have the resources, education, and ability to train you. Start by inquiring with the Audubon Society or Nature Conservancy in your area.

Be humble. Commit yourself to a period of apprenticeship before starting your own group. You will learn more this way and eliminate the chance of making mistakes. Always work with scientists—botanists and biologists—when doing a restoration project. You need all the expert help you can get.

Spread the word. Share news of your work with friends and family members. Even those who cannot help physically might be able to help financially or by telling others about your new commitment. You never know where help will come from.

RESTORING THE CHICAGO RIVER

"It was nice and it was a lot of fun. I love going through the city like that!"

"There's no other race where you can go through and see all the skyscrapers and things like that. It's different. It's cool."

"I'd say it's just exploring Chicago and it's a nice day. It's fun and you get to see from a different vantage point!"

"A great day and a great river!"

—CANOEISTS AFTER A DAY ON THE CHICAGO RIVER

Margaret Frisbie remembers the time she threw a barbecue for friends and colleagues who work with her grassroots organization. "I was setting up our picnic in a park, unloading bags of charcoal, and some people wandered by and asked me what I was doing. 'We're having a barbecue for Friends of the Chicago River,' I told them. And they looked at me and said, 'Oh, that's great, but where is the Chicago River?' I pointed over my shoulder. The river was flowing *right past us* in that park and they didn't know it. That's the problem we face every day. People don't know that Chicago even *has* a river! And you can't save what you don't know."

Frisbie's job is to help change all that. She's fond of telling people that the river everyone takes for granted is the reason Chicago exists at all. In general humans have always been drawn to watery locations, intuitively grasping that these places best support life. The original settlers selected Chicago's site because it was close to major waterways. But the river today looks nothing like the wilderness Marquette and Joliet would have seen as they paddled their fur-laden canoes in the seventeenth century. But neither does the river look as it did in the 1970s, and Friends of the River has had a lot to do with that.

The river's rebirth began in 1979, after a local magazine railed about the river's sorry state. "It was a complete dump," confesses Frisbie. "What you'd see was pretty despicable."

Even from the city's earliest days, people and businesses dumped garbage and sewage into the river. The water whisked it out of sight and mind. At that time, the river flowed north and emptied into Lake Michigan, from which Chicago drew its drinking water. As the city grew in population, city officials realized that this practice was untenable. In 1900, a massive engineering project reversed the river's flow, now sending water down the Mississippi River. This was fine for Chicago, but bad for its neighbors downriver, who complained about the refuse that now flowed past them on the way to the Gulf of Mexico.

As late as the 1970s, the river continued to be a site of illegal dumping. Rusty chain-link fences and concrete walls obscured river access. "Because it was so unpleasant, it was

Events hosted by Friends of the River throughout the year raise awareness and appreciation of river restoration efforts.

barred off," recalls Frisbie. Sewage treatment plants had cleaned up their act but still did damage. Runoff, treated with chlorine, destroyed plant and animal life. If you were nutty enough to paddle down the river back then, you would have felt like you were coasting down a stinking no-man's-land littered with trash and overrun with weeds. Wildlife was exceedingly rare.

Friends of the River took a look at all this and dreamed of a 156-mile river park, flowing past fifty or so towns in the Chicago area. They tackled the work on two fronts: a physical cleanup job and legislative efforts to get scofflaws to stop dumping trash on riverbanks and pollutants into the water.

Easier said than done. As Steve Packard knew, the native plant species had been beaten back over the years by exotic plants that were brutally tenacious. Friends of the River began recruiting people out to the river on weekends to help cut down invasive trees and replace them with native vegetation. It was slow, painstaking work. Local groups

Chicago's Flatwater Classic canoe race is an annual favorite.

interested in wildlife, the environment, and activities for children invited Friends out to their meetings to talk about their work. Slowly, momentum built. Some groups signed on to "adopt-a-river"; they'd promise to clean up a specific site through all four seasons. If something was awry, they immediately reported it. Along the way, they mapped out walking trails, put up interpretive signs, and knit that piece of the river into their daily lives.

During that time, the federal government also got stricter. The Clean Water Act, signed in 1972 by President Nixon, put severe limits on waterway dumping. Previously, we thought nothing of dumping factory effluent into rivers to be washed out to sea. As a result of this legacy, our waterways signaled their contamination in the most outrageous ways. The Cuyahoga River caught fire. Lake Erie was declared dead, unable to support marine life. In drier regions, the carcasses of dead wildlife littered the banks of small streams and arroyos, where creatures had drunk their last. The Clean Water Act required anyone who released water into a stream to get a permit and to treat the waste before releasing it at all. For many, the cost of such treatment was too much to bear, and it forced them to become more efficient about how they ran their operations. When sewage treatment plants stopped putting chlorine in the water they released, nature rebounded. Fish became more noticeable, and birds tended to linger.

As the river began looking better, people wanted access to it. Some of the old fencing was torn down to provide access for recreational groups. Today high school and college rowing teams use the river regularly. A canoe and kayak rental company has sprung up along the path. The city's parks department is busy buying up parcels of land to incorporate into the grand vision of a river park. And some developers have actually built condos emphasizing the river view.

Today Friends of the River holds events during the year to introduce newcomers to the river and welcome back old friends. Chicago River Day, held in May, is a one-day cleanup blitz. The Chicago River Flatwater Classic, held in August, is a river race for canoe paddlers. Another favorite is the "Voyageur" race, featuring huge, twenty-five-foot canoes modeled after the ones used by Marquette and Joliet.

As someone who knows the river in all its seasons, Frisbie can tell you that there's more work to be done. Concrete walls and stands of buckthorn still block access in spots. The river teems with sixty-eight species of fish, but some of them are exotics, and anglers are still warned not to eat their catch. "All in all," she says, "it's the beginning of what could be wonderful."

Today there are rumors that otters have returned to the river. If true, it would be a tremendous harbinger, since otters require slightly purer water conditions than other mammals. For a while now, Friends of the River has had to teach people how to behave around beaver, which have returned to the river in startling numbers. "There were no beavers years ago," Frisbie gushes, "but to hear that they're back and to watch out, because if you plant some trees a beaver might come along and chew on them, is fantastic!"

CALUMET RESTORATION

When tourists descend on Chicago, they tend to focus their excursions in the city center. Visitors come to behold the view from the Sears Tower, troll the tony shops on the Magnificent Mile, take in the museums, catch a Cubs game, and try real deep-dish pizza. It is safe to say that few have put the Calumet region on their to-do list. This long-neglected region, situated on the city's southeast side, gets its name from the seven-hundred-acre Calumet Lake and the nearby Calumet River, but historically its reputation is far from natural and pristine. Calumet was once home to Chicago's steel industry. Smokestacks belched

Victor Crivello (left) and Aaron Rosinski envision a future in eco-tourism for the lands in the Calumet region that they have helped restore.

blackness into the sky twenty-four hours a day, and the landscape was forever altered by the mounds of molten residuum, called slag, that was dumped outside the factories. Hot slag was bright red, and as it cooled it hardened to a thick slab as hard as concrete.

Times and economies change, and one by one the steel mills moved out of Chicago. Once this region employed eighty-six thousand men; today not a single one makes his living pulling steel. The old factories that brimmed with productivity are now silent, motionless giants. Refineries, steel mills, landfills, and railroads dot the area, most of them decrepit and abandoned. "For Sale" signs, rusty pipes and Dumpsters, scattered slabs of concrete, and endless oceans of slag are all that remain. The highest percentage of Chicago's vacant industrial buildings is

found in this region, and for years it was the city's biggest eyesore. A dumping ground, a place to forget or else cover up. There was nothing here worth saving.

Or so it seemed. What few realized or appreciated was that in the absence of humans, the original marshes and prairies of the lake and river were rebounding. Wildflowers sprang up in abandoned parking lots and in chinks of the tough slag. Herons, egrets, and cranes stalked fish in the Calumet's murky waters. People thought some early environmentalists strange when they suggested the area was actually a rare jewel worth saving, a piece of Chicago's natural history that had managed to withstand more than a century of punishment.

Today, the activists are not alone. The city, state, and federal governments have joined the effort to preserve the nearly five thousand acres left of the region's natural spaces and attract less harmful businesses to the area. Some, like environmental engineer Victor Crivello, envision a day when the toxic dumps are cleaned up, slag is irrelevant, waterways run pure again, and tourists come in droves to enjoy the water, wildlife, history, and views.

"The Calumet is less polluted than its reputation," says Crivello, who has spent his career inspecting and rehabilitating industrial areas. "There were nine steel mills within the city of Chicago that have closed, and the major chemical plants and refineries have closed, so there are some historical problems left by those industries. But Lake Calumet never had any major industrial discharge into it. Calumet has pretty high water quality, and the sites we have identified with problems are like any sites in the country with those same problems."

The Calumet is being rebuilt in two different ways. To transform the slag fields, the state is spreading sediment from Lake Peoria—largely topsoil that washed away during years of poor water management—on the slag fields to create a base for planting. Next, biologists seed the fields with alfalfa and rye grass, two crops that grow quickly, root deeply, and will help prevent erosion while sucking excess moisture from the wet soil. The roots can also penetrate existing cracks in the slag. The next year, biologists shape and landscape the area and plant a large part of it with native plants and smaller areas with grass more suitable for foot traffic and other park activities. At the same time, volunteer organizations like Crivello's Bold Chicago invite citizens and students into the reclaimed areas to help them cut down invasives and plant new native vegetation.

"I have a group that I work with, from three high schools, and eight Saturdays a year we'll put kids out in the fields doing biodiversity natural air restoration work and water sampling," says Crivello. "These are city kids, these are kids that most people have given up on. But the kids that return to my program are engaged—they love it—and they want to have the sense of accomplishment and they need a mission. Bringing back Calumet is very alluring."

The Calumet region was once Chicago's densest industrial area.

Crivello expects that the region will grow on two levels. Eventually, he thinks, the Calumet will attract companies that are looking for real estate in pristine settings. Then, too, he thinks the area will lure birders, anglers, and boaters who see the place as the perfect recreational setting. Soon the Calumet will boast bicycle trails, public access to the wetlands area, and an active environmental center.

But there are those who see that success as shortsighted, and perhaps misplaced. A truly revitalized Calumet, they say, won't happen until industry plays a major role in the region once more. William Alexander, a steelworker who was employed at Acme Steel and was a former president of the local union, puts it on the line: "I hear a lot around here about beautification and everything. Beautifying is great, but this area

Ed Sadlowski (left) and Ted Stalnos, two retired steelworkers.

needs jobs. They talk about how they can beautify this area and make it really look nice, but the stores, like the Burger King down the street, go out of business. How often do you see a Burger King go out of business? The reason they went out of business is because the people in the area don't have money. Beautification, parks and all, that's nice, but this area needs jobs."

Another man, Ted Stalnos, thinks a lot these days about the dollars and cents that were sucked out of the community when the plants shut down. "The average service industry job pays $19,000 a year," the former steelworker says. "The average manufacturing job pays $35,000 a year. I'm really focusing on the economic end, and we've been enriched by unionized manufacturing. I was able to raise children. Bill

[Alexander] raised his children and sent them on to college. One of my sons teaches high school across the street. That's because for fifteen years here I was paid a good wage with good benefits. I'm really positive about what can happen here from the industrial end, so I guess I'm looking at it from a different standpoint. We all want a clean environment, but I also want the economic engine to be able to supply the kind of jobs we need."

Clearly, then, there are no easy answers, though activists like Crivello insist they also want jobs to return, albeit the kind that won't devastate the landscape and create unsafe work and living conditions. "The reason we're standing here right now—the reason we *can* stand here right now—is because we're on some solid ground. Industry did help the area in some respects. If industry never came through, if the railroad tracks never came through, residents living on the south side of Chicago would be unable to come here and enjoy this unless they could pay a guy to come out here in a canoe."

Indeed, the new strategy among environmentalists is to include the remaining local companies in the dialogue about the future of the region. "I believe in ten years you can come back here and it will be a different region," says Crivello. "You'll know it immediately when you get out of your car."

MARIAN BYRNES: CONSCIENCE OF THE CALUMET

If you're going to take a walk with Marian Byrnes, you need to bring along three things: a walking stick, some good shoes, and your conscience. Nothing less will do.

One morning recently, the seventy-nine-year-old woman sets out on a walk to show a visitor some of the wild places in her neighborhood. The ground under their feet shifts from asphalt to pavement to grass in a matter of minutes, and soon they have left Marian's Jeffrey Manor neighborhood behind. Birds sing in the trees, and the grasses rise as high as your hip in spots. Marian has insisted for decades that she is no naturalist, and yet she calls out the names of plants as she passes, saluting them as if they were old friends: wild parsnips, wild roses, wild strawberries, fleabane, wild oats, vervain, squirrel grass, and catnip. "Well, since I started work to save the prairie I learned as much as I could from experts and wildflower identification books," she confesses.

Marian stands straight and has a good spring in her step. Her hair is white and her voice, when she speaks, is soft and raspy. She grew up on a farm in Indiana and longed for open spaces, even after she came to Chicago to teach school and raise a family.

"I moved here because of the prairie," she says. "I was a widow with three boys to raise, and when we went house hunting and came to the house that I live in now they said, 'This is the house we want!' They hadn't even been inside. They were running toward the prairie. Kids used to come from all over the South Shore to play army on the prairie. The realtor told me that it had been a government land grant to the railroad on the condition that it never be sold, that it was supposed to be a buffer between the railroad and any kind of development. But obviously that changed."

In 1979 she came home from teaching school to find a note in her mailbox saying that the Chicago Transit Authority planned to build a bus garage all over the northern half of her family's beloved Van Vlissingen prairie. "Naturally I was very upset about that, and I went to the public meeting and found a number of my neighbors there who were also upset about it. So we formed an organization, the Committee to Protect the Prairie, to keep it open, and we somehow managed to succeed in doing that for twenty years until the city also decided it was a good idea and took over the project."

In twenty years, Marian and her growing number of friends—the committee has since morphed into the Southeast Environmental Task Force and draws its strength from thirty area organizations—have thoughtfully prodded the city to do the right thing a number of times in the Calumet region. They defeated a proposal to build a dump at Big Marsh, a major birding site. They opposed construction of a garbage incinerator on the site of an old steel mill. And they defused the mayor's plan to build the city's third major airport in the region. At the time, the city thought it was the best solution to years of toxic waste: blacktop it over. There are countless other projects, or threats of projects, that have sent residents back into the meeting halls.

Eventually area residents forced the city to stop thinking of the Calumet as a dumping ground. The turning point came in 1998, after the National Park Service announced the Calumet was suitable for designation as a National Heritage Area. Two years later, the city and state announced they would allocate funds to save the area. At first they split the acreage down the middle: three thousand acres of the best land to be preserved for nature, three thousand acres of the already damaged or denuded fields to be set aside for appropriate industrial use. (The preserve area has since grown to 4,800 acres.) Much of the discussion these days is about how to find the right industries, ones that would add value to the region, not harm it in any way. Part of what makes Marian such an effective crusader is her acceptance of this sensitive balance. "I think we all now agree and accept that industry has a right to be in the region. That's what made the Calumet. But it has to be done intelligently."

Marian is pleased that younger environmentalists who started on local grassroots organizations have since moved up the ranks in city government themselves, paving the way for a smoother passage of environmentally friendly legislation. And an even younger generation is learning to love the area that is being saved.

"School classes come here for field trips, and the kids have a wonderful time because they can gather anything they want to. There's no restriction on gathering," Marian says. "Kids find things here that I've never seen, that I knew were here but had never seen. Last time I brought a group out here, a little boy found a Western frog, a little tiny brown frog, and caught it. We examined it for a while. So it's a really important educational resource."

Recently project leaders have set up ten experimental plots, treating each one differently to find out which method works best for prairie restoration. The results will help scientists fine-tune their treatment of the area. At the same time, area residents have started meeting with local factory managers and discovered they too are committed to open dialogues with the community.

Marian steps gingerly around the edge of a small pond and spies a small frog and some tadpoles in the water. It's a rare thing to get a private tour with her these days. At an age when most people would consider slowing down, Marian attends at least a meeting a day, shuttling to each on public buses. "It's hard to say what keeps me going," she says. "But there's always something else to do."

But just how has she done it? Marian says she has managed to be an active and powerful voice for so long because she never lost hope. From the very first meeting she attended, she learned something she has never let go of: "I found that there were plenty of people just like me who felt the same way. My own neighbors. If you put us in a room and got us talking, something would happen."

She continues, "I think we're a fairly classic model of how things get done through activism. So far as I can see we followed the same model that citizen activists have adhered to all over the country in getting what they wanted. It's a fairly simple and fairly classic model. Anyone can do it if they put enough energy into it. It doesn't require any great degree of intelligence. It does require a great deal of activity, but anyone can do it."

For a while, she thought she would be able to give up her work, now that the city has finally seen the wisdom of saving the Calumet. But she has since amended that notion. The city needs to hear the voices of its people—including Marian's soft but firm one—or it will lose touch again. Much has improved since she became an accidental activist, but she still grieves for what was lost.

She gestures at the land around her. "I'm sorry, I'm probably going to cry. The Eden lost is what used to be here," she says. "I mean, where we are now was all cattail marsh. I have friends who remember going out with their fathers in the 1930s in a rowboat, where Van Vlissingen prairie is, fishing among the cattails, because it was all cattails, and now it's all filled. The Eden found is the restored prairie. So the Eden found can be considered superior to the Eden lost. The birds, especially the big birds, have managed

Marian Byrnes and the organization she helped form, the Southeast Environmental Task Force, have successfully championed the restoration of the Calumet region for the past twenty years.

to survive. They've become accustomed to this territory, and they persist in returning even though their habitat has shrunk and shrunk, and there definitely are less of them than there were in the original Eden."

Like one of those rare birds, Marian continues coming back to the land and the bargaining table, again and again, to raise her voice. Ultimately, she feels, her flock will triumph.

"I'm hopeful for the future of this area because the city of Chicago and the state have made this pledge to save thousands of acres of land for permanent preservation, and I think they will hold to that pledge. It makes me feel very happy, wonderful."

And she heads back home through a field of thistle, daisies, and wild strawberries.

YOUNG PEOPLE IN URBAN NATURE

"He's a community activist, he's a nature man, he's a construction worker, he's a teacher, he's a preacher. Yes, he does everything. He never stops."

—ARIEL HOWARD,
ON HER FATHER, MICHAEL

One June night some years ago a Molotov cocktail crashed through the window of Michael Howard's bedroom at 2 AM, as he and his family lay sleeping. Seeing the flames, Michael jumped up to protect his family—his wife Amelia and five children—running to get a fire extinguisher and to call the police. Even as he was fighting the flames, Michael was shocked, but not surprised, that drug dealers in this Chicago neighborhood of Fuller Park had made him a target. Just the day before he'd found a poorly made bomb in his mailbox.

Michael, a big man with a big heart, had spent his life trying to help others help themselves. A successful building contractor and a devout Christian, Michael persuaded his

family to leave their affluent Beverly neighborhood in 1992 to return to their old neighborhood, Fuller Park, a poor African-American neighborhood on Chicago's south side. They moved back, in fact, to the house where Amelia, a teacher, had grown up. Almost immediately, Michael was troubled by what had become of their once-proud neighborhood. Daily he griped about kids selling drugs on the corner. "I kept telling my wife, 'Somebody's gotta do something about this!' And she challenged me a little bit. She said, 'So? Whatta you gonna do about it?'"

That line, coming from a loving wife who knew her husband was incapable of doing nothing, spurred a man to action and transformed a neighborhood.

Michael Howard has never been one to stand still. He joined the army as a young man and reveled in three years of discipline. Fresh out of the army, he thought he'd take some time off. He was bored before the week was out. With the help of a friend, he landed a job as a stock analyst, where he met Amelia. Michael always enjoyed working with his hands and so left the dull office gig to train as a carpenter. One project led to another, and soon he was buying and rehabbing buildings all over Chicago. He'd buy 'em, fix 'em, and sell 'em. It was good work—highly profitable work—but Michael wanted to help his community. In 1986, he closed his business and joined a local ministry program, dedicating himself to

Michael Howard with his wife, Amelia, and their children.

using his talents as a speaker, preacher, singer, and contractor to locate and create affordable housing for members of his church. Now, having moved back to his old neighborhood, he was being handed another huge challenge. Could he really stop drug dealing in Fuller Park?

He thought back to his days as a contractor. Not a day went by when someone didn't hit him up for a job. Usually, the asker didn't have employable skills. All over Chicago, general contractors needed plumbers, electricians, carpenters, and the like. Michael called some of his friends in the trades and asked if they would consider teaching classes to students, if Michael could find a place to train them. The result was the South Point Academy.

"It was a battle from the beginning," Michael recalls. "I was going out to the corner every chance I had and tried to recruit students. I'd say, 'What are you doing this for? Why don't you come learn a trade and then you can get a job?' See, there were no other alternatives for these kids. Eighty percent of them couldn't read. Ninety-five percent of them were high school dropouts. I remember one time I got one guy into our literacy program, and one morning two guys came to the door in class and just stood there. He got up without a word and left, and a few days later I saw him back out on the street. I went out to talk to him, and he said, 'Please, Mr. Howard, you're going to get me in trouble.' After that, he ended up in jail and then he was back on the corner."

But for every setback like that, South Point Academy racked up another success. More than three hundred students did avail themselves of Michael's trade school education and graduated with employable skills. "I have a lot of star graduates," he says. "We have some who have gone on to start their own businesses. We have some who have actually rehabbed the house right around the corner. One young lady rehabbed a house for a Chicago police officer who moved back into the community. So that was really a good story to hear. I had a young man come into my office a month ago. He's been working since he graduated and he just bought a house a block away from me. So, we've got a lot of stars that are really doing well."

The firebombing happened early in Michael's tenure in Fuller Park. He could have given up and pulled up stakes. But he stuck it out. He worked closely with the police, who managed to conduct more and more effective raids on drug houses. Whenever a house was vacated, Michael moved in to help rehab the structure. His knowledge of finance and property law came in handy as he helped neighborhood residents avoid predatory lenders, apply for favorable mortgages, and buy their own homes. The neighborhood steadily improved, and drug dealing appears to have declined.

Things were starting to come together, but many challenges remained. Michael read a report that said that Fuller Park—the city's smallest neighborhood, with the least clout

Residents of Fuller Park worked together to transform a city block into Eden Place, a wildlife preserve and nature education center. Eden Place provides both a refuge and a natural education for students who live in the fast-developing community of Fuller Park.

at the polls—had the highest lead levels in the city. A disproportionate number of residents were dying of various cancers.

"I started wondering, 'My house is rehabbed. So where was the lead coming from?' So we went out and had the water tested." They found that many of the water lines in the neighborhood dated to the days of the great Chicago Fire in 1871! The pipes were either wood or lead. It was very expensive to change those pipes, so without waiting for the city to get around to doing it, the neighborhood held a fund-raiser to buy their own water filters. Next, they tested a nearby debris-strewn block and found it too was contaminated with lead and asbestos. The EPA confirmed it, but

neither the city nor the feds would do anything more.

Michael organized the neighbors and phoned contractor friends, who donated earthmovers, dump trucks, bulldozers, and backhoes. Together they picked the block clean, sending the refuse—including twenty-three tons of concrete—to a certified waste disposal site. Then, using about $3,000 earned in the fund-raiser, Fuller Park residents bought several tons of topsoil and used it to cap off the existing soil. Slowly they began to transform the block into Eden Place, a wildlife preserve and nature education center, complete with its own prairie, wetlands, nature pond, savanna, Indian village, farmyard with farm animals, and extensive vegetable garden.

Michael Howard's many roles include that of mentor.

At every step, Michael forced himself to learn more and more about nature in order to teach neighborhood kids. He became a certified master gardener and learned to train raptors, and he and Amelia became certified tree keepers. "A lot of us in the African-American community think of the green movement as a white movement. We need to teach them that we all live in nature. It's part of all our lives," he says.

"I came up an avid camper and avid fisherman, and I gained a true love for nature. And I took people to the boundary waters all the way up to Canada to expose them to what I had found. When I can share nature, when I can share all of the science, the beauty, the art, even the reading that you can find in nature with children, I really see a light go on and there's a connection. And for our community I think it's a great healer."

Today Eden Place is a magical place for students to learn about nature in their neighborhood, Illinois, and the world beyond. Fuller Park has become a thriving community again. "This year, for the first time in forty years, we finally got a new home built," says Michael. "We've got our first major development: a one-hundred-unit senior retirement home. Also the first in forty years. We've got new businesses coming into the community. We finally got three gas stations. Now, that may not seem to be a big deal to you, but can you imagine living next to an expressway and no gas station? Thirty years with no gas station, and now we've got three! And so we've got a little economy coming in, we're working on some job issues for next year. We hope to put ten families in business. Developers are moving in and we want to be able to buy these new homes being developed.

"There are a lot of times when I really feel overwhelmed," he admits. "There are some days when I'm working with South Point Academy students and they bring so much weight that they're trying to overcome and they focus it in on me. And you can imagine having twenty-five people pulling at you for sixteen weeks. There's times when I just say to Amelia, 'Would you be mad if I just quit and go to the country, where I really want a barn so I can build furniture all day?' That's really all I want to do. And she says, 'I'd be disappointed because that's not what you want to do.'"

"I get tired all the time," Michael says. "I'm tired right now, but I can't stop. I can't give up, you know, it's just too much to do. And I really think it's important to teach your children how not to give up just because you're tired. If you just stop for every roadblock that's going to come in your life, you won't ever succeed and you won't make any progress."

Amelia thinks he will keep on keeping on, because he knows how high the stakes are. "Michael doesn't see anything small. There are no small visions. And we're always telling him, 'Well, can't you do it this way?' And he'll say, 'No, no, no, I see it with *this* and I've gotta have it.' I think that's what I love most about him. Because he says, 'Why shouldn't my people have this?' Or 'Why shouldn't my kids enjoy this? You know they deserve it.'"

"Michael is a dreamer," she says. "He can look at an empty field and see a whole city. And I think because of his dream and because of his vision and because of his excitement and enthusiasm, he can get you to catch the dream too."

"When I joined South Point Academy I was an active addict, which means that I drank and I drugged and I abused my body. My mind and my spirit were shot. When I joined South Point Academy, it made me want to be sober in the mornings so that I could go and learn."
— TIANA R.

"When I came to the academy I was basically homeless. I had nowhere to live. I attended the academy, but I came to the academy every day from some abandoned building or some friend housed me the night before. The academy gave me hope. It was hope for me and that was one of the reasons I was there every day. It opened doors. I learned this much from the academy: that any doors that had to be opened, I had to participate. I couldn't wait for somebody to do it for me."

—FRANK S.

"When I first came to South Point Academy, I came here looking for a direction, to fulfill some of my goals, and I found that here. I got a lot of help from here. I really like the school now. They've been putting me on the right track and I finally found something that I would like to do and can succeed in doing. Now that I'm leaving South Point Academy, I'm leaving with a new attitude, a new person with new goals and hopefully to open up new horizons."

—MALICK C.

ADVENTURES AMONG TEENAGER AMERICANUS

About ten years ago, a young woman named Deborah Perryman landed a job as a science teacher at the high school in Elgin, Illinois, a working-class community in the Chicago area. Behind the school was a thirty-five-acre stand of woods, which Deb has since transformed into a magnificent nature trail. The classes vary: She taught her students about water,

Deborah Perryman worked to create a nature trail in the thirty-five-acre stand of woods behind the high school in Elgin, Illinois, where she began teaching ten years ago.

where it appeared on the earth, and how they could tell whether it was ocean water or fresh. She made them take samples of their local stream to test its chemical content. How could they tell if the water was improving?

One day in 1997 Deb found herself being summoned to the principal's office. "Hey Deb," the principal said when she showed up to find a handful of people in his office, "these folks are from the school district. I was wondering if you could take us on a tour of that place out back."

"Sure," Deb said. She had no idea what was going on. But it had to be important if she had been called out of class. Out the door she went, the district delegation in tow. In the woods she began rattling off some of the features of the site. "This is a rare wetland,"

The Sustainability Game

Deb Perryman uses this game to teach the principles of sustainability to her students. The game is perfect not only for kids but for adult team-building experiences.

You'll need ten poker chips or counters per player, some paper plates, a portable stereo with some music, and some tantalizing treats: cookies, fresh fruit, or chocolates.

Break up the gathering into groups of three to six players each.

Place a paper plate in the middle of each group, and place ten chips per person on each plate. Announce that this is each group's "carrying capacity." If there are six players, the carrying capacity is sixty chips. Explain that when you start the music, players should reach for as many chips as they can get. When the music stops, you will award one treat per every ten chips in a player's possession. One last rule: Team members are allowed to communicate, but not by talking. Body language, notes, et cetera, are permitted.

Start the music. Let it play for a minute or so. Then stop.

In most groups, the first round of play is marked by a ferocious scramble for chips. Go around the room and award a treat to every person holding ten chips, and collect those redeemed chips.

Extra chips go back into the plate. Announce that you will double whatever is left in the plate up to the group's prior carrying capacity. Do this now. Groups that have no chips left get nothing—tee-hee! Then announce that it's time to play again.

In some gatherings, this announcement will engender discussion. "We can't play another round," people tend to say. "We don't have any more chips!" Use this opportunity to discuss why they don't. Why do some groups have enough for another round, and other don't?

If the groups seem to have absorbed the lesson—that cooperation ensures that everyone gets a treat in subsequent rounds—start the whole game again to see whether it produces a different outcome.

The game is an excellent model of what happens in the real world. If a single person in each group depletes a resource, everyone loses further down the line.

---

she'd say. "This is a fen. This is an endangered forest. This is a floodplain."

The group seemed to stop dead in its tracks at the mention of floods.

"Do you mind if I ask something?" she said. "What is all this about?"

"We need soccer fields," one of the men said.

Deb was stunned. She knew if she didn't say anything she might lose this precious plot of land. "Why can't you use the other fields?" she asked. "The school already has two."

That question engendered some chuckles, and the group launched into a conversation about the merits of using different fields to play different sports. A football field was a football field. It couldn't be a soccer field, in other words. Deb couldn't believe what she was hearing.

"You mean to tell me you would cut down three-hundred-year-old oak trees for nothing but grass?" she asked, taking them to task. "If you ask me, that's putting athletics before academics, and I think it should be fifty-fifty. I will fight you to the end on this," she announced calmly.

She glanced at her principal, who was secretly smiling, his tongue firmly in cheek. She knew in that moment that he had purposely asked her to give this tour. Who else would be a more eloquent spokesperson for the woods?

As she stalked out of the woods, Deb had a revelation: So far, she had used the woods to teach her own students. Few others in the community knew how wonderful the Elgin woods were. "I knew I had to get other people involved on the trail," she recalls, "and that was the beginning of the Mighty Acorns."

Today the Mighty Acorns program for elementary school kids is going strong. From April to May, Deb's students run one or two field trips a day. The program is so popular that busloads of little kids are starting to come from outside the Elgin school district for this two-and-a-half-hour nature experience. For some of these kids, it is the only experience they have ever had in woods of this kind. When a visiting school calls, Deb assigns one of her students as a point person. It's that student's responsibility to figure out which science standards will be taught that day. Then the other high schoolers pitch in to teach recycling, say, or the principles of clean water and air.

Something must be working. The desperate need for a soccer field seems to have sorted itself out. The idea of leveling the woods to build an athletic field died. In fact, when an adjacent acre of woodland was offered for sale, the school district bought it and added it to Deb's nature trail.

How to Design a Nature Trail

Once you have permission to use property:

Determine the goal of your trail. What will the trail feature or highlight? A historical perspective or unique ecosystem?

Who will visit your trail? Mainly adults, school-aged children, or the general public?

Obtain aerial photos of your property (they may be photocopied) and draw different trail possibilities on them. (You can get such photos from your local Soil and Water Conservation Service, or maybe even on the Internet.)

Once you are happy with the path, it is time for the work. Organize workdays and invite volunteers via local media. Most newspapers are very generous to grassroots organizations. You will also need equipment. Contact local conservation groups; they may have equipment they would be willing to lend you. If your trail will need wood chips, contact local utility companies. They often have tons of wood chips that they need to get rid of, and most of them are so happy you asked for them, they will even deliver. Don't forget to reward your volunteers. I find that having treats and water on hand keeps your troops happy. Remember, you want them to return!

You never know until you ask! Have a special need for your trail? Just ask someone in the community. Each time I have gone to the community needing a supply to make our trail a special place, enriched with hands-on, multisensory activities, my community has met our need. I think this is true because from the beginning, we "billed" the trail as a community resource.

—Deb Perryman

especially need teachers like that, because kids can sense insincerity a mile off.

Deb's passion comes from her own love of the outdoors and from watching that passion unfold in her students' lives. She loves when students take what they've learned into the community. "Service learning," she calls it. "I think we need to give young people opportunities to actually practice being leaders," she says. "We're always telling them to be leaders, but I don't find very often that we're giving them enough opportunities to actually lead. I find that if I get my kids doing one service learning project, I can't keep them out. I cannot keep them out of the community, they are everywhere doing all kinds of things.

"My kids are poor," she says. "My kids can barely speak English, some of them. But every day I give them a problem and they solve it, and that's where our hope is and that's why I can't ever be someone who says, 'We can't,' because every day they do it. And despite everything, it's powerful. As a teacher, you don't always feel supported, but if we could find a way to do that, it would be powerful. We have such a powerful opportunity, and I hope that you will remember those young people that are in your communities. Please bring them to the table when you're planning things, and don't pick just the A-plus students. Pick the students who just want to make a difference, the ones who have those bright eyes but are sitting in the back and they're shy, and include them in all of our power. That's how we're going to turn all of this around."

There are only two postscripts to the story: In 2004 Deb Perryman was named Illinois Teacher of the Year, and the woods outside her school were named the Deborah Perryman Nature Trail and Outdoor Classroom.

Some people would call Deb a rabble-rouser, the kind of passionate individual who kicks up the dust and gets in people's faces. But so what? We need people like that; we

Art: Think Before You Dump

Deb Perryman always likes her students to follow up coursework with some kind of an action project. One year they used stencils like these to remind people not to dump toxics—paint, motor oil, food wastes, et cetera—in storm drains. The town was happy to have them do it. Here's one you can use to spread the message in your community. Photocopy this page and cut out the lettering with a sharp knife. With your town's permission, place the stencil on the ground near the drain and paint over the letters.

Photo by Jack Ramsdale

PHILADELPHIA

The Holy Experiment

"William Penn might, with reason, boast of having brought down upon earth the Golden Age, which in all probability, never had any real existence but in his dominions."

— VOLTAIRE

Like a prophet winging out of the desert with a fever in his eyes, William Penn came to the New World in 1682 to build a new kind of city. In his hands he clutched a charter from King Charles II of England granting Penn a massive parcel of land west of the Delaware River. Penn dreamed of a place where people could live free regardless of their religious beliefs. Back home in London, he and his Quaker brethren had been harshly persecuted for their religion. Quakers couldn't be bothered with churches or clergy; they sought a personal relationship with God and believed that a person's conscience shaped his or her morals, not the Bible. Penn had caused trouble for himself and his staunch Anglican family ever since he began spouting these ideas in his twenties. His father's position as an admiral in the Royal Navy may have protected the young man until then, but family connections went only so far. To young Penn, the king's offer must have seemed like a godsend, proof that his convictions were finally bearing fruit.

This 1681 engraving by John Hall depicts William Penn's treaty with the local Native Americans. Courtsey of the Library of Congress

The king no doubt saw it another way: finally, London would be rid of this trouble-maker once and for all.

Once in America, Penn embarked on his "holy experiment" in a place called Pennsylvania, or "Penn's Woods." The city he founded, Philadelphia, "the city of broth-erly love," was the first in America to guar-antee all citizens equal rights under the law, regardless of race, gender, or religion. As governor he proclaimed his lands open to free press, free enterprise, trial by jury, edu-cation for both sexes, and religious toler-

ance. Penn's progressive vision included even the local Native Americans, whom he won over without weapons and to whom he insisted on paying a fair price for their land.

In his description of the government he envisioned, he wrote, "No one can be put out of his estate and subjected to the polit-ical view of another, without his consent."

Today, Penn's words seem like common sense to our ears because in essence he

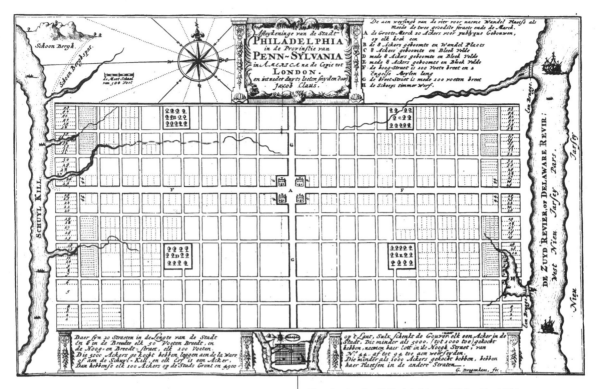

Penn's plan for Philadelphia, published in 1684. Courtesy of Princeton University Library

summed up what America was all about, although almost one hundred years would pass before his ideas would be echoed in the Declaration of Independence, written and signed in the city he founded.

Penn was ahead of his time, not only in his notion of liberty but in his environmental concern and city planning as well. As he laid out his city he recalled the highly combustible wood-frame housing of London and mandated that houses in his city be built of brick. He stipulated that owners build their homes in the center of their lot, to allow room for gardens on each side. He would never forget the squalid slums of London and worked hard to avoid replicating them in his new paradise. If you had

enough green space, he believed, you could prevent the diseases that ran rampant in big European cities. And so he laid out grand parks in his city—the first public ones in North America—and encouraged all homeowners to tend their gardens. He called Philadelphia his Green Countrie Towne and called for one acre of trees to be planted for every ten acres developed.

From that moment on, Philadelphia became the intellectual and horticultural center of the New World. Philadelphia's John Bartram, the first horticulturist in America, built the first botanic gardens and sent exotic New World species back to England. For a time even Ben Franklin financed some of

Philadelphia's rich horticultural heritage is manifest throughout the city. This site, the Spring Gardens, is one of Philadelphia Green's "keystone" gardens—long-term, high-profile gardens that have become centers for their communities. Courtesy of the Pennsylvania Horticultural Society

Bartram's expeditions. Still later, when President Thomas Jefferson sent Lewis and Clark on their western journey, the pair departed from Philadelphia, and they sent all their specimens back to Philadelphia's

Academy of Natural Sciences for study. In 1819, the city began work on a series of beautiful classical buildings at the edge of the Schuylkill River that would become the Fairmount Waterworks. Later in the century, as sections of the river became dumping grounds for industry, the city realized that the only way it could ensure the purity of its drinking water was to set aside a massive plot of land as a watershed. This 4,180-acre holding, just up the river from the Waterworks, became the largest landscaped park in the United States. The park—which today has holdings that number 9,100 acres—was a prescient commitment to the environment early in the city's history.

All this shows that Philadelphia had a long legacy of incorporating nature into the fabric of city life. But why does that matter?

Penn's city went on to become the great intellectual center of a young nation. The seat of America's Enlightenment. The city of the Liberty Bell and the Declaration of Independence, and the birthplace of American freedom. It was also a major manufacturing hub. A steam- and coal-fired, piston-charged factory boomtown, and for a while the largest textile maker in the world. The city became a major publishing town on the East Coast, home to the Curtis Publishing Company's *Saturday Evening Post* and the J. C. Lippincott book company. Nearly every major industry that characterized the American industrial revolution—breweries and confectioners, tobacco makers and ice cream factories, drug companies, shipbuilders,

and train yards—all made their home in the Philadelphia of old. And then, like a balloon pricked with a pin, it all went bust.

Blame the American dream. After World War II the GIs returned home and headed to the fast-growing suburbs with their young families. Two-thirds of American cities lost population from the 1970s through the 1990s. In the phenomenon known as "white flight," middle-class families fled cities in droves, believing that urban areas had become too big, too noisy, too expensive, or too crime-ridden and unsafe. After all, the American dream was to own a home, a car, and a yard enclosed by the archetypal picket fence.

In 1950, Philadelphia's population peaked at 2.1 million. Today, it stands under 1.6 million. More than five hundred thousand people just picked up and left, and haven't returned. The outlying suburbs grew while the city shrank. In Philadelphia, the loss of those people, their incomes, and their potential tax revenues was devastating. Poverty, crime, and drugs soon filled the void.

Philadelphia has struggled in the past fifty years to stop the slide and turn itself around. Despite its problems of abandonment, poverty, and a challenging tax structure,

Sommerton Tanks Farms utilizes half an acre of Water Department land near the center of the city.

Philadelphia's residents, its leaders, and the thousands of people moving back into its downtown area believe in its future. With its solid and historic architecture, excellent location along the Northeast corridor, extensive public transportation system, and bustling cultural scene, the city is poised for a renaissance. The model of the Center City District is beginning to spread to other commercial areas and neighborhoods throughout the city. Significant efforts are underway to improve the public school system. Philadelphia continues to shift its economy from being a manufacturing giant to having its base in service and tourism,

with a flourishing health-care system, a growing technology base, and several major universities and colleges.

Environmentally, the city is already far ahead of other cities in implementing best practices on a variety of fronts. Fairmount Park's educational programs teach thousands of Philadelphians the value of city-based wilderness. Many of those citizens later volunteer in a number of public stewardship programs designed to restore the park's varied ecosystems. The city's Water Department has embarked on experiments in urban agriculture as a way to reduce the environmental impact of maintaining its vast lawns. Its first venture, a partnership with Sommerton Tanks Farm, has already turned a profit growing delicious, healthy food on a mere half acre of Water Department land in the heart of the city. The city's stormwater infrastructure is old and fast approaching replacement age. To lessen the impact on these pipes, the department is implementing the methods of natural drainage that we talk about throughout this book. It's helping to install porous asphalt at local schools and rain gardens that absorb water on school playgrounds. It's also spearheading an effort to use the city's numerous vacant lots to capture and purify precious rainwater and reduce toxic runoff into local waterways. "We have a saying at the Office of Watersheds," says Howard Neukrug, director of that office. "'Clean water, green city.' As we have a green city and we bring back quality of life and green trees and green communities into Philly, that is going to improve the quality of the water in the city."

These are wonderful efforts, but a massive challenge remains. Philadelphia must remake its old inner-city neighborhoods, which have been hit hardest by the downturn in fortunes in recent decades. Mayor John F. Street's Neighborhood Transformation Initiative is the boldest effort to date addressing this significant problem. In gardening parlance, it's a very long row to hoe, but positive signs are emerging—such as suburban developers starting to build market-rate housing, new

Howard Neukrug, director of the Office of Watersheds, has pioneered numerous alternative methods of improving water quality in Philadelphia.

small businesses, and vacant land being turned into attractive spaces with grass and trees surrounded by wooden fences. In many neighborhoods, residents are working together to make community gardens and reclaim derelict parks.

In this chapter, we'll meet people who are committed to helping Philly live and thrive again. Many of them, you'll see, are among the strongest, most dedicated women you will ever meet. For guidance and inspiration, they are looking to the past. Philadelphia's salvation appears to lie in the dreams of the idealistic Quaker that first breathed life into it. Today's heroes, today's visionaries, today's William Penns have hit upon a winning formula:

To clean the city, to dream the city, you must green it.

SAVED BY FLOWERS

Each year, as winter draws to a close in March, thousands of people flock to the Pennsylvania Convention Center to get an early dose of springtime. There, they wander the aisles of the great exhibit halls and feast their eyes on orchids, daylilies, delphiniums, daffodils, hybrid roses, and millions more in the pantheon of color. Vendors come from across the nation. Some exhibitors are big landscapers who treat passersby to outdoor-indoor fantasies: an inviting fern forest complete with rocks and waterfall, a Japanese garden with its bamboo fountain and raked sand, and gorgeous bulbs that have been coaxed to an early bloom. Some are small mom-and-pop businesses selling from tables laden with cacti or bulbs.

The Philadelphia Flower Show, presented each year by the Pennsylvania Horticultural Society (PHS), attracts more than two hundred sixty-five thousand, including the fourteen thousand or so PHS members who automatically get a ticket to attend. In fact, you could say that Philadelphia's Flower Show is *the* event of the year. Even if you don't have a green thumb, you may come to experience the unofficial start of spring—and when you do you are helping Philly back onto its feet.

While the Philadelphia Flower Show attracts more than 265,000 visitors each year, its contribution to the culture and public spirit of the city might be even greater than the economic benefit it brings. Courtesy of the Pennsylvania Horticultural Society

To understand how that works, you need to step back in time to 1827, the year PHS was founded. Its earliest members, fifty-three men, were wealthy Philadelphia landowners who were devoted to the "highly instructive, interesting science" of horticulture. Philadelphia would eventually become the site of major seed companies such as W. Atlee Burpee & Co. and J. Landreth. Two years after they created the society, the group's founders sponsored a plant show to introduce new cultivars to members. One of the strange new plant introductions that debuted in 1829 was a plant with red leaves—the poinsettia—a Central American native that few Americans besides the society's well-to-do members had ever seen. A photo from the 1930s shows just who had joined PHS: well-dressed women in cloche hats and mink stoles.

And then, in 1963, the society picked a new president. Ernesta Ballard, a former greenhouse director and author of gardening books, had a tony Philadelphia pedigree and the soul of an activist. She looked out the windows of her office and saw a city where so many people, particularly city kids, didn't even know that their food came from the earth. Ballard wanted to change all that. Each year, after the Flower Show, the society had a little extra money left over. She wondered whether they could do something with those extra funds to give back to the community. They started with a few small programs: a summer camp for kids, and a vegetable garden program on

As president of the Philadelphia Horticultural Society, Ernesta Ballard began many of the community programs that have transformed the city.

vacant lots for which the society donated plants and supplies.

"We had one very fundamental rule," recalls Ballard, now eighty-four and retired from the presidency, "and that was that we didn't do anything for anybody on any block unless 85 percent of the people living on the block agreed that they wanted to be part of the program. They all had to put in a little money. Maybe it was one dollar. I forget the amount. It wasn't very much, and it took off. We had very, very few failures."

The field staff from the Pennsylvania Horticultural Society soon began to help residents with window boxes and wine barrels

grow flowers and trees to green the row house streets. Then it was siting gardens on vacant lots and eventually undertook the revitalization of neighborhood parks, gradually cleaning empty lots around town and planting beautiful new landscapes. "In the early 1970s when this all began, we didn't have a lot of drugs on the street and there was only a little bit of vandalism. Sometimes people would snitch a plant, but very little, really, and the whole thing was very successful," recalls Ballard. "We sat around one time and said we have to think of a name for this program. We all thought the name Philadelphia Green was wonderful, and it just sort of took off from there."

Today, thirty years later, under the dynamic leadership of Ballard's successor, Jane Pepper, who took the reins of the Pennsylvania Horticulture Society in 1981, Philadelphia Green is the remarkable engine behind Philadelphia's green transformation. Each year, PHS takes the profits from its Flower Show—usually about $1 million—and pumps it back into the local community to provide

Since 1981, when she became president of the Philadelphia Horticultural Society, Jane Pepper has expanded the enormously successful restoration program called Philadelphia Green.

training, plants, tools, soil, and the general know-how needed to positively impact urban areas. Besides the funds raised at the Flower Show, PHS has received grants for many years from two major local foundations, as well as longtime funding from the city's block grant. In 2003, Philadelphia Green entered into a partnership with the city to expand its work, using about $6.5 million in operating dollars over two years.

HOW IT WORKS

Philadelphia Green begins its work on two levels. First, it tries to find people who want to work hard to make a difference in their communities. Next, it focuses on vacant lots. At last count, Philadelphia had somewhere in the neighborhood of forty thousand vacant lots in neighborhoods plagued with crack dens, drug pushers, gunfights, and overt prostitution.

How did it get so bad? Traditionally, Philadelphia was a city of neighborhoods where workers lived in row houses that encircled local factories. After the 1950s, the workers started moving out to the suburbs, and factory owners were lured to the American Southeast with the promise of low taxes and cheap labor. As each factory fell silent, it hushed yet another neighborhood. Over time, many of those old row houses were abandoned, fell into disrepair, and were appropriated by people engaging in negative activity. Occasionally the city would con-

In his first term as mayor John F. Street championed the cleanup of 40,000 vacant lots and partnered with the Philadelphia Horticultural Society and other groups to maintain and plant trees on abandoned property throughout the city.

demn a dangerous building, demolish it, push the rubble into the basement, and cover it with "fill," inviting passersby to dump whatever they liked on the property.

When Mayor John F. Street took office in 1999, he undertook a massive campaign—the Neighborhood Transformation Initiative—to do something about those trouble spots in his city. Street, who grew up on a 110-acre farm outside Philadelphia, had a strong sense of the importance of green space in urban environments.

"When I took over," he recalls, "We had thirty to forty thousand vacant lots. Some hadn't been cleaned in twenty-five years. In my first term we cleaned every vacant lot in the city of Philadelphia twice—every single one. The city entered into contracts with neighborhood groups, as you know, with the Pennsylvania Horticultural Society's Philly Green to help us keep our lots clean, and to help us train people to garden on those lots and to green those lots. We planted over seven thousand trees in neighborhoods. We changed the wording in demolition contracts so that sites would be left better prepared for grass and trees."

In the past, as the mayor explains, when a building was condemned and demolished, wreckers were permitted to push the rubble into the basement and cover it over with a thin layer of poor dirt. Many of those structures were lead-contaminated from paint, and old industrial sites were polluted with other contaminants. Often, the city would later have to pay for expensive cleanups. Now, much of the debris is hauled away to an appropriate landfill and a several-inches-deep layer of topsoil is placed on top of the demolition site and planted with grass and trees. A side-yard program allows property owners to apply for and acquire a lot adjacent to them to use as a green space or parking area.

The mission of the city's $295 million bond-funded Neighborhood Transformation Initiative (NTI) is to halt the decay of vacant lots around town by planting green spaces.

Under Mayor Street's watch, the wording in demolition contracts now requires preparation of the site for planting of grass and trees. Courtesy of the Pennsylvania Horticultural Society

The land may someday be sold for development, but for now, it must be transformed into a "clean and green" space, to begin to change the perception of the lot, the block, and the entire neighborhood. It's called creating "curb appeal." When NTI takes over a lot, it's eventually planted with grass and trees and its boundaries gently defined with wooden fences.

The "clean and green" lot program of NTI's work in neighborhoods has been one of its most visibly successful aspects. Headed up by Director Patricia L. Smith, NTI works with a number of minority contractors and

The sprawling Glenwood Green Acres in north Philadelphia is now twenty years old and boasts more than ninety garden plots. It has hosted intergenerational projects on the heritage of Southern agriculture; crops of tobacco, cotton, and peanuts are still grown there. In 1997 the garden was preserved as a permanent open space by the Neighborhood Gardens Association. Courtesy of the Pennsylvania Horticultural Society

with nonprofit neighborhood groups, through subcontracts with Philadelphia Green. The lot-cleaning program has created jobs for more than seventy neighborhood residents. "When I became the mayor, there were neighborhoods where you couldn't give away this vacant land," says Street, "and now we have people sometimes standing in line bidding on it."

One afternoon, as Smith walks in northeastern Philadelphia, in a neighborhood that has suffered from decades of disinvestment, she says, "When I came back to this city, after having lived in Washington for about five years, we were faced with the challenge of having more than nine thousand dangerous buildings in the city of Philadelphia. That was the spring of 2000. That summer, because of the excessive wet weather, vacant buildings were collapsing at an extraordinary rate."

Using funds that Philadelphia raised through issuing bonds, NTI was able to pinpoint the most dangerous buildings and demolish nearly seven thousand of them over a five-year period. Like all efforts in the public sector, the program has its critics, some of whom decry the wholesale eradication of old row houses. Some would rather see the buildings "harvested," that is, picked clean of their valuable architectural details. Supporters of the program counter that since many of these buildings were constructed as worker housing, they were plain structures to begin with and have little architectural merit. NTI prefers to focus on the safety issue. "Recently," says Smith, "even though we had a very wet summer, there were only three unanticipated collapses of buildings. The program is working."

After a building is demolished and the lot prepared according to the new demolition specifications, neighborhood contractors hired by Philadelphia Green step in to create beauty out of blight. The before and after photos of these transformations are astonishing.

"As with all journeys," says Smith, "you have to take that first step. Yes, the scale is significant. Philadelphia is a large, older American city. In many ways it's one step at a time, one neighborhood at a time, one block at a time. But if you don't take that step you won't make progress. We're hopeful. The challenge is great. We do believe we can make progress."

She stops a moment and gestures to a new housing development over her shoulder. Pretty porch-front homes extend in a row down a tree-lined street. This is Pradera Homes, built two years ago by a community development corporation known as the Association of Puerto Ricans on the March. It's one of the first mixed-income tracts of housing built in this part of north Philadelphia for many years. Its fifty units practically create a whole new neighborhood. It's also two blocks from a supermarket, and there are plans to build a school.

Smith smiles as she tells this story. It wasn't so long ago that this land was vacant yet filthy, useless in the eyes of most developers. "Now," she says, "it represents the type of neighborhood that we want to see in this city."

Blaine Bonham, executive vice president of PHS, agrees. "Now, the Association of Puerto Ricans on the March has a much better sense of attracting people and attracting investment in that area. We conducted a vacant land study in 2000 and found that if the city did nothing proactive to address vacant land issues, eventually, because of crime, drugs, and decreasing property values, the hidden cost in the end would cost the city more than if they decided to own the problem and address the issue. And that's just what Mayor Street decided to do through NTI."

WHAT MAKES A CITY

Philadelphia is not like the other cities in this book. In many ways, its challenges are greater, and its potential payoffs more exciting. The City of Brotherly Love does not have the deep pockets of Seattle, Los Angeles, or even Chicago.

"I speak of Philadelphia as a city on the cusp," says Susan Wachter, professor of real estate at the Wharton School at the University of Pennsylvania. "A city on the cusp of remarkable potential and growth, or of continued decline. Both these alternatives are in front of us and they are futures that we can choose depending on what we do as citizens."

Wachter is one of a new breed of researchers who are analyzing cities and defining in perceptive new ways what makes them tick. Thanks to their research, city leaders now understand that for a city to thrive and attract new businesses, it must address aesthetics. Sure, there might be more jobs available, but that doesn't make the city desirable or more livable. We all know cities where no one wants to linger after work or visit on a weekend, or where everyone flees to the suburbs at 5 PM each afternoon. A vibrant city hums because it has four things: jobs, home ownership, culture, and public places that anyone, rich or poor, can enjoy.

The American dream changed in the 1990s, possibly because a generation of people who had grown up in the suburbs returned to cities seeking excitement, opportunities, and homes with character that couldn't be found anywhere else but in urban areas. "We have had a remarkable turnaround of cities in the 1990s," says Wachter. "But there were winners and there were losers. New York won, Philadelphia lost. Cities like Baltimore and Detroit continue to decline."

Now, we stand on a threshold of a new city boom. Because New York is so expensive, cities like Philadelphia are great places to land real estate deals. Rents in Benjamin Franklin's old city are about one-third of those in Boston, Washington DC, and New York. Intrepid homebuyers can find century-old brick row houses with enormous potential for restoration and appreciation for a fraction of what they'd pay in hotter cities. Philadelphia has booming neighborhoods right downtown, adjacent to its commercial district. "Philadelphia is a city of homeowners," says Wachter. "Because of our amazingly low interest rates, homeownership is now more accessible than ever before."

Wachter and others, like PHS's Bonham, feel that Philadelphia is finally starting to experience a renaissance. "We have a growing and thriving Center City," Bonham says. "We have the third largest population of any downtown in the country next to New York and Chicago, with eighty thousand people living there right now. We have a heavily used parks system, and while it's been underfunded for many years, it has new leadership and

direction. We have a vibrant shopping district and we have the largest number of preserved historic buildings in the country, along with some dramatic skyscrapers. So, our city is beginning to reinvent itself from the inside out."

FOR THE WANT OF A TREE

With ownership comes a desire to protect one's investment and increase the value of that property. One of the simplest ways to boost the price of a row house—and indeed the entire neighborhood—is to plant some trees. Fifty years ago, city leaders, realtors, and homeowners themselves would have scoffed at that assertion. Today, researchers like Wachter can calculate and compare the cost of a home before and after a tree-planting initiative with great precision. The

numbers are remarkable. She completed a study in 2005 that quantified the effect of greening vacant lots and planting street trees in the New Kensington neighborhood. "Planting a street tree increases the value of nearby homes by 15 percent," she says. "Turning a blighted vacant lot into a clean and green space increases the value of adjacent homes by 30 percent."

So do the math: If you bought a house for $100,000 in a neighborhood containing other similar properties and planted some trees on your block with your neighbors, each of you would have boosted the value of your home by $15,000. If you and your neighbors devoted some weekends to building a garden in a nearby vacant lot, you'd boost the values of your homes by $33,000. Imagine: instant equity for the cost of plants and landscaping.

Building a garden or park is a little like the old saying:

For want of a nail, the shoe was lost;
For want of the shoe, the horse was lost;
For want of the horse, the rider was lost;
For want of the rider, the battle was lost;
For want of the battle, the kingdom was
   lost,
And all for the want of a nail.

Each sapling or seedling in your garden is a crucial link that can either make or break a city. "We all recognize beauty when we see it," says Wachter, "but a green space is not just beautiful, it affects the bottom line." Gardens and trees raise property values in urban areas, which in turn raise the property tax base, which gives cities greater tax revenues, which they can reinvest in the betterment of the city.

"Look at what happened in West Philadelphia in the past ten years," says Wachter. "You would be amazed at the transformation." In a single decade, the West Philadelphia Initiative, spearheaded by the University of Pennsylvania and its partner neighborhood organizations, has embarked on a massive planting program. "We are now an extraordinary urban city in a garden," says Wachter. "Crime has fallen dramatically, the schools are improving. There are all sorts of positive things, not only for the faculty and students, but for the neighbors as well."

Can it be that green spaces hold down crime? The Harvard criminologist Dr. Felton Earls has actually documented this phenomenon. One study, based in Chicago, found that there were 56 percent fewer violent crimes and 48 percent fewer property crimes in public housing apartment buildings when they were surrounded by landscaping as compared to apartment buildings where there was no landscaping. It's not so much the planted spaces as much as what they stand for. A well-tended area broadcasts to passersby that people care about what goes on in this area. If you litter, it will be picked up. If you engage in negative activity, it will be reported. The last thing a criminal wants is a pair of watchful eyes.

Besides the effect on property values and the crime rate, there's something else that happens when green spaces are planted in cities. If you do the job alone at first, you will stand out. You'll attract attention, possibly for the first time since you moved to the neighborhood. If the project is a large one, inevitably some neighbors will offer to help you. Little by little, the act of planting knits people together as nothing else can. This simple, communal act builds community, and strong communities can transform entire cities.

Acting together to create something seems to be a basic human drive. "For the first time in the history of the world, we will be an urban world," Wachter reminds us. "The globe, for the first time, will have more than half of the population living in cities. In a period where we have telecommunications and the Internet, it would seem as though we can all live out in the wilderness and communicate

Studies have consistently shown that "greening" a neighborhood can significantly raise property values and reduce crime. Courtesy of the Pennsylvania Horticultural Society

over the wires and over the Internet. But something's missing. What's missing is people together in place, not one on one, but one on one in groups. Creativity and innovation happen best when people are working together in interest groups. People want to be with people, not only to create, but to recreate. They want to be together in beautiful places that they help build."

Cities are public places. In order for them to be beautiful, people must work together. Cities are not malls, they are not gated communities, they are not subdivisions bought, developed, and sold by one person or corporation. When a single entity designs something, everything about that space looks and feels alike because a single "mindset" created it.

No one person can create a city. When you walk down a city block, every shop is different, every building unique, every street corner exceptional. Old city houses enchant our eyes because each has a different look, built at a different point in history, by a different builder or speculator. The pavement itself changes under our feet from cobblestone to brick to concrete. The greatest of cities are palimpsests, old parchment written upon, erased, and written upon again. The result is a wondrous thing that can never be duplicated.

"The beauty of a city is its lack of planning," says Wachter. "You do something, your neighbor does something, and together it works as a whole. Each is creative and beautiful on its own and makes the city seem interesting. Something about us humans craves diversity and variety."

MEET PHILADELPHIA'S URBAN WARRIORS

"He that plants trees loves others beside himself."

—THOMAS FULLER

Philadelphia Green is made up of people who didn't believe they had what it took to round up their neighbors and get them committed to a task. But little by little, these urban warriors found the strength to inspire others.

Doris Gwaltney is one of them.

Gwaltney grew up in West Philadelphia around the Carroll Park neighborhood, named for a then glorious four-acre park built, owned, and maintained by Eugene Carroll, a wealthy realtor. When Doris was a little girl, she played in the park with her brother Donald. She grew up hearing stories about how her parents used to meet for dates there in the 1930s. It was beautiful place back then, with a massive flower bed in the center, and the edges of the park lined with proud Philadelphia row houses.

The neighborhood was made up mostly of Irish and Italian families, though some African-American families like Doris's were starting to move in. It isn't pretty to say or to think about, but it's very common: the more African-Americans moved in, the more whites moved out to the suburbs. Within ten years, the character of the neighborhood had changed entirely.

Doris's family stayed. They settled into their old family home and watched the decades pass in Carroll Park. Mr. Carroll turned the deed of his wonderful park over to the city of Philadelphia. No sooner had the transfer been completed did the maintenance begin to slip. In the 1960s, the city ripped out the flower bed and installed a spray fountain, which families enjoyed in summers. But even as they came and went, they could see that the trees were beginning to look overgrown, the remaining shrubs hadn't been tended, and weeds were piling up in the beds. For a while, a neighborhood association composed of local elderly people tried to take care of things, but as each member died there were fewer and fewer residents willing to take their place.

The park went to hell. Drug dealers and prostitutes held sway. Longtime neighbors learned to avoid the place. "It just wasn't a safe place to be," says Doris. "It was just something that was there and you didn't really think about it anymore."

Occasionally, neighbors would complain to the Recreation Department, which would send out a crew from time to time, but as soon as they left the criminals moved back in. "I tried to pick up trash in there from time to time," Doris recalls. "But it was just too much. It was wall-to-wall glass in there."

In 1993, PHS started a program to begin to resuscitate neighborhood parks around town. They called a meeting at a local church, which Doris—who was well on her way to becoming a community activist—attended. There, for the first time, she met neighbors like herself who desperately

Joan Reilly, Director of Partnership Development at Philadelphia Green (left), with Carroll Park community leader Doris Gwaltney (right).

wanted to see "the element," as they called the pushers and prostitutes, gone for good.

"So, we went to the church to see what everybody had to say about Carroll Park once again. We went to the church and there was a young woman making a presentation. Once again, they're going to save Carroll Park. So, we're sitting there skeptically, at least I was. Well, how are we going to save Carroll Park this time? And the presenter said, 'We have $30,000 for you through the Pennsylvania Horticultural Society's Philadelphia Green program.' The ears pricked up. 'Ah, they have the money.' This is what made the difference. Carroll Park's time had come."

Doris Gwaltney (second from right) with fellow Carroll Park neighbors on a cleanup day. Courtesy of the Pennsylvania Horticultural Society

In the summer of 1997, residents came into the park with brooms, rakes, and paint for a day of work. They painted the benches, painted the spray pool, and painted the storage-shed building. At the end of that day the transformation of Carroll Park had begun.

"It was a hard day's work," recalls Doris, "but the community knew, that's a new group over here taking back Carroll Park and that is true."

That was the beginning of an extraordinary relationship. All it took was knowing that there was hope, that someone from the outside cared enough to come up with the money, and that others who lived nearby were willing to put in the time to make something beautiful. Money in hand, the neighborhood came together. Those days in the park, says Doris, you could practically feel the sense of satisfaction that something was *finally* being done. Philadelphia Green lent the expertise; Carroll Park residents provided the manpower.

It's never easy reclaiming a park. The key, experts agree, is for law-abiding citizens to make their presence known, day after day after day. Joan Reilly, director of partnership development at Philadelphia Green, calls it an uphill battle. "These folks like Doris are like warriors, and I think Philadelphia Green provides warrior support. If Doris and her group of women stop coming out here, in a matter of time it will revert back. Neglected spaces like parks become havens for negative activity, and that preys on a community."

Doris and the others were out there regularly, even when it wasn't exactly comfortable to do so. "I spent the winter of 1999 in Carroll Park," she boasts. "I came out here every Monday at four o'clock in the afternoon to pick up trash. Even in the ice and snow I was out here. I was out here picking up trash because every Monday at four o'clock I wanted the neighbors around here to look out their windows and see that crazy woman is still out here picking up trash. I wanted the neighbors to know that we were here and we were here to stay."

That was seven years ago, and Carroll Park is now the hub of a thriving community. "We have a little group that gets together every Monday at 4 PM to pick up trash," says Doris. "And then once a month to do the bigger chores."

On October 10, 1998, residents built an entire playground in a single day. At 6:30 AM, a huge flatbed truck showed up with a load of steel parts. "They looked like big Legos," says Doris, giggling. A few neighbors who were ironworkers started welding, and by nightfall, with the help of others who joined in, says Doris, "they had slapped that puppy together."

With time, they cleaned up the spray pool, planted flower beds, and began the arduous task of tending or replacing all the old trees first planted in Mr. Carroll's day. Landscape architects from Philadelphia Green helped the

Tree planting ensures the long-term viability of a community park while simultaneously contributing to purification of the city's water. Courtesy of the Pennsylvania Horticultural Society

Philadelphia Green's Mindy Maslin (right) teaches youths about the benefits of trees. Courtesy of the Pennsylvania Horticultural Society

community pick out the species—maples, oaks, hawthorns, lindens—that were right for the region. One day, the news spread around the neighborhood that the local Citizens Bank would donate the last twenty-two trees the park needed to round out its planting. The president of the bank himself was on hand at the next planting day to help install the trees.

"One of our participants at a park conference likened a three-way partnership to a three-legged stool," Doris says. "If one of the legs on that stool is broken, that stool is useless. So everyone must do his and her part to keep the partnership alive and vital."

These days, even local children are invited to take part in that partnership. After school on Wednesdays, the park sponsors a Park Patrol class for kids, who pick up trash and participate in environmental education classes. The park is home to Earth Day festivities every April and a concert series in the summer, and it is, of course, the site of meetings for the local garden club.

Folks here are proud to report that property values have risen steadily since the revi-

This New Old Green House

As neighborhoods become desirable again, so do the old row houses that have managed to remain standing for a hundred or more years. The people who snap up these structures have their work cut out for them, and upgrading with environmentally friendly products may mean that their old house is more energy-efficient and sustainable than homes only a decade old. Following is a sampler of possible "green" products:

Tiles: Many manufacturers are creating beautiful ceramic tiles that are made with up to 60 percent recycled glass.

Lights: Look for compact fluorescent light bulbs, which last ten times as long as Edison's incandescent bulbs and drink up about one-fifth of the energy to light the same space. These bulbs are also cooler to the touch, so they're not painful to change in a pinch.

Heat: Most old houses use radiators, while newer houses use blown hot air, but the best technology is probably radiant floor heating, in which flexible hoses are attached under the floorboards and more directly warm humans, animals, and plants standing above them. Heat rises, which means it takes longer for radiant heat to escape a room. Radiant heat is up to 40 percent more efficient than other heating systems.

Insulation: Okay, polyisocyanurate doesn't *sound* terribly organic, but it is more effective at slowing heat movement between rooms than fiberglass and other types of insulation. It's becoming the insulation of choice for people refurbishing chilly brick walls.

Caulk: Not terribly cutting edge, but definitely useful for sealing holes around service lines, where precious heated air can escape.

Finishes: Choose from a wide variety of biodegradable, low-toxicity strippers, stains, and paints.

Roofs: Thermoplastic polyolefin (TPO) is recognized as the best flexible roof covering. It will better reflect the sun's rays and reduce the urban heat island effect.

Skylights: Skylights can be tricky to install but well worth the effort. They eliminate the need for extra lighting in certain spots and will even admit moonlight on certain nights.

Windows: Old single-pane glass windows are notoriously drafty and are costly to replace with the new standards: low-emissivity, double-paned windows filled with argon gas. There's no rush to replace your windows, however. A good insulation job on all exterior walls will go a long way toward eliminating waste.

talization of the park. "I know one woman was moving out to New Jersey," says Doris. "She put a sign out in front of her house on a Monday and two days later it was gone. I thought she had changed her mind. 'Oh, she's staying after all.' But no. That's how fast she sold. Another house was sitting here around the park boarded up for years. But someone came along, bought it, and rehabbed it, and now there's a young family living there."

Along with the obvious changes, there were some intangible ones as well. Doris wasn't a gardener before this experience, but she's since taken courses at Philadelphia Green on perennials and trees and is now qualified to prune any of the trees in the park. Today, at the age of sixty-six, Doris can say she has spent her whole life watching the seasons come and go in Carroll Park. In fact, she still lives in the same house

with her mother, who is ninety-one and remembers well those days when she went courting around the big flower bed.

"The young people are still dating in the park," Doris is happy to report. "Oh yes, indeed! Just like old times."

A FAMILY'S PAIN BECOMES A NEIGHBORHOOD'S GAIN

"Take care of the land and the land will take care of you."

—Hugh H. Bennett

Michael Elliss was the neighborhood's go-to guy. "Michael, can you fix my door?" "Michael, can you go to the store for me?" "Michael, can you take me shopping?" No matter what people asked, Michael did his best to help. Unfortunately, when *he* wanted something done in the neighborhood, he did it alone. He didn't like the idea that his kids had to walk ten blocks to the nearest playground, so he decided to clean up a vacant lot across the street from his father's house. The place was huge by city standards—seven building lots, almost an acre.

On weekends, Michael would wander over from his house around the corner, leading his kids—three boys and one girl—in a little troupe. They'd spend a few hours in the lot, picking up trash, pulling the weeds, and hauling out debris. The lot was like so many others in big cities. A building got demolished, and the rubble stayed behind.

Weeds sprung up, obscuring the remnants of the old structure. And little by little, the lot began to broadcast to passersby that anything goes. When people remodeled their homes, fixed their cars, or worked in their yards, they dumped the ensuing junk in the trunk of their cars and waited till dark. Then they'd drive it over to Belgrade Street and dump it in the dead of night, ostensibly when no one was looking. The lot was a sorry state, but what could you do? This was life in the big city; you couldn't police a vacant lot 24/7.

Michael thought otherwise. He and his kids collected that trash and tossed it in receptacles. They'd find and dispose of dead animals, too. Michael carefully planned how to get rid of the more unwieldy stuff. Off to the side he'd set blocks of concrete, rusty metal, and car and house parts, and then find Dumpsters in town where he could drop them off. This too was not exactly "kosher," as his father says, but at least the trash was finally going to a dump where it belonged. Belgrade Street wasn't a dump. It was a dream in the making.

Michael's dad, Ed, watched these cleanup brigades from his stoop across the street. "What the hell're you doin'?" he'd ask his son. "Why waste your time? That's not your lot. Forget about it." Ed was in his sixties. He'd been a Navy radar man for twenty years and thought he knew the score about the neighborhood. "I didn't know my neighbors, and they didn't know me," he recalls. "They minded their business. I minded my business."

With the help of the New Kensington Community Development Center, Ed and Loretta Elliss turned a trash-ridden vacant lot into a superb example of the power of citizen-city partnerships to improve and transform neighborhoods.

Then, before anyone knew anything was wrong, Michael was gone. Dead. A thirty-three-year-old man snuffed out in his prime. His wife left without a husband, his children fatherless. Michael, you see, had had a drug problem that few could help him with, least of all those closest to him.

"Well, there are a lot of good things to say about Michael," says Ed. "We can go on and fill five books, volumes of them, libraries of them. There are a lot of good memories to remember about Michael. Ask the neighbors around here. There isn't one of them who could say a bad thing about him or would say a bad thing about him. At his funeral there were more than two hundred people. People I didn't know who knew

Michael. So there are a lot of good things to say about Michael and he was a damn good father to his kids. His children came before he did, and yes, they came before his drugs too. The only thing that kept him alive as long as it did was his kids because surely that drug would have got ahold of him."

Ed and his wife Loretta took their son's passing hard. Some days it was all Ed could think about. He puttered around his backyard, working on different projects, trying to numb the pain. He had a large yard, with a small pond and about a dozen ducks and some chickens. In his grief he doted on those animals, and some days, when his work out back was done, he'd sit on the front stoop and stare across to the vacant lot where his son's eye had alighted.

"I would watch over there and of course without anyone to pick up the trash, the yard started going back to the way it was," he remembers. Some mornings he'd come out and see that another errant dumper had strewn the lot with junk in the night. "One day I was sitting there and I just thought, 'No, no, no! I can't have that! He thought enough to do it, to clean that place, and I'm going to finish the job.'"

Ed got up, walked across the street, and started where Michael had left off. After that, he was out there every day, weather permitting. People would look at him funny on the way to work, as they drove past in their cars. He was the old guy with maybe too much time on his hands. But a funny thing happened. One miserably hot day a guy stopped by, driving a tractor mower down the middle of the city street. "Hey," the guy asked, "what're you doing?"

"I was reluctant to tell him anything," Ed remembers. "It wasn't my lot. I wasn't supposed to be there. I didn't want to get myself in trouble, you know?"

But the man worked with a local organization called the New Kensington Community Development Center (NKCDC), which was helping people fix up lots just like this one. The guy told Ed all about various groups in town that would be willing to help him

transform that lot into a park—if he was willing to go the distance. "If you need help sometime," the guy said, "give me a call."

"Well, the next week, he came back and cut those weeds down, and then you could see that it was a nice big place and there was a lot more work to do." Ed followed his gut and went to talk to a few of the man's friends at NKCDC, who were connected with PHS's Philadelphia Green program. "They said they could help me out, but they wanted me to get the neighbors together and see what they said. . . . Well, I didn't know my neighbors. I didn't know anybody. So I knocked on doors. I told them what I was doing and why I was doing it and how Philadelphia Green was involved and what we hope to do. So two years and many cups of lemonade later we developed the plan."

It was two more years before the first plant was put in the ground. In most of those early meetings, the neighbors spent time getting to know each other and sharing their ideas for the park. Everyone liked Michael's earlier idea—a playground for the children—but they couldn't see any way to pull it off. A park like that would need insurance, in case a kid got hurt. It would be expensive to install playground equipment, and the location was just too close to passing traffic. But everyone liked the idea of a garden. A place where they could all pass by, spend some time and enjoy nature— which was sorely needed on Belgrade Street.

Those endless meetings were tough for Ed, but he stuck it out and noticed a change in his behavior. "I spent twenty years in the Navy. I'm a military man. I expect things to be the way they're going to be. You make up your mind and that's that. But that wasn't the way it was. I had to find a whole new way of dealing with people. It really developed my leadership skills; you know what I'm saying? I had to learn to speak and relate to people."

In the end, a partnership was formed among the residents of Belgrade Street, Philadelphia Green, and a number of other local organizations. The big groups arranged for a backhoe to dislodge some old billboard pilings and stanchions that were virtually impossible to remove by hand. When all the old construction rubble—bricks, concrete, old timbers—was carefully picked away, one of Philadelphia Green's landscape designers came out to the scene, listened to the neighbors' ideas, and made some sketches. Then Philadelphia Green sent over a massive assortment of plantings. In a single weekend, the neighbors planted fifty-four roses and trees and more than 280 perennials. Overnight the Belgrade Street Park and Garden was born.

"It's nice, it's peaceful, it's pretty," says a local schoolteacher who brings her class out to the park whenever the weather's nice. "We come, we play, we bring our books and sit down and read and have a little picnic, and we don't have to go too far. It's wonderful to have a garden in a community, and if we can get even more space, we'll be even more appreciative for that because we'd like to start our own orchard."

There are always big plans surrounding the garden. Now the neighborhood is planning to create a dedicated area for a kids' garden. "Not necessarily peas and carrots and corn and stuff like that," says Ed. "I want them to know what a heliopsis is, how to mix the colors of plants, and things like that." The neighborhood has also started a garden club, which hopes to run a plant exchange program. People will bring in plants that they want to exchange for others. Or they'll buy plants that they want to see in this park and everyone will plant them.

The garden has transformed the way everyone relates to each other. "We have

Ed Elliss at Belgrade Street Park and Garden. Courtesy of Ed Elliss

block parties now," says Ed, "where we never had them before. We'll put chairs and tables out in the street and have music. We're able to deal with each other on a personal level. We're friends, in other words. I have a big backyard and people now use my backyard. I got a storage shed and people use my shed too. The kids in the neighborhood come around now too. The rule is, if you eat your peas, I'll take you to see the ducks. People even bring me stuff to feed the ducks. Or when they use up their aluminum cans, they throw them over my fence, and I take them in and get a few bucks, $8 or $15 a month, which I use to buy materials for the garden."

If you go out to Belgrade Street most days you'll find Ed. Mostly he's upbeat, but now and then his thoughts return to his son and the dream that galvanized a neighborhood. "Michael would've appreciated this park as much as he would a playground," Ed believes. "This park, what it's done for the community, I didn't realize it, but it's amazing. My daughter-in-law came to visit us yesterday and brought two of her friends. They just came from a bridal shower and a woman said, 'Oh what a beautiful park, and I'm getting married next summer. Can I get married in your park?' People come here graduation day. All the roses are in bloom about this time of the year. They stand out there and take pictures of their kids. We have people from companies down the street and they come up, throw a blanket down, and eat their lunch here in the park. They're

using it for everything nowadays. A woman, her brother passed away last summer. They set up chairs out here and had a memorial service for him in this park."

"If something's really bothering me," Ed says, "I come out here and pitter around the garden a little bit, or clean it up or rip the bushes apart and put them in again and change it around. I don't let it get me down. You just keep fighting on. Well, you have to if you want to live. We all have our trials and tribulations. We all get up and go and make each day better than the day before. That's the way we do it."

CITY OF MURALS

She calls herself a wall hunter. Most days you find her prowling the city in her car, looking for vacant lots and the huge, graffiti-spattered brick walls that come with them. Jane Golden is the director of Philadelphia's Mural Arts Program, a fascinating organization whose members are determined to rescue the old, ugly, beat-up spaces between buildings and use them to make stunning visual art.

Earlier, you heard about what the city's doing to rid itself of dilapidated buildings. Sometimes NTI comes in and marks a building for the wrecking ball. If the land is taken over by a community group for a garden—or even if it is not—there's always that adjacent two- or three- or four-story brick wall to contend with. What do you do

Jane Golden, director of Philadelphia's Mural Arts Program.

with it? Since 1984, Philadelphia has dealt with those extraneous bits of architecture in an innovative manner.

Enter Golden, who works out of a studio space in the artsy part of town, Northern Liberties. "We're a program that's dedicated to bringing art to every citizen in this city," she says. "I think it's special because this is art as a part of city government. I think it's special because people who wouldn't have access to art have access through this pro-

gram. I don't buy into the notion that art belongs solely on the walls of galleries and museums. I don't know who made that rule. Murals level the playing field of where art should and shouldn't be, and I think that's extraordinary."

Back in the 1980s, when Mayor Wilson Goode was elected, he made good on a campaign promise to reduce graffiti throughout the city. Taking a lesson from what had been

Vibrant colors and imaginative shapes have injected a much-needed dose of art into many Philapdelphia neighborhoods.
Courtesy of the Mural Arts Program

done in Los Angeles, he vowed to paint out bad graffiti and work with truly talented graffiti artists to see if they could come up with something more attractive than splashing one's name in gaudy letters on every blank wall in town.

Muralist Golden had lived in Los Angeles and was hired by Philadelphia to undertake this mission. At first she was skeptical of the city's motives. It sounded like all the city really wanted was a cleanup program and to rehabilitate graffiti artists by channeling their expression down another avenue. Golden wasn't about to do arts and crafts, and she took the work of the graffiti artists seriously.

"I'm a muralist," she says, "so I came with a mural bias, and I realized that these graffiti writers have extraordinary talent. They've been stealing magazine art, they've been sneaking into museums, they love abstract expressionism, and they love mural making. We have lots of skills in common. They are great wall hunters, they like painting large, and they don't mind working outside in the weather."

When she began working in partnership with neighborhood groups and community

Common Threads, mural by Meg Saligman at Broad Street and Spring Garden. Courtesy of the Mural Arts Program

Through the Cracks in the Pavement, mural by Paul Santa.
Courtesy of the Mural Arts Program

Metamorphosis, mural by Josh Sarantitis on Ridge Avenue.
Courtesy of the Mural Arts Program

organizations, suddenly her modest program took off. "It was wonderful to see our organization going from one tiny mural to suddenly two-story to three-story murals. It was like a renaissance happening throughout Philadelphia."

Much of this chapter—indeed this book—has been about building and greening. We've seen how incredibly those things shape and change a city, but the way Golden saw it, art had a bigger role to play.

"You can rehabilitate housing and you can enforce laws and fix potholes," she says. "All those things are important and they sort of make a city go. But the heart of community revitalization is in our ability to touch people's hearts and souls, and I think that art can do that. Art has a profound impact on people. So when you talk about neighborhood and community rejuvenation, I don't know how you leave art out of that equation. If you don't have beauty, then I wonder where you are, because I think that we all, at the end of the day, have an intuitive desire and need to have beauty in our lives, to create meaning, to say, 'We are here!' And murals do that."

The mural at Aspen Farm. Courtesy of the Mural Arts Program

Many times, Golden will be riding along in a friend's car and suddenly yell for him or her to pull over. "I'm a wall hunter, you know; I notice great blank walls," she says. "People are like, 'Why?' And I would say, "Look at that wall!'"

Walls are an obsession for Golden. She tries to fight the urge to line up another project because, frankly, she has way too many as it is. At this printing, the office had a waiting list of a thousand people who want murals. A thousand citizens in the city who want art in their lives.

At the beginning, when the program was young, no one knew about it and things were a little looser. You want a mural? Fine, someone will design and paint one for you. No problem. Today, things have become more formal.

"We have this waiting list," she says, "we have mural *applications*. People fill in an application and twice a year we put together a panel and we'll review these applications. They're moving, they're poignant, and today, when there's such an emphasis on technology, the media, it's sort of interesting to me that people take this time to write essays about why they want art in their lives.

Color mosaics and murals enliven the Village for the Arts and Humanities, a community arts center.

There's something very intimate and wonderful about it, and when you read these applications you just want to do murals for everyone, but you can't. So you challenge people to make a really good case about why we should come and create art in their neighborhood."

But that's only one way Philadelphians land a mural. The second way is tied to an after-school or summer program that the mural project runs. At last count, the after-school program was attracting 1,100 kids who don't receive art education in their daily class schedule but would commit to weeks of instruction outside school.

"I think if we're serious about reaching kids who've fallen through the cracks," says Golden, "then we need to think outside the box, and this is one way of reaching them, because for many kids this is how they articulate themselves, through art."

Besides schoolkids, the program reaches out to prisons, detention centers, and shelters. Through all these programs, they manage to paint 120 to 130 indoor and outdoor murals a year. No other mural program in the country or the world accomplishes that much. Since the program started, more than 2,500 murals have sprung up on Philadelphia walls, and they are amazing examples of creative minds at work. Gone are the one-dimensional images most often

Tribute to Grover Washington, mural by Peter Pagast on **Broad Street.** Courtesy of the Mural Arts Program

Safe and Sound, mural by Roldan West on Susquehanna Avenue. Courtesy of the Mural Arts Program

equated with outdoor art. Some of these are three-story masterpieces worthy of exhibition in the Philadelphia Museum of Art.

Somewhere in Golden's mind is a map of the entire city, warts and all, cataloged according to walls. She boasts sometimes that she knows all the walls in town, and yet she is always on the lookout for more. She won't take just any wall. She has her criteria. The wall has to be in good shape structurally. The roof can't be poorly drained, or it will ruin the artwork—and ultimately the building too. No, a good wall is one that pops up on a major road and cuts through several neighborhoods. A wall that many people see every single day. That's a good wall.

One day, she hops in her car and drives around with a visitor, explaining how the process works. If she likes a wall, she'll leave a note in a mail slot for the nearest resident. After a day like this, she is giddy and excited, especially if her program has been freshly funded and she has money to spread around town. "Half the people of Philadelphia wake up to a note from me saying, 'Hello, I love your wall. Please call our office and, with the city of Philadelphia, we can do something really beautiful here.' And you know what? People call back! It's so great when the system works. I'm like, 'Oh my god, they're calling!'"

"I don't say that what we do is a silver

bullet or a magic potion," she concedes. "I am saying that what we do shows us the powerful catalyst that art can be in healing the wounds of a city. When I came to Philadelphia it felt right to me. Twenty years later, I feel that this is not *just* the right city, it's a city where the dynamics are in place to create a renaissance, and there is a mural renaissance going on here. I believe it with every bone in my body. Now this is spreading throughout this country, and I think ultimately we want this world to be better. I think that healing the world is a common task. It belongs to all of us. For me, it's a privilege to do this work."

Her foot taps the brake. The car slows. She stops talking for a second. Her eyes are glued to a wall ahead. She pulls the car over and without a word she's leaping out and hurrying over to a man who seems to be digging a garden in a large lot.

"Hi, how are you?" says the Great Wall Hunter of Philadelphia. "I have a question. Do you know who owns this wall?"

SHE FELT THE FEAR AND DID IT ANYWAY

Lily Yeh is a painter, a scholar, an educator, a mystic, and a dreamer. She's a petite woman who speaks in the halting accent of one for whom English is a second language. Lily was born in Taiwan but calls Philadelphia her home. She came here nearly forty years ago to study art and never left. Inspired by traditional Chinese painting, Lily has spent her life and devoted her art to a single mission: creating enchanting places. To explain what she means, she sometimes tells stories, because just explaining often isn't enough.

Imagine, then, that you are looking at one of her paintings. Before you is an idealized scene of Chinese pastoral life, reminiscent of an old tapestry or a piece of fine china, and Lily is telling you a parable.

Once there was a fisherman who one day docks his boat and decides to wander along a hidden road. He passes impassable rocks and slips through dark places, and just when he thinks he has reached the end of the road, he stumbles upon a place full of cherry blossoms, healthy farm animals, and happy people

Lily Yeh founded the Village for the Arts and Humanities, a community arts center.

dressed in the garb of yesteryear. The fisherman is astonished. He asks the people how they came to be in such a wondrous place, and he learns that years ago, to escape warfare, they came to this remote place and never left. The fisherman is so entranced that he decides to stay a little while himself. But after a time he begins to miss his home and family. And so he heads home, but not before he marks the road, thinking, "I will tell everyone about this paradise." Of course, once he returns home he cannot find the road and must search for it all over again.

The story is a popular one in Chinese lore and one that Lily feels sums up her life's work. She accepted a challenge twenty years ago to create a park in the heart of desolate North Philadelphia and has been making art and building parks—and lives—ever since. "It is about the mundane," she says. "We live in the mundane and sometimes there are the sparks of inspiration and light, and we decide to explore. It's like coming to North Philadelphia and this abandoned lot and we explore it. In taking on the journey there are many roadblocks, but if we continue and follow the voice inside us, we are led to this paradise, to this very beautiful, pristine place, which is the park we built. But we cannot stay there forever, and we have to come back to the mundane and rediscover it through another journey. And that's what I think my work is like."

After completing her studies at the University of Pennsylvania, Lily got a job teaching at the University of the Arts. On the side, she continued to paint and exhibit her work. One day in 1986, Arthur Hall, founder of the Black Foundation Center, asked her to create a small garden in the abandoned lot behind the center's building. Lily had never done such a thing. She hesitated. Deep down, she feared that she was out of her element. She was a trained painter. She knew nothing about gardening, knew nothing about carpentry, and possessed no outdoor skills whatsoever. To make matters worse, when she approached her artist friends and others who had actually built gardens, they did everything they could to dissuade her.

"People said, 'Kids will destroy everything you do.' 'You're Chinese and this is an African-American neighborhood.' And then the city leveled ten houses next to the lot and the project got bigger. I had a little bit of money, but suddenly it became a huge lot. Everyone I knew said, 'You must not do that.' And I said, 'Well, you know, the experts must be right.' As I was deciding to withdraw I remember distinctly the voice in me said, 'You must rise to the occasion, otherwise the best of you will die and then the rest will not amount to anything.' I think that was very powerful because I didn't want to look at myself and see a coward in the mirror down the line."

She went out to the lot one day and thought, man, this is a mess. It's chaotic and disorienting. How can I do this? She had no background in designing spaces, but she had

Yeh relies on volunteers whose community pride and neighborly relationships are often strengthened by working together.

one great insight: "To transform a chaotic space into a place of order we need a center and we need a boundary. And so I picked up a stick from the ground, I drew a center in the middle of the park, and I said this is where we're going to start building. When I look back, that center, the physical center, it's a reflection of my own inner center and that's where the energy, inspiration, and the light guided me through the whole path, I think."

She used her small budget to buy cement and shovels and began by working with a local man, JoJo, who helped her build many of the structures in the lot. Local kids would wander by after school to see what they were doing, and little by little, the kids began helping. She contacted Philadelphia Green, who supplied trees and soil and worked with the children to teach them about gardening. That inspired Lily to run a simple art program for children. But in a few months, the park was done, and Lily prepared to head back to her teaching job, to the world she knew best, the one she had prepared for all these years. She would go back to painting, writing reports, trying to land a show at galleries or museums.

Back at school, she wandered the halls feeling haunted. It was a feeling she could never explain to her colleagues. "That was a calling," she says. "I didn't know what it was, but I said 'No, I'm not ready,' because I knew if I responded to it, it would be my life and would be all consuming."

"I couldn't shake off the images," she says. "Something gripped me. Then I realized that I needed to go back and understand what caused me to do that. And so I went back, and it's been eighteen years since. I really feel my life unfolded with the doing of the project."

Her experience with the lot led to the formation of the Village for the Arts and Humanities, a community arts center that Lily founded. Children and adults come here to learn about different types of art. Like the center point she drew in the dirt of that very first lot, the Village has become the center of an entire community. People who feel the system has forgotten them, people who have never been encouraged to express themselves before, now have a place to go and an enthusiastic teacher in Lily. From that unusual place, they can take what they have learned out into the surrounding neighborhoods, creating park after park.

If you can pinpoint any one "style" in the Village's creations, it would have to be its colorful mosaic sculptures. "At the very beginning we wanted to buy trees," Lily recalls, "but we didn't have money to buy trees so we built cement trees. And then we painted them and we eventually mosaicked them."

One day, she takes some friends out to see her work. One by one, they wander through the neighborhood, visiting the new parks, checking out the sculptures. Lily drops the names of her neighbors into conversation easily, along with their accomplishments. "Those were done by children with me from three-and-a-half to thirteen years old, and they're still here. The benches went through different stages, we have to repair them, but they are so important because they are the beginning. See the benches there? Those were done with recycled materials. We saw some metal frames in a dump truck. So I pulled them all out and then we put them together, we put lath wire and then cement, and Big Man [*the neighborhood's nickname for Village volunteer James Maxton*] and the children constructed this. Big Man never did any artwork before, but he became a master mosaic artist." (Mr. Maxton passed away in 2004.)

In another park, they come across Lover's Lane, so named because the row of trees looks so romantic. After the Flower Show one year, the Pennsylvania Horticultural Society donated small trees. Local residents diligently watered them, even in the hottest of summers, and now they are gigantic. Another park features a mural of beautiful angels

A wall flower painting at the Village for the Arts and Humanities.

standing atop columns. This is a memorial to the sixty-four local graduates of Edison High School who later died in the Vietnam War—the highest number of that war's casualties from any one public school in the nation.

"When we build a park," Lily explains, "I have a concept, I have a basic design, but what I try to do is get as many people from the community as involved as possible, especially our young people. Our parks are all open. The way we protect them is by engaging people directly in building the park and transforming their land."

Leon Saunders, a local resident, stops his work long enough to explain how he got involved. "I started with Lily when we did our first wall over here, the big rainbow. I was one of the artists. I painted whatever Lily wanted to be painted, and it came out beautiful. It was my first mural. When I was doing the mural with Lily I had some problems. I wasn't working. I mean my life was going downhill. Now, whenever I can I come down here and I help out. I'm just here for the community, this is where I came from."

After all these years, no one has defaced the mural in the slightest. "I think people respect beauty," Lily says. "Beauty has a lot of power and energy. Also, when it's painted with quality, it means 'This place is occupied.' People respect that."

One park features a mural of a magical kingdom, where dragons fly across the sky. Another features sculptures of creatures Lily calls the Guardian Birds, whose wings envelop and protect the neighborhood. In another space, a group of stone lions stands sentinel over the street. The stone lions came from China, but once the artists got hold of them, they were retrofitted with more colorful mosaic chips. Another sculpture, of a woman with outstretched hands, gets Lily giggling. She runs over and spread her arms in front of it.

"This is me," she proclaims.

The pose and place of honor seems appropriate. Clearly, she has found a home here among the residents of North Philadelphia that will last forever. "Philadelphia is where I lived my adult life, so it's very dear to my heart. I spent forty-seven years here, more years than I have in any other place. Philadelphia's the place I call home."

Art, she says, is about understanding what matters to you. For Lily, the Village became a special place where she found like-minded people and an environment in which she could thrive and grow. At first she feared it, but like a lot of the people in this book, that fear was a pivotal moment, a time of reckoning.

PHILLY EATS WHAT PHILLY GROWS

Philadelphia is also home to thousands of "farmers" who would rather plant a tomato plant or a handful of carrot seeds than a flower or a tree. Most do this as a hobby, but for others it's a living, and a tough one at that. Farming is hard enough in the countryside, where you have open space, fresh air, and the camaraderie of fellow farmers. Imagine trying to farm in the soil of row-house Philadelphia, where you stand out like a sore green thumb and everyone thinks you're nuts.

That's pretty much Mary Seton Corboy's life. On St. Patrick's Day, 1997, she started working a sizable plot of land in the Philadelphia neighborhood of Kensington that was formerly the site of a galvanized steel plant. Mary doesn't pull any punches. When she talks about that period in Philly's history, she looks like she's about to pick a fight.

"At one point in American history, industry was the salvation of this neighborhood," she says. "Nobody saw the long-term downside of industry. All they saw was that it gave them jobs and put bread and butter and beer on their table, but the long-term effect of it was the complete decimation of this neighborhood. I mean utter decimation of this neighborhood. The captains of industry are long gone, and the grandchildren of the people who built the captains of industry are still living here and are still struggling."

The land here was so badly contaminated that it qualified for federal "superfund" money to clean it up. Ordinarily, you would not grow conventional crops in land like this, even now. But Mary did not want to run a conventional farm. She thought she could grow crops hydroponically, in specially formulated water, where the roots of the plants could suck up their nutrition without the need for soil.

It's been tough. Very tough. Ask Mary if her farm is an Eden, lost and found, and she quips, "It remains to be seen if I'm Eve."

"I didn't come up with the idea of farming on a brownfield," she says. "I recognized early on that the land that was available wasn't going to be everything that I hoped it would be, so I spent some time working on developing a hydroponic system that I thought would really work in the city. Why an urban farm? I live in the city and I didn't want to live in New Jersey, in a rural area. I wanted to live in a city and I wanted to

Mary Seton Corboy founded Greensgrow, an organic farm on the former site of a galvanized steel plant that utilizes hydroponic technology, which is not as dependent on soil as traditional farming.

The site of Greensgrow Farm before and after Mary Seton Corboy transformed it into a highly successful urban farm. Courtesy of Greensgrow Farms

pursue a green business, producing food for restaurants. At one point I had been a chef and so I knew that restaurants, even in the middle of the Pennsylvania growing season, weren't getting Pennsylvania produce, so one thing led to another."

It's one of the weird things about our supercharged industrial society: the food we eat has been shipped, trucked, or flown in from another part of the nation or globe before reaching our plate. Most of us can accept this in the depths of winter. If you want to eat a tomato in December, you must make peace with the fact that the little round orb either came out of a hothouse or was flown in from a warmer climate, be it Florida, California, or South America. But why is it that we're still eating that hothouse tomato in July, when all of the United States should be able to produce their own? Why, when apples are being freshly picked in the orchards around Philadelphia, are local supermarkets stocking Granny Smiths flown in from Washington State? Probably because it's still weirdly cheaper and more efficient than buying local.

The organic foods movement has sought to correct this strange economy by emphasizing locally grown produce. "Buying food from local farmers has a huge impact on the region," explains Judy Wicks, a restaurateur and activist who runs the now-famous White Dog Café, a remarkable eatery found on Sansom Street in West Philadelphia that serves up music, ideas, and a dash of politics with its delicious fare. "First of all, it supports the small family farms that have been going out of business at a frightening rate and selling out to developers. So by making small farmers

> The White Dog Café is the first business in Pennsylvania to have 100 percent of its electricity come from windmills.

economically viable we're saving farmland from developers and keeping the family on the farm."

When Mary first started Greensgrow, she thought the local residents would just quietly accept her, although she expected they might think that what she was attempting would seem outrageous. What she didn't count on was how quickly she would become attached to the community.

"When I started, it was just about growing lettuce and selling it to restaurants in Center City. When you work outdoors like I do, you see the world of Kensington pass you by every single day. A lot of people still walk here. They walk to the store, they walk to visit each other, they sit on their stoops, they hang out of their windows, and so you hear this whole life that's going on around you. Quite honestly, it wasn't a life that I was familiar with."

Over time, Mary stopped growing exclusively for restaurants and starting growing for her farm stand, selling her food and plants directly to her neighbors. Along the way, she was able to explain to people about the importance of eating local, about organic food in their diets, and ultimately, why she has chosen such a difficult way of making a living.

"I would like to think that we're an important part of the neighborhood," she says. "Our goal is both to educate people about food and to provide access to the food—the highest-quality food for them. The same is true for our nursery in the spring. I think it's important that people, particularly in this kind of cement environment, have access to beautiful living things. So we pride ourselves on the fact that we provide really high-quality locally grown plants."

Mary now has a great deal of affection for her adopted city. "I say it's a city that loves you back but hates itself. I'm not a native Philadelphian. I moved here, and so most of my friends are people who moved here. I think that we, as a group, are much more optimistic about Philadelphia than native

Greensgrow Farm, which originally supplied produce strictly to restaurants, is now open to a grateful public and offers customers a firsthand experience of organic farming. Courtesy of Greensgrow Farms

Greensgrow Farm tomatoes ripening on the vine. Courtesy of Greensgrow Farms

Philadelphians. Maybe that's the case everywhere. I'm from Washington DC, which has certainly had its problems, but they were different problems. There was no industry there, so DC didn't lose manufacturing jobs and there was none of this decimation of neighborhoods. But Philadelphia has all of the resources to be a really great city. It has still the buoyancy and the elasticity to come back. If you can play some role, however miniscule, in making it be all that it can be, then you've done your job."

Some days, though, Mary is not even sure whether she'll be able to live up to that promise. "If I had had any indication at all of how hard it was going to be," she says, "the truth is I wouldn't have gotten started. It's interesting: People say you're a pioneer. *Now* you're a pioneer, initially you're just a nut case. I don't think that I was really cut out to be a pioneer. After a couple of years when things didn't always go exactly the way I wanted, I really could have just dug my heels in at that point. Now, it's pure obstinance that keeps me here. It has nothing to do with optimism or belief or anything else. I'm just determined I'm going to beat this thing. I don't care what it takes."

AN IRIS BLOOMS IN NORRIS SQUARE

"He who plants a tree plants a hope."
—LUCY LARCOM

William Penn cast an eye on the Norris Square area of Philadelphia and fell in love. Back then, trees sprouted from the earth as far as one could see. "The land is good," Penn wrote of the place, "the springs plentiful, provision easy to come at."

Two decades ago, the Norris Square area would have broken his heart. Syringes littered the ground, drug dealers had the run of the place, and gunfire was as common as TV violence. City fathers seemed to have given up on Norris Square. Like much of the greater Kensington area, it was filled with derelict factories and warehouses, dilapidated homes, trash, traffic, and poorly lit vacant lots.

Among the largely Latino population were numerous residents who wanted to take a stand to reverse the area's decline. They formed an organization called the Norris Square Neighborhood Project and began doing simple things to help stabilize the neighborhood. Many of the volunteers were women, mothers who didn't want to lose their children to the violence that was encircling them. One of them was a Puerto Rican woman named Iris Brown, who, among other things, liked to garden and cook.

When she came here from New York, Brown says, "this neighborhood was paradise. It was beautiful, beautiful. There were a lot of old ladies, senior citizens from Germany

Building a Rain Garden

The opening up of so much new vacant land within Philadelphia's city limits is allowing the city's Water Department to use those parcels to capture precious rainwater. In nature, the soft, permeable ground under trees acts like a giant sponge, capturing and holding vast quantities of rain. In cities and even suburban backyards, pockets of absorbent soil are hard to come by. One of the easiest ways to remedy this is to build a rain garden. A number of schools, city facilities, recreation centers, public rights of way, and redevelopment projects throughout Philadelphia already have one. At the Penn Alexander School in Philadelphia, workers created one by excavating a forty-foot-deep hole, filling it with gravel, and planting water-loving plants on top. Rooftop drains feed into the gravel pit.

Your backyard rain garden doesn't have to be that labor-intensive. Start by studying the way water drains off your property. Do you have rainspouts leading down from your roof? Spots where the spouts discharge might be a good spot for a rain garden, provided they are thirty feet away from your foundation. Also, look at how your yard is sloped. Are there natural depressions that typically remain moist after a rain? This is also a perfect spot for a rain garden. Improve drainage in these areas by excavating a trench or square-shaped hole a few inches or even a few feet deep. Fill the hole with a layer of gravel, and top it with a portion of the excavated soil mixed with fast-draining materials such as compost, sand, or peat moss. On top of the filled hole, plant a selection of moisture-loving plants. A good nursery can help you select plants appropriate to your climate and hardiness zone.

Norris Square Park during renovation.

and other European countries. And you would see the ladies just going to church and going to bingo games and sitting down in the park. No trash whatsoever, no crime. I'm talking about thirty years ago. Later on, the ladies started moving out because they were very old. They were dying. Their families were taking them to senior centers or retirement homes, and other people started moving in. The neighborhood changed, and later on is

when we started having problems. Little by little. It took us by surprise, but the neighborhood was totally infected by drugs. Then that was our situation, that was our nightmare."

At first, Brown didn't do much to help the neighborhood. Her grasp of English was not good. She stuck to the job the neighborhood association had assigned her, cleaning up litter on vacant lots, which she enjoyed. Others met with police or boldly confronted drug dealers at the corners where they plied their trade. Brown couldn't bring herself to do that. "I am a chicken," she says frankly. She was not alone. At the time, drug sales and prostitution were openly carried out even in City Center, within sight of City Hall. The problems got so bad in all of Philadelphia that the police finally started cracking down.

In 1989, the local news reported that drug business was so brisk that area drug lords were actually bidding on and renting street corners from each other for as much as $30,000. The high price was justified by the fact that on a good day, a well-organized drug corner operation could rake in hundreds of thousands of dollars.

This story broke just as the Norris Square neighbors were preparing to ramp up their gardening efforts with a new partnership with Philadelphia Green. With Brown as garden coordinator, the group had submitted a proposal asking to be Philadelphia Green's first Latino Green Countrie Towne, and they were accepted. But res-

Iris Brown (left), who, with other neighbors, founded the Norris Square Neighborhood Project.

Murals like this one were commissioned for Norris Square Park.

idents decided that before they could go on gardening, they had to do something to shut down the drug trade. They knew they were stronger in numbers, so nine different neighborhood groups got together for weekly antidrug rallies. Working with agents from the federal Weed and Seed Program, they used the same approach as all inner-city "Take Back the Night" events: the more law-abiding citizens patrol the streets at night, the less drug dealers will want to be there. Most illegal activity takes place under the cover of darkness. Shine a light on the negative activity, and it will disperse. Many

antidrug vigils are ineffective because they're one-time events, but Norris Square residents were persistent and called the police whenever they spotted illegal activity. Little by little, the neighbors made it increasingly difficult for criminals to rule the streets.

One day, recalls Brown, police swept the neighborhood and arrested nearly sixty people, many longtime residents. Standing on the sidelines, Brown says, "I saw the suffering. We wanted the neighborhood to change, but then I saw the other hand. I saw the suffering of the mothers and the children and the wives of the people who had been arrested. Then those people were not in the community, so we were not winning."

This was the beginning of a marvelous transformation: the blossoming of Iris.

"I think what made me change from being a follower was I couldn't speak any English," she says today. "I didn't want to go to meetings because I didn't understand anything." Then, when she *did* begin to understand what others were saying, she had opinions but didn't know how to express them. This conflict—a yearning to speak up, to be heard—galvanized her. "After I learned a little bit of English, then I started speaking and nobody was making fun of me. It was like taking the lid off the can. And after you do that, it's like there's no stopping. Then I became a little bit *too* bold."

Bold doesn't quite get to the heart of Brown's courage.

In the summer of 1990, Brown and a group of her garden volunteers walked straight into enemy territory in the daytime. The 2200 block of North Palethorpe was known as a particularly bad drug street. Calmly, resolutely, Brown and her friends seized control of a vacant lot on the block and proceeded to paint a mural, plant fruit trees, and install a small swimming pool. They had brought their children along, and when other neighbors heard the kids' laughter, they showed up to help as well.

A few years later that land became a unique park called Las Parcelas, where park benches are painted bright island shades of yellow, blue, and pink. The walkways are covered with gravel. Herb gardens and ornamental grasses sway in the summer breeze. The focal point of the garden is a *casita* ("little house"), which is modeled on the traditional vernacular homes still found in Puerto Rico. La Casita, as it's known, is a kind of heritage learning center, where children born and raised in Philadelphia can learn a little about their Puerto Rican ancestry. (This program is directed by Grupos Motivos, a club Brown started that is aimed at preserving Puerto Rican culture.) On display inside are musical instruments, rare spices, work tools, and various arts and crafts. The place is run like a hands-on museum, where kids are allowed to smell, taste, and touch all they like. Outside, families maintain their own vegetable and flower gardens. At a small outdoor food stand, neighbors serve traditional foods on special occasions.

Norris Square Park itself, once part of Penn's Green Countrie Towne, has been so remodeled and restored that families are actually moving back to the "needle" park they once shunned. The park looks good as new, with new trees, a new playground, and a new pergola used often by residents of the nearby senior center.

One day, always-on-the-go Brown shows some friends one of the abandoned buildings the project is rehabbing. "This is going to be our restaurant, Bambalea Sea Ya," she says. "The name is Spanish, but it doesn't have

Much of the restoration work in the park was successfully carried out by volunteers.

any meaning. It's part of our African traditions. What we're going to do here is rescue all these recipes, dishes from Africa that are still in Puerto Rico, and teach and share them with people from the community and all the parts of the planet. We also want to have a little store, and we are inviting people from the community to come and bring their arts and crafts."

The restaurant, when it opens, will sponsor cooking classes and allow diners to go out back and actually pick the greens and vegetables for their salads. It will be a delicious tribute to three cultures, three different races that came together to create the Puerto Rican people: Spaniards, Africans, and Natives. "If you go to my basement, I have all these things there just waiting for these walls to be ready. African masks and pictures from Spain. It's going to be gorgeous."

In 2005, Iris was honored by the Yves Rocher Foundation in France with its first annual Terre de Femmes ("Women of the Earth") Award, presented to outstanding women from all over the world who make the world a greener place. Most people are astonished to learn that Brown, who slowly came to realize her natural capacity for leadership, helped transform fifty abandoned lots in Norris Square into six award-winning community gardens in eighteen years.

Back down the stoop, as they wander back to Las Parcelas, Brown pipes up, "I'm not going to lie to you and say that it's easy. It's hard work, it's a lot of challenges, and we have learned many, many lessons. Patience is one of them, and also learning to ask for help from the community. We have learned so many lessons and I think we could do it again. We encourage people to try to make their communities better because there is no choice. We are here to stay. Now other people are moving to our community."

This last, in fact, has had an unexpected side effect. "The only thing that we don't like is the taxes," she admits. "The taxes are going up and that means that the value of the properties is going up. But we have many, many politicians moving to the community. It's a good sign, and you see, we feel safe because we know everybody, everybody knows us. And we can walk freely in the community."

GAMBLE'S GAMBLE

"The time is always ripe to do right."
—Martin Luther King, Jr.

Philadelphia rocks—and in more ways than you know. Some of the greatest names in rock and roll got their start in Philadelphia. Frankie Avalon, Chubby Checker, and Patti LaBelle all hailed from the City of Brotherly Love. In recent years, the city has encouraged the flowering of rappers such as Jazzy Jeff and the Fresh Prince. The "Prince" is the famous actor Will Smith, who went on to star in a hit TV show and a string of Hollywood films. But when people talk about Philadelphia's born-and-bred sound, the Philly Sound, they can talk only about Kenny Gamble and Leon Huff, who shaped the sound of soul that characterized the music of the O'Jays, the Soul Survivors, the Intruders, Harold Melvin and the Blue Notes, Archie Bell, and the Drells.

One day a ruggedly handsome Kenny Gamble appears at the site of some houses in Philadelphia's south side. In the past twelve years Gamble has begun acquiring parcels of land here at a ferocious pace, announcing that his real estate development company, Universal, plans to rebuild the entire community and generate as many as two thousand new homes in his old neighborhood.

Today, Gamble is hanging out at the site of the former Martin Luther King projects on Twelfth and Catherine streets where a new city park—the first in decades—will be built. "This is the beginning of a brand new life for a community that was at one point almost devastated," he says. "The public housing that was here had been here for about forty years and it declined into such devastating conditions. We're creating a whole new neighborhood here that's going to give new life to this community."

Gamble's company will rent some of these new units, but the chief goal is to sell a good chunk of the units, since home ownership is the quickest way to make someone care about the community. "We believe that once people own their own homes, they have a lot more at stake and the community is guaranteed to be cared for because its citizens have a stake in the community. We have a homeowners institute at Universal, which along with Fannie Mae, a federally backed mortgage/insurance company, works to prepare people to own their own homes."

Real estate is not exactly the field you'd think a musician would get into. Gamble's aware of this, but he says that much of his early work was shaped by what he saw in the ghetto. "Many of my songs were written about the conditions of the communities. We used to write songs about the neighborhoods and how devastated the neighborhoods were. One thing led to another, and I believe that being involved in community development work and working along with the community is sort of like reliving my songs."

Musicians like Curtis Mayfield and James Brown all had messages in their songs, he points out. "What I'm doing now is a continuation of that. It's almost like making the music real by really being in the community to work and develop a better quality of life. In my view, you got to make every day count, you got to make everything you do count, not only for yourself, but for the future. The future of Philadelphia, the future of America, depends on all of those who are living right now."

Gamble has had a number of opportunities to live elsewhere, but he's always returned to Philadelphia. "At one time the music business wanted us to move to Los Angeles, but the one thing you have to remember is that our music was called the Sound of Philadelphia. Well, you can't have the Philadelphia Sound in Los Angeles or in New York. The Philadelphia Sound experience is the life and times of Philadelphia, and how radio and street life and all of that combined together. That's what we wrote about. Life here in Philadelphia. Our perspective of the world from the Philadelphia view."

Musician Kenny Gamble's company, Universal, provides new housing in some of Philadelphia's neediest neighborhoods.

Universal Companies' Martin Luther King Jr. development under construction.

Working with the old community hasn't been easy for Gamble, whose ambitions have been criticized by area residents, who say his political connections have allowed him to take advantage of real estate opportunities not available to ordinary citizens. Gamble has tried to listen to the concerns of citizens.

Now, he points to an area behind him. "That, behind us, is a small recreation center that had a lot of meaning to the residents and the people who lived here because Martin Luther King spoke there. We were going to tear it down, but we decided to leave it there, and we're going to rehab it and rebuild it. This whole neighborhood here will be beautiful housing. We're working along with the school district, we're working along with many people, so we can improve the education in this area because that's really the crux of Universal Companies: making it better for everyone."

Universal is a private entity that has worked with Philadelphia Green to identify which spots in its holdings would be best for public green spaces. The new development Gamble's visiting today will also feature a new park, built by the company and designed in a partnership with Philadelphia

Green. "We're very proud to have partnerships like this," Gamble says.

"I love what I'm doing," he adds, smiling, "because it's one thing to think about doing something, but it's another thing to be able to do it. People, many times, ask me what I get out of it. And I say I really can't explain it, because it's a soul-satisfying feeling. When your soul is satisfied, when you actually feel that you are doing what you were born to do, that your life is really worthwhile, then life becomes something that's worth living."

FLOWER POWER

If you were a young architect, artist, or landscape designer, you could do a lot worse than to head to Philadelphia. Where else can you find such a vibrant, relatively inexpensive blank canvas waiting for your talents?

Joan Reilly, director of partnership development at Philadelphia Green, comes to each project with an activist's-eye view. In the 1960s and 1970s, she and her husband, Mike DiBerardinis, were among the early antiwar demonstrators in the Philadelphia-Camden area. The pair has steadfastly chosen to remain in their old Philadelphia neighborhood through thick and thin, believing that social justice was linked to

> Since 2000, Philadelphia Green has stabilized more than 3 million square feet of vacant land. That equals ninety-four football fields or sixty-nine acres.

their choice. If another family flees to the suburbs, it's as if you have turned your back on something you love. Human beings are fascinating creatures, and Reilly particularly enjoys what happens when a bunch of them gather in one place to work on a garden.

In the Carroll Park project, for instance, she says, "all of our lives got knitted together in a way that changes everything for you. We come together to transform the land, but ultimately it's about the people and the way we live our lives together. The park gets transformed, the neighbors get transformed, and the neighborhood gets transformed."

Blaine Bonham, PHS's executive vice president, says the organization has looked at studies from the University of Illinois that document the decrease in violence around public housing where green landscapes thrive. If young people are invited to participate in the design and planting of an area, they will grow up learning to respect that area, because they know just how much work went into it.

Beyond this, there might be some powerful natural allure that tempers our hearts when we're around green things. Bonham, who grew up in the Philadelphia area, remembers the joy he felt as a kid visiting his grandmother in her garden. "One of the fascinating aspects of horticulture is its ability to affect how people feel about themselves, and it's one of the reasons I've been involved in this work for so long," he admits. "It feeds the soul, it feeds the personal soul, and it also feeds the soul of a community. It can

Joan Reilly, director of partnership development at Philadelphia Green, and executive vice president Blaine Bonham.

feed the soul of an entire city. It still gives me a thrill to talk to people who've been involved in a new project—of planting a new garden and planting trees, in changing a vacant lot to a green space—to see how excited and interested they are in how they've been able to come together with their neighbors to effect the change. You can hear it in their voices, you can see it on their faces: they become zealots overnight."

At the beginning, no one at Philadelphia Green wanted or expected more than the renewal of their beloved city. The idea that sustainability could be achieved in the mainstream was a far-off dream. Today, when all city planners are trying to figure out ways to manage water and air quality, the work of Philadelphia Green now appears in hindsight to be remarkably prescient.

William Penn, that canny old Quaker, was right after all: green spaces are better and healthier for cities.

The Pennsylvania Horticultural Society operates the largest comprehensive urban greening program in the nation. These kids are doing their part with plantings they picked up at the Willard Street plant sale. Courtesy of the Pennsylvania Horticultural Society

The Colorado Street Bridge in Pasadena. Photo by Photo-Dave, ShutterStock

LOS ANGELES

Dream a Different City

"They call Los Angeles the City of Angels. I didn't find it to be that, exactly, but I'll allow as there are some nice folks there."
— *The Big Lebowski*,
JOEL AND ETHAN COEN, 1998

The first Europeans who beheld the future site of the City of Angels were entranced by the land's natural beauty. Father Junipero Serra and Captain Gaspar de Portola, both Spaniards, led an expedition north out of San Diego in search of good spots to build future settlements. The year was 1769, and Father Juan Crespi, the expedition's diarist, took pains to describe what he saw. His were the first words ever recorded about this part of the American continent:

> We set out from the valley in the morning and followed the same plain in the westerly direction. After traveling about a league and a half through a pass between low hills, we entered a very spacious valley, well grown with cottonwoods and alders, among which ran a beautiful river from the north-northwest, and then doubling the point of a steep hill, it went on aftwards to the south. . . . This plain where the river runs is very extensive. It has good land for planting all kinds of grain and

The Los Angeles River near Sepulveda Basin today.

seeds and is the most suitable site of all that we have seen for a mission, for it has all the requisites for a large settlement.

After crossing the river, the expedition found fields of wild grapes and roses. "All the soil is black and loamy," wrote Crespi, "and is capable of producing every kind of grain and fruit that may be planted. We went west, continually over good land well covered with grass."

Crespi named the river El Rio de Nuestra Senora la Reina de Los Angeles de Porciuncula, which means "The River of Our Lady the Queen of the Angels of the Little Parcel of Land."

The name was a mouthful, but in any culture, the land Crespi described would have been regarded as a utopia. Twelve years later, another party set out to build a pueblo nearby. The pueblo, which took its name from the river, was the beginning of the city we know today as Los Angeles.

No city possesses a more seductive allure than the City of Angels. Los Angeles signifies the conquering of the American West, the completion of the mad rush to settle the American continent. All those wagon trains, all those cattle driven west, the hopes and dreams of the pioneers—it all culminated in this, the brash, bold capital of the West

In the early 1900s, the Los Angeles River provided recreation for residents and visitors alike. Today, a concrete basin encases the entire fifty-one-mile length of the river. Courtesy of La Historia Society Museum

Coast. Los Angeles is the city of flawless weather, of sun and palm trees. It's also the city of dreams, where thousands flock each year in the hope of becoming stars. Like it or not, Hollywood is the nation's great publicist, broadcasting to all the world what it means to live an American life.

Indeed, Los Angeles is one of the most storied, mythical, and wondrously modern of American cities. Along with the dream of fame and wealth that draws people to it, Los Angeles lends itself to the American dream—a house, a car, and boundless energy, culture, and sunshine. The young, growing America of the twentieth century believed that its future lay not in cities but in the suburbs. Los Angeles seemed to have it all: pristine detached homes and wide open spaces as far as the eye could see. What could be more perfect than this paradise by the sea? And yet—something has gone terribly awry.

In discussing the demise of Los Angeles's natural beauty and suburban promise, focusing on one problem inevitably draws attention to another and another and yet

The combination of deforestation and dependence on automobiles have contributed to Los Angeles's infamously poor air quality. Photo by Ricardo Aguero

another. A dialogue on suburban sprawl leads inevitably to the region's overdependence on automobiles, lack of decent public transportation, horrendous traffic, and deterioration of air quality. As we'll see, it's impossible to divorce the issue of strained water resources from the endless cycle of drought and flood, and so on. On its own, each of these is a massive issue. Fused together, they become unmanageable. No wonder they persist. Their very complexity seems to resist analysis and resolution.

Once upon a time, El Rio de Los Angeles—the very river that inspired the city's birth—had tree-lined banks and a soft dirt bottom. In the early days of the past century, kids swam in its cool, sandy waters. But today virtually every inch of the fifty-one-mile river is encased in concrete, the natural river transformed by well-meaning engineers into a kind of vast man-made culvert.

Now, the river excels at ushering rainwater out of town as quickly as possible to prevent flooding. But the greater Los Angeles area desperately needs that water for drinking. As its population grows, fresh water is becoming harder and harder to find.

The interconnectedness of Los Angeles's problems only reinforces how elegantly nature solves so many problems. If the river weren't "channelized," as engineers describe it, much of that water would seep into the ground and replenish the parched aquifers under the surface. Los Angeles would then be better able to meet its own water needs without having to buy river water from other states. It is a painful irony that the "delightful" river that first enchanted Los Angeles's founders has today been so altered, so hidden, and so violated that most Los Angelenos understandably would not be able to identify it.

If there is one theme to the story of Los Angeles, it is this: the human subversion of nature always causes bigger problems down the line. If you build a housing development far from a shopping area with no sidewalks, people will be forced to drive. If you build many subdivisions along this model, more and more cars will end up on the road, and eventually everyone will complain of traffic, smog, poor air quality, and more precious time wasted in traffic snarls. Each planning disaster begets the next.

"Los Angeles is the most enigmatic human environment ever created," says architect Dan Rosenfeld, whose company, Urban

A view of downtown Los Angeles over a garden along Freeway 405. Photo by Rodolfo Arpia, ShutterStock

Partners, is leading a movement toward more sustainable development in the city's center. "Some places are poor and barely scraping by. But here we are, in a beautiful natural environment with fifty miles of beaches and more human talent than anywhere else on Earth and a very accommodating environment. Yet everything here is disorganized and inefficient: the roads, the schools, the parks. There seems to be an almost psychological resentment against natural pleasantness that's at the heart of Los Angeles."

How can we reverse that trend, and why should we? There are many in this country who take an unkind view of Los Angeles. The city has gotten what it deserves, they say. But this is shortsighted. Los Angeles, for all its faults, for all its problems, is truly emblematic of many places in America. What happens here will ultimately happen where the rest of us live. The U.S. population is growing, not shrinking. The small American city of one hundred thousand will be two or three hundred thousand in a few years. Cities of more than five hundred thousand will top one million and keep growing. We must be able to intelligently solve the problems that come with larger populations, and we must know how to do it in the sprawling suburban cities that have become the norm throughout the United States.

Luckily, there is new awareness afoot. The younger leaders of today's Los Angeles grew up harboring a sense of skepticism about the city's relentless sprawl, growth, and progress.

Cindy Montanez, who was elected to California's state assembly in 2002, has actively championed efforts to restore the natural environment of the region.

Some of them grew up loving the intimacy of the city's downtown and are working to make it more livable. Others are spearheading a remarkable number of grassroots initiatives to reverse poor planning and design, encourage responsible development, and harmonize the city with its natural surroundings once again. "I've lived my whole life in the northeastern part of the San Fernando Valley in communities like Sun Valley and Paquoima and San Fernando," says Cindy Montanez, the youngest woman ever to win a seat in California's state assembly. In 2002, at the age of twenty-eight, she was elected to the Thirty-ninth Assembly

District seat by voters in the nine communities in the San Fernando Valley. "These are communities that have historically been disproportionately impacted by landfills and other polluting industries, a lack of open space, and a lack of recreational space. I remember growing up in that area and we didn't have the beautiful parks and we didn't have the beautiful trees and we didn't have the beautiful coastline, but we did have beautiful people, and now we're going to go back and we're going to create those riverways, parks, and recreational fields. We're going to be able to ride horses or walk with our family and have a place just like anybody else does—a place where we can just go outside, enjoy the environment, enjoy the beauty of the trees and parks and the natural environment, and ultimately make home a better place where we want to stay."

The heroes of this chapter feel that they are playing for keeps with all the world's eyes upon them. "If we can't come up with a sustainable city with all the advantages and resources and money in Southern California, what hope do others have?" asks Paul Brown of CDM, an environmental engineering firm that consults with all the cities in this book. "If we can't do it, the world is doomed."

THE BIGGEST MISTAKES: GOODBYE WATER, GOODBYE TREES

"Los Angeles gives one the feeling of the future more strongly than any city I know of."

—Henry Miller

Before we can understand the challenges facing Los Angeles, we need to understand some of the choices the city's twentieth-century builders made—specifically how those early Angelenos treated the water and the trees.

Although Los Angeles's roots stretch back to 1769, most people still regard Los Angeles as a "young" American city. In our collective imaginations, the Los Angeles of yore didn't really start percolating until the birth of the film industry in the early twentieth century.

The reason for this disconnect is simple: Until 1848, California was still Mexican territory, and its vast lands were held by wealthy rancheros. Americans were still considered "immigrants" in this largely Spanish-speaking world. But that would soon change. The discovery of gold in 1848 sent legions of easterners to the West in search of their fortunes. California became a state in 1850, but the railroad—the most important link with "American" culture and technology—didn't arrive in Los Angeles until 1876, sparking the birth of the citrus-growing industry. Los Angeles was tied into the American "grid" for just

Early in the century, a plan to import water from the surrounding mountains turned an otherwise untenable city into a mecca for booming business enterprises of the 1930s, including the film industry.

one hundred years when the United States celebrated its bicentennial in 1976.

By 1900, Los Angeles's population had grown to one hundred thousand people, a huge number for the time. (In 1860, forty years earlier, the city boasted merely two thousand three hundred.) Many of the teeming throngs of newcomers had come on the advice of newspaper editor Horace Greeley, who spurred the settlement of the West Coast by famously exhorting, "Go west, young man!"

In 1900 Los Angeles was nothing more than a beautiful, up-and-coming place with inadequate water resources. The Los Angeles River—the reason the old pueblo had been built on this site—couldn't possibly supply the needs of the growing city. A young engineer named William Mulholland visited the verdant lands to the northeast, in Owens

Valley, and returned to his office at the water bureau with a hot idea: he would build an aqueduct to bring water from the mountains to the city, where it was needed.

Back then, this bold plan made a heck of a lot of sense. Owens Valley was a sparsely populated agricultural area and Los Angeles was growing rapidly. Mulholland's idea was hailed as a brilliant move, the work of a visionary. Today environmentalists and others often excoriate his work. (In fact, the 1974 movie *Chinatown* appropriated elements of this story and cast the whole plan in a sinister light.) Still, Mulholland's achievement was monumental. Less than a decade after his original idea, Los Angeles was importing water from the Owens River to the tune of twenty-six million gallons a day. The city's future was assured.

By 1930, the city had grown to two million people and was home to the film, oil, and aircraft industries. The employees of these booming businesses needed homes, and the city rapidly built more and more housing to meet the growing need. Concerned about how unchecked growth would affect the city's quality of life, the Los Angeles Chamber of Commerce hired the Olmsted Brothers and Bartholomew Associates, renowned architects, to create a master plan for the city. Their report, *Parks, Playgrounds, and Beaches*, was a masterful description of the city-as-Eden. The plan called for the creation of a powerful parks department that would buy up and designate large parcels of land along the Los Angeles River as parkland. The idea was smart, because during the winter, when

Southern California got its fair share of storms, the river often flooded. It had, in fact, killed nearly one hundred people in recent years. The Olmsteds and Bartholomew envisioned a massive fifty-mile park along the river that would act as a buffer or floodplain when the rains came. They sited parks throughout the city so that beautiful green vistas would tantalize the eye as citizens drove their cars out to the country or shore.

This grand vision for Los Angeles never came to pass. Word is, the Chamber of Commerce got nervous when they read the report, because the large parks department the Olmsted-Bartholomew plan called for would almost certainly wrest power away from the Chamber. Although the Chamber had spent $80,000 on the plan—nothing to sneeze at in 1930—they quashed the report. So few people ever heard of Los Angeles's master plan that today copies of the report are exceedingly rare documents and survive only in rare-books libraries.

It would be wrong, however, to say that Los Angeles grew without any plan at all. At every step, city and local governments made policy decisions—albeit sometimes at the behest of wealthy developers, campaign contributors, and well-paid lobbyists—that promoted the building of freeways, encouraged sprawling development, and favored cars over mass transit. Few would argue that those decisions were best for the city in the long run.

Poor planning affected the course of the Los Angeles River. Looking to create jobs during the Depression, the county enlisted the help of the U.S. Army Corps of Engineers, which swept in and encased the entire Los Angeles River in a concrete basin. The idea was well meaning: they wanted to make a basin high enough and deep enough so that the river would never, ever, ever, ever overflow its banks and kill people again. They wanted to make sure that any water that fell in Los Angeles would flow swiftly to the channel and be whisked out to sea.

Seventy-five years later, the results of this choice, and others equally misguided, are hard if not impossible to reverse. Today the "Los Angeles metro area," as defined by the U.S. Census Bureau, has grown to more than sixteen million people. The Owens River supplies more than 525 million gallons today, and it is still not enough. The region gets still more water from the Colorado River, two hundred miles east of the city, and other rivers closer to home. The Los Angeles River, where children once splashed and played in the safe season, is now a massive, two-story crevice in the earth whose sole job is *to get rid of freshwater*. How massive are

Original advocates for paving the basin of the Los Angeles River with concrete hoped to thus prevent flooding, an approach that we now know has far-reaching, unfavorable consequences on both water management and water supply. Courtesy of LAPL

Decorative palm trees, which line many of the city's shopping and business streets, are insufficient to significantly improve Los Angeles's air quality. Photo by Ricardo Aguero

these concrete basins? Fans of action films will recall Arnold Schwarzeneggar riding a motorcycle through one of the river's tributaries in the film *Terminator 2*. This is actually one of the *small* basins!

Elsewhere Los Angeles has become a city of asphalt and concrete, where the natural world has been completely encased, erased, or eradicated. While you can find small parcels of land or landscaping and Los Angeles's signature palm trees are everywhere you look, these green spaces and palm icons are not nearly enough to mitigate the city's heat island effect, smog, and flood events.

Parkland is limited; Los Angeles has 0.9 parkland acres per person, compared to a national average of 10 parkland acres per person. The other cities we look at in this book—Chicago, Seattle, and Philadelphia—all have more parks than Los Angeles. Even New York City, the classic example of a cramped, crowded metropolis, has more green space per person than Los Angeles.

Bizarrely, that was the plan. The dream of Los Angeles, indeed, the dream of California, countered models of eastern and midwestern industrial cities. At the very

beginning, Los Angeles's builders simply chose to imagine their city in a different way. Although Los Angeles is now one of the densest metropolitan regions in the country, due to densification of already developed central city areas and older suburbs, officials wanted a horizontal-looking city with low-density housing and ample surrounding space.

"Many of the older cities such as Chicago, Philadelphia, Boston, and New York City had an emphasis on urban design and making sure that there were large open spaces right around the most densely populated areas," says Jennifer Wolch, a geography professor at the University of Southern California and the director of the Center for Sustainable Cities. Wolch has helped design the Green Visions Plan, a joint venture between the University of Southern California and the region's land conservancies, including the Rivers and Mountains Conservancy, Santa Monica Mountains Conservancy, Coastal Conservancy, and Baldwin Hills Conservancy. The Green Visions Plan provides a blueprint for how the city can identify, rescue, and knit together vital pieces of open space to create a "living green matrix" for the Los Angeles metro area.

"Boston had its Emerald Necklace, and so on, and many smaller cities have ample parkland. Los Angeles grew up in an era in which people expected to have a backyard and a garden, and city officials and developers were disinclined to dedicate public open space, so

Jennifer Wolch played a key role in developing the Green Visions Plan, which advocates for creating more open spaces in Los Angeles.

not many areas were set aside for parks. Given rapid growth and increasing population density in Southern California, lack of parks and open space has become a severe problem."

This is one of the issues that concerns California's former state public health officer, pediatrician Richard J. Jackson. "Two-thirds of the kids in Los Angeles cannot walk to a park," he says. "If they don't have a place to walk or run around, we have no business telling our kids to get in shape. Three-quarters of the kids in California cannot pass a basic fitness test, which is running one mile in twelve minutes. These are ninth graders that can't run a mile. So we've allowed our kids to get out of shape. You want to give your children sequential challenges. Their sense of adulthood, their sense of who they are, comes out of the sequencing of various victories in their lives. And yet many of them cannot go out, they cannot get on a bus and go where they want to go. They cannot get on their bike and bicycle down to the church or the library or a store or anything else. They can't even walk home from school. Years ago, more than half of American kids walked or biked to school. Now, it's less than 7 percent of our kids. I think we're cheating our kids."

Now, to save the city and its children, a new generation of planners, designers, and builders must dream a different dream—not just in terms of bricks and mortar, but also by thinking long and hard about what humans truly want in their souls. Time and again, the answer to that question has been "To be around other people. To feel connected. To feel a sense of belonging."

Old-growth trees on residential streets are a visual oasis in a city known for its urban sprawl and pavement. Recent years have seen a massive increase in tree planting throughout the area. Photo by Ricardo Aguero

Dr. Peter Whybrow, the renowned UCLA psychiatrist and author of the book *American Mania: When More Is Not Enough*, sees Los Angeles as the ultimate bastion of individualism. "It's a migrant city in a migrant land," he says, "and all migrants are survivalists. They learn quickly how to get ahead in their chosen society. But human beings were not designed by nature to act alone. The human race became dominant by cooperating. You can't kill a woolly mammoth by yourself."

Now, after a century of rampant growth and individualism in Los Angeles, Whybrow says, "the pendulum is swinging in the other direction. People are realizing, 'I need a park. I need my neighbors. I need a place where I can be with my children and get to know those around me.'"

That is the heart of the new Los Angeles, and that is what this chapter is all about.

Growing a Green Vision

The Green Visions Plan is an excellent model for how communities can pull together green areas even if their city is already heavily developed. The long-term goals of the Green Visions Plan include the following:

- Protect and restore natural areas to ensure the growth of native biodiversity and reintroduction of historically accurate natural plant communities.

- Restore natural function to the hydrological cycle to maximize groundwater recharge, improve storm-water quality, and minimize flood hazards.

- Increase and ensure equitable access for residents to a range of open spaces and recreational opportunities, and thereby reduce socioeconomic and geographic disparities in present-day patterns of access to these types of resources.

- Maximize political and financial support for the Green Visions Plan by proposing multiple-use facilities wherever possible to meet the goals of habitat restoration and conservation, restoration of hydro-ecological function, and creation of more recreational open space.

To achieve these goals, the plan spells out the opportunities and constraints that could arise as projects related to habitat conservation and restoration, open space acquisition and recreation improvements, and protection of watersheds are proposed and implemented. The plan helps local agencies and organizations attract public funding or allocate their own resources, reduce the fragmented approach to regional resource planning, and promote projects that will ultimately be more successful because they are part of a larger, scientifically grounded vision.

THE MAGIC OF TREES

One of the buzzwords in city planning today is *urban forestry*. The phrase refers to the new national understanding that cities thrive best when they have a green infrastructure built into their grids. No one would find it surprising to hear the mayor of a city say, "We need to invest in our roads and bridges" or "We need to invest in our schools" or "We need to invest in our older and younger citizens." All these statements sound perfectly reasonable because everyone understands that a city depends upon people, schools, roads, and bridges to survive.

A green infrastructure is now being recognized as equally necessary and important. In previous chapters we've detailed how trees cool off cities, reduce energy usage in summers, and help purify air. In the Philadelphia chapter we learned that trees also reduce crime and elevate property values of entire neighborhoods.

In recent years, researchers have discovered other benefits of trees in urban landscapes. For example, they have discovered that people would rather shop in downtown areas where trees are present. That is, if given a choice, people are more likely to stop and browse downtown areas that seem wooded, shady, and inviting. For some reason, people prefer to eat and shop on tree-lined avenues. A city that understands this interesting human quirk can help create attractive downtown settings—and serve the public good—at the same time.

In addition to beautifying its surroundings, a single mature urban tree reduces the amount of carbon dioxide (CO_2) by about 115 pounds per year.

Another cool finding: Drivers tend to speed when tooling their cars down treeless streets. They tend to *slow down* when driving down tree-lined streets. There's an interesting theory about why this happens. On a treeless street, drivers have few landmarks to gauge how fast they are going. But a driver who zips past eight big trees in a minute quickly senses that he's going too fast. It may also be that drivers are instinctively more cautious when their visibility is reduced. Or perhaps tree-lined neighborhoods appear friendlier to the eye. Maybe drivers slow down because they want to drink in some of that atmosphere.

These are just a taste of the findings by psychologists working at the University of Washington and the University of Illinois. Taken alone, they are simply quaint findings that point to interesting features of human personality. But in seeing these findings coupled with everything else we know about trees in the urban setting, there's not a city manager alive who could resist encouraging more green space in cities. "It's not just about the trees," says Susan Mockenhaupt, an expert in urban forestry who works with the U.S. Forest Service. "If it's just about trees we will lose the battle in American cities."

Andy Lipkis planted his first tree in 1970, when he was fifteen years old, and discovered what would become his lifelong passion and professional work. Andy's organization, TreePeople, had planted more than 50,000 trees in the Los Angeles area by 1980.

TREES CAN SAVE LOS ANGELES— BUT ONLY IF WE LET THEM

"A city no worse than others, a city rich and vigorous and full of pride . . . "
—RAYMOND CHANDLER

Andy Lipkis has been thinking about the plight of trees—and the humans who depend upon them—for more than thirty-five years. When he was only fifteen years old and attending a summer camp in the San

Bernardino Mountains outside Los Angeles, a naturalist told the group of kids that the pine trees in the local forest were dying a slow death because of smog. The naturalist predicted that in twenty-five years the forest would be entirely gone. Andy and the other kids were horrified. Andy asked whether anything could be done to save the forest. The naturalist noted that native smog-tolerant trees could be planted in place of the dying trees, but that would take a superhuman effort. Thousands of these special trees would have to be planted by hand to offset the dying ones. Who could do such a thing?

Well, Andy. His efforts are a study in the power of persistence. At first he tried to interest local companies and banks in helping him, but to no avail. He almost gave up, but a few years later, when he was in college, he hit upon the idea of getting other summer-camp kids to help. The camps he approached were willing to help, but when Andy phoned the California Division of Forestry to order some baby trees he discovered that he had to pay for them. The amount wasn't much, only $600 for twenty thousand seedlings, but every business he approached for a donation said no. To make matters worse, the California Division of Forestry had a policy of plowing under and killing each crop of unsold seedlings at the end of the season to

TreePeople, at its inception and now, depends on the work of volunteers.
Photo courtesy of TreePeople

make room for a new batch. (They weren't set up to take care of older trees.)

The situation infuriated young Andy. Here he was, volunteering to reforest entire swaths of California's National Forest, and the state wouldn't give him the trees to do it! They wanted him to pay for them, and if he or no one else bought them by a certain date, they would discard all these trees.

Andy hit the phones. He called the offices of local newspapers, politicians, and famous actors who had taken a stand for the envi-ronment. The newspapers and one politician offered to look into the situation. No sooner did they phone the California Division of Forestry than the state announced it was willing to donate the trees to Andy, provided he could plant them. Andy knew he had the manpower—all those kids—but he would need more than $600 to pull off such a huge project. Each of those seedlings would need to be transplanted into milk cartons and

kept alive until they were transported to the proper site and planted. He'd need dirt, shovels, trucks—where would he get the money to do all that?

One of the local newspapers wrote an article about Andy's encounters with the California Division of Forestry. Andy had told the reporter that all he needed to plant one tree was fifty cents from a willing donor. This tiny, quite reasonable amount of money caught on with readers everywhere. After that, letters starting pouring in. Grade-school kids, teenagers, and senior citizens all sent him a few bucks out of their pockets. As the cash started flowing in, the publicity about the adventures of California's Tree Boy grew. When donations reached $10,000—more than enough money to get those trees in the ground—the executives of a few of the companies Andy had first approached now saw that he was a legitimate organizer and activist. They started writing checks themselves. Andy didn't know it then, but he was well on his way to a life of activism. His organization, TreePeople, was born, and before 1980 its members had planted more than fifty thousand trees.

"I heard about Andy in the early 1970s and started sending him some money," says noted actor and activist Ed Begley, Jr. "I didn't have a lot of money back then, but I sent him ten dollars, fifteen dollars when I had it, and twenty-five dollars when I had that. I very much liked what he was doing. Then in the late 1970s when I started to work more and became more successful, I sent a little more money. I met him at some function and thought, 'Wow, this guy's incredible. He's about my age and he's done this incredible thing. Look at the contribution he's made with his lifetime. He's planted so many trees, he's affected so many people, his work will continue.'"

Andy's story is told in the pages of a children's book called *Tree Boy*, published in 1978 when Andy was only twenty-four years old. Today he's an energetic fifty, with elfish good looks and boundless enthusiasm. TreePeople still plants trees, but its mission has matured greatly, along with the vision of its founder. Andy is one of the foremost environmental thinkers on the topic of green infrastructure as the pathway to urban sustainability. As we said earlier, it's not just about the trees.

"For some people, urban forestry is about managing trees," Andy says. "To me, it's both a real thing and a metaphor. A city like Los Angeles is two-thirds paved. That paving, the concrete, covers a living, functioning ecosystem. Because we paved over that ecosystem, we now have to pay a lot to recreate the benefits that would be free if the ground weren't encased in concrete. I'm talking about free things like water, like natural cooling, like flood prevention, like oxygen."

Los Angeles could meet half of its water needs if it could somehow capture and retain its rainfall each year. Instead, 85 percent of

Ed Begley, Jr.: He Walks the Walk

"You know, sometimes the word *sustainability* bothers me," confesses Ed Begley, Jr. "I'm not sure I want to have a sustainable marriage. I want something more exciting than that, but I accept the term and I use it a lot. You want something that will last for a long time, something that's not just a short-term gain or a quick fix."

Begley, the tall, blond actor known for his long-time role in TV's *St. Elsewhere*, not to mention quirky turns in movies such as *This Is Spinal Tap*, *Best in Show*, and *A Mighty Wind*, is arguably Hollywood's most visible environmentalist. He's usually spotted driving around town on his bicycle. At night he plugs in his electric car. He composts. He lives in a solar home. He plays a major role in the Santa Monica Mountains Conservancy. Today, much of what Begley stand for is accepted and applauded. But when he first started out, he says his strong beliefs were sometimes misinterpreted and got in the way of his career.

In the early 1990s, his agent and manager pulled him aside and told him that his views were costing him work. "People think you're a wing nut," he recalls being told. "People don't want to hear about electric cars or you riding your bike around. They just want you on the set on time. I don't think I was ever blackballed, but I know I gave people the creeps, because they just weren't sure about all this. 'What do you mean, live with less? We're a business about more. That's what this whole industry is based on: more, more.'"

He recalls shooting a film once that required him to drive a car down a driveway. His employers apologized profusely for having him drive a gasoline car. "I was legitimately confused," he recalls. "They said, 'We know you won't drive a gasoline car.' People thought I was so strict that I would make their job difficult on the set, which wasn't the case."

These days, it's totally different. "I go on a set now and people are better at recycling than I am," he laughs. "They have all sorts of bins set up and they're way ahead of me, they don't need any help from me to do the right thing environmentally."

His advice to anyone who wants to make a difference is tinged with pragmatism. "I always stress that people pick the low-hanging fruit first," he says. "That's what I did. I couldn't afford solar way back when. I bought energy-efficient light bulbs. I got a smart thermostat. I put good insulation in my home. I got a home garden so I could grow a lot of cheap food with compost that I made myself. All these things I did are very cost-effective. Taking public transportation, riding my bike to and from work, it was good exercise. I didn't have to pay for a gym because the world was my gym. And all this stuff that I did was so good for the environment, but it was also good for my pocketbook. It's not like I have a vast amount of money now. I'm not a millionaire, I never have been a millionaire, but I don't need a lot of money because of the decisions I made many years ago. All this stuff was good for the environment, but it was also good for my pocketbook."

Photo by Sebastian Artz, Getty Images

Volunteers are taught not only how to plant trees but also how to care for them—something most residents who've personally helped re-green their neighborhood are motivated and eager to do. Photo courtesy of TreePeople

that water slips out of the city's grasp, washed out to sea and never seen again. "Because we don't save that water," Andy says, "we have to buy water that falls in Salt Lake City. It's the height of absurdity."

"California is the sixth largest economy on the planet," he says. "So the implications are enormous. In Southern California we've got 1.2 cars for every person, which means this urban region is one of the largest sources of global warming in the world. It seems that good people who want to do

good are unwittingly having a huge effect on the environment. Did you know, for instance, that half the water used in Los Angeles is for irrigation [*watering plants, lawns, et cetera*], not drinking or cleaning or showering? And 40 percent of our waste stream, the trash we throw out and pay to haul to landfills, is green waste—grass clippings, tree branches, leaves—that would do us all more good being mulched and spread around our plants instead."

Green waste has the potential to mitigate, prevent, or lessen flood conditions. In the forest, green waste isn't waste at all. It is the essential factory of nutrients, soil, and habitat and acts as a giant sponge lying on the floor of the woods, absorbing and cleaning water. But if you remove from your property everything you cut, rainwater rushes off your property. If citizens mulched all that waste instead, their city would save all that money driving big trucks around neighborhoods picking up clippings and hauling them back to a landfill.

Sometime in the 1980s, Andy took a good hard look at the work he had accomplished in the first ten years of TreePeople. He'd helped plant tens of thousands of trees. But were the trees living? Yes and no. Trees survived best when they had humans to look after them during their most vulnerable period, the first couple of years in the ground. Some trees, it seemed, lucked out. They had managed to attract human "owners." Those that didn't died.

Andy realized TreePeople had to revamp its strategy. In the past, a community would approach the organization and say, "We want trees." "Great," Tree People would say, and they'd rush out to plant them. Andy saw that it was smarter to bring the trees to those people instead, to show them how to plant them, *but let them plant the trees themselves.* "When we did this, we found that they devel-

oped a sense of ownership over those trees and protected them," Andy says. So far, more than two hundred community leaders have been trained as part of TreePeople's Citizen Forester program. These days, 95 percent of the planted trees are living after five years.

TreePeople's twentieth anniversary occurred close to a pivotal event in Los Angeles history, the Rodney King trial and subsequent riots. Those turbulent days brought Andy's life of activism to a crisis. After all, the trees were supposed to lead to

TreePeople volunteers in Sun Valley. Photo courtesy of TreePeople

an improved quality of life for Los Angelinos. Nothing he saw around him indicated that his work had fulfilled its purpose.

"What do we need to do?" Andy asked himself. "We had to change our mission again. We were out to make the city livable versus pretty. Our work was supposed to be about improving the health of Los Angeles's citizens, the health of the city."

Sociologists looked at the problems leading up to the riots and concluded that Los Angeles needed about fifty thousand more jobs for urban youth. The city was at a loss as to how to create those jobs. The most intelligent estimates said the city needed a half billion dollars. The whopping figure seemed too big to ever become a reality.

TreePeople tried to create programs to help, such as the Urban Greening Initiative. But federal management of the program directed the bulk of the $13 million to a program that employed only four hundred people who rode buses out to the forest and worked their butts off. It was cool, Andy thought, but what happens when that funding runs out and the jobs end? Much more was needed to address the city's needs.

Andy despaired. He was exhausted, hurt, and unsure how he could make his organization relevant.

Andy and others had tried for years to increase green space in the city itself. It was tough going. So much of Los Angeles was paved over that it was difficult to insert new green spaces into the urban matrix. Frankly,

it was easier in a city like Philadelphia, where vacant land could be assembled out of the remains of abandoned buildings. Los Angeles was still too young, too vibrant to lose sections of valuable real estate, and where the city had run-down areas, it lacked the political leadership willing to make vacant land an important issue.

As we saw earlier, each time you try to solve a problem in Los Angeles, you are inevitably forced to grapple with another. Many had tried and given up. This Gordian knot seemed unbreakable, until Andy started to think about how elegantly nature solved many of these problems. There was never too much water in woods because the water always had someplace to go. There was never any polluted water because plants and dirt filtered it before it reached natural underground reservoirs. Wasn't there some way to mimic nature's example? Andy wondered.

After the riots, he read in the papers that the U.S. Army Corps of Engineers was planning to raise the concrete walls of the Los Angeles River yet again to prevent flooding. "This is insane," he thought. "We should be removing asphalt and concrete from the land and lowering those walls."

When Andy read further, he saw how much the county was about to spend on those walls: a half billion dollars!

The lights went on in his head. If the city could come up with a more sustainable solution to its water problem, it would have all

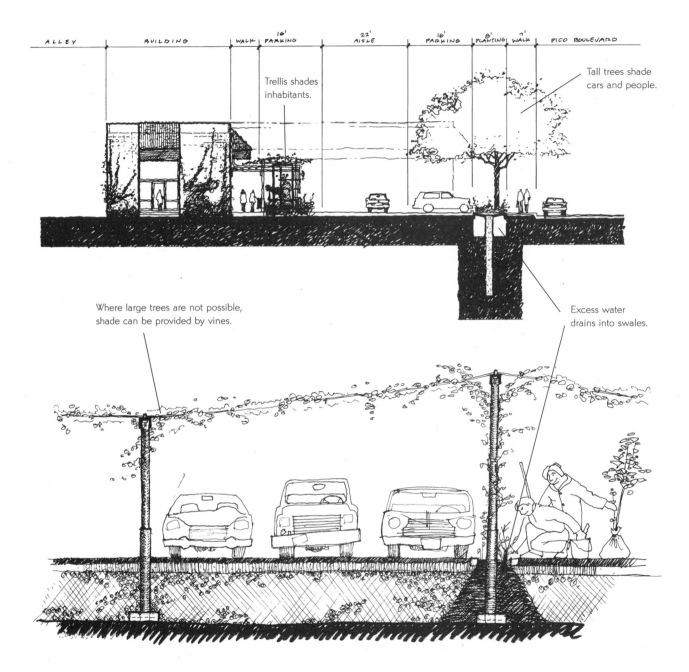

As Los Angeles lost its tree cover, storm-drain management emerged as a major problem. The root systems of trees act like cisterns, absorbing rainwater and replenishing underground water reserves. Artificial cisterns can be created that mimic nature's solution to water drainage.

the money it needed to help employ its citizens. "From my perspective," he says, "we're hurting people because we're spending that money on water."

Andy had an idea that could help.

On a visit to Australia he had seen how citizens used cisterns—underground tanks—to capture runoff on that parched continent. Cisterns are hardly a new concept. The ancient Greeks and Romans used them more than two thousand years ago. They carved chambers into solid rock and built their homes or gardens above them. Modern cisterns can be enormous, capable of holding enough rainwater to fill a swimming pool. Back on his home turf, Andy started designing his own cisterns, large and small.

He sat in on Los Angeles County water meetings. At the time, no one at the county Department of Public Works was thinking in terms of a watershed. Los Angeles was separated into two different camps. One agency, the Los Angeles County Flood Control, was responsible for managing floodwaters. The other, the Department of Water and Power, was responsible for buying water from other sources. The flood folks' priority wasn't to save water but to get rid of it. The faster the better, for safety reasons. Neither party had ever given much thought to the benefits of *capturing* water. The idea of installing millions of cisterns all over the city, or building swales to absorb the water into the ground, seemed foreign, ridiculous, and expensive. It was cheaper to keep doing what had always been done.

Look, Andy told them, if you install cisterns now, you pay a lot up front but you'll have flood and water protection and water forever. If you do it the way you've always done it, you'll *never* have water and you'll be buying it forever to the tune of billions of dollars a pop.

Andy wasn't the only one upset about the river wall project. He and a few other environmental groups sued the county, accusing it of squandering the citizens' water resources, which is prohibited by the state's constitution. Andy and his partners eventually lost the suit, and the river project went ahead, to the tune of a quarter of a billion dollars. One good thing came out of it: the county and the corps learned a new word, *watershed*, and promised to begin thinking of Los Angeles in terms of watershed management.

After that, Andy wanted to make it obvious to everyone that trees, swales, and cisterns could be cost-effective. He launched the Transagency Resources for Environmental and Economic Sustainability, or TREES, project. With $1 million in funding, he pulled together a team of experts—scientists, economists, and others—who designed a "natural" retrofit for Los Angeles. They even created an elegant software program that could show you what different green infrastructure scenarios would cost as well as the benefits they would offer.

TREES needed a test subject: a small, single-family house that they could remake in their own image. A woman named

Rozella Hall offered her little bungalow-style home in South Central Los Angeles. Andy's crew descended on Ms. Hall's eighty-year-old house and installed a dry well at the end of her driveway. Rainwater rolls down the driveway to a small grate and falls into a chamber, where it is filtered and then released into the ground. Drain spouts that had expelled rain into the street were repositioned so they send water into Ms. Hall's newly landscaped garden. The edges of her front yard and backyard were raised to form a bowl shape. Water collects here and gently seeps into the earth. In the backyard, TreePeople installed two 1,700-gallon cisterns made of recycled plastic. The two green rectangular boxes huddle against the side fence, collecting water from a drain spout that runs down from the roof. The yard looks pretty much the way it did before TREES arrived, except that the flower and shrub beds have been more amply beefed up with mulch.

When the house was ready, Andy called in the press and invited the same public works officials that he'd sued years earlier. They watched as workers lugged fire hoses to the top of Ms. Hall's roof. Officials in suits stood by, watching from the safety of their umbrellas. Someone gave the word, and the water gushed from the hoses, soaking the guys on the roof and spewing a heavy, simulated flash flood over the entire house. Two tons of water came down, but none of it ended up in the street. Every drop trickled into the cisterns or the ground.

Redesigning the New American Backyard

No matter how large or small, your plot of land constitutes an important part of your city's watershed. You can help replenish your city's groundwater resources by slightly altering your backyard. In California, TreePeople proposes the following:

- Build a 6- to 8-inch-high berm, or hill, around the perimeter of residential properties to keep water from rolling off slopes and into the street. Rainwater will pool up in these natural basins for a few hours after a storm and slowly seep into the earth, where it belongs.
- If soil is impenetrable or drainage is poor, a cistern can be installed above or under a section of your backyard to capture water. Later, this water can be pumped out when needed to water plants, lawns, et cetera. A lower-tech solution is to install rain barrels under rainspouts.
- Replace asphalt driveways with porous ones, such as gravel, which allow water to seep into the earth.
- An asphalt driveway can be graded to drain water into a swale, a rock or mulch creek bed that slows water down and allows it to be absorbed.
- Run all grass clippings, tree trimmings, and leaves through a wood chipper or mulcher and spread the resulting mulch around trees, shrubs, and flower beds.
- Strategically plant trees to shade your home during summer but allow sunlight to heat your home during winter. Trees can also shield your home from strong winds. Your state department of energy or your local cooperative extension office can help you choose the best sites for energy-saving landscaping.

A panoramic view of Sun Valley's watershed system today.

When the hoses were shut off, Andy invited everyone out to the backyard, where he turned on the water sprinkler, which was hooked up to the cistern. It started spraying away.

The press loved it.

"How much is this gonna cost?" a reporter asked.

Andy told him that they projected a cost of $10,000 per house.

One of the public works officials—the same guy who had fought Andy's proposals years before—interrupted. "Yeah," he said, enthusiastically, "but we could do it for cheaper if we really sat down and thought about it!"

That was the first inkling that Andy's message was beginning to seep in, like water into Rozella Hall's lawn.

Four days later, Andy got a call from the same man. "I'm sorry," he told Andy. "We didn't understand. We think you've cracked it. I disagree with you on the time it'll take and the cost, but it's got to be done. We have to do it throughout the county and we have to start *today*."

Sitting at his desk at TreePeople's office, Andy finally felt vindicated. He'd been waiting for this phone call for six years.

"Listen," the official said, "I have a project about to go out to contractors for bid. We were planning to build a $42 million storm drain in Sun Valley. But if we can apply and prove your technology, you can have this money to do it."

Andy realized he was being offered a tremendous opportunity. In all of Los Angeles, there was no better test ground for his ideas than Sun Valley. The neighborhood was a lower-middle-class to middle-class Latino area renowned for some of the worst flooding in the city. Every time there's a huge storm in Los Angeles, news crews dash out to Sun Valley because they know they'll get dramatic footage. County Supervisor Zev Yaroslavsky says the flooding issue is "a vortex taking the community down."

"The water comes out of the mountains during rainstorms," Yaroslavsky explains, "not even heavy rainstorms, and it gets into the sump, which is in the urban core of the

Before and After At Sun Valley Schools

TreePeople's plan for two schools in Sun Valley offers a good example of how to retrofit large complexes with outdoor space. Such a plan might include the following:

- Adding natural outdoor learning areas
- Planting trees and other vegetation
- Removing asphalt playgrounds and installing grassy ball fields
- Installing stormwater collection systems to reduce flooding and tying these into the campus's irrigation system (see illustration)
- Installing porous pavement in parking lots, or sloping the driveway to direct water toward a swale area (see illustration)

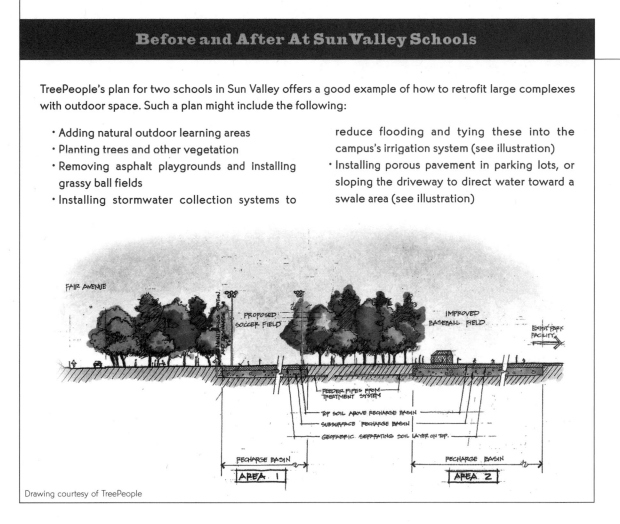

Drawing courtesy of TreePeople

San Fernando Valley, and it floods. Intersections flood, cars get into accidents, cars stall, they get damaged. Kids can't go to school because they can't cross the streets. As a result of kids not going to school, the school loses the income it gets from the state because they get it on the basis of attendance. If the kid doesn't show up, they lose money for that kid, and the kid doesn't get an education."

"It's ironic that it's called Sun Valley," says Cindy Montanez, the state assembly member whose Thirty-ninth Assembly District encompasses the community. "You would imagine a beautiful place with a lot of sun and hills and trees. But it's an area that historically had fourteen operating landfills. There's probably no part anywhere in the western part of the United States that had as many operating landfills as Sun Valley. Schools are literally located across landfills, animal cremators, and incinerators. You have rock quarries, auto dismantlers, and chrome platers. But Sun Valley is very much engaged right now in turning its community

Shaping Your Own Ideas: Sponsor a Charrette

TreePeople encourages communities to plan their own brainstorming retreats, or "charrettes," to talk about how they could implement some of these ideas into their communities. The format for a charrette is simple: Citizens with expertise in various areas of local planning get together for a day or weekend and split up into groups to draw sketches, draw up wish lists, and make plans about how they would retrofit major public places in their towns or cities. When time is up, they present their ideas to the other groups regardless of how spontaneous or well thought out they are. Among architects and designers, charrettes are a time-honored way of getting lots of ideas out into the open, where they can be critiqued and absorbed by the group. Charrettes tend to generate their own momentum, and the energy and ideas will filter down into later civic projects.

around and making it a greener place, a more environmentally healthy place, and a community where kids can play at a local park without having to be exposed to many contaminants."

Andy's plan would contribute to that grand plan. In the fall of that year, the county's public works department agreed to investigate the cistern-and-swale technology for use in Sun Valley. A two-year study concluded that Andy's method would cost $100 to $300 million—two to six times the cost of the original storm drain. That sounded steep, until you looked at the numbers. Doing it Andy's way would put $200 million worth of water in Los Angeles's underground water

supply. Mulching green waste at people's houses and leaving it for their gardens instead of hauling it to the dump would save the county $30 million alone!

Not long ago, Sun Valley broke ground on the first project, a big infiltration system that will be installed under a park.

Andy Lipkis, the grown-up Tree Boy who is neither a scientist nor an engineer and refers to himself as a college dropout, got his start thirty years ago inspiring people to care enough to plant a single tree. The idea was so simple that it could not be ignored. His ideas are still just as powerful: Plant a tree. Plant strategically. Take ownership of it. Be bold enough to remake the place where you live into a little watershed.

"We think you've cracked it."

What did the official mean by that? What is it about Andy's ideas that offers such hope?

Andy's plan addressed each of the major air- and water-quality problems facing Los Angeles. Instead of one problem leading to another, each *solution* led to another. Each link in the chain was *integrated* with the next, a perfect model of something called integrated resource management.

Consider the following:

- The problem of green waste? Solved: Residents and schools would mulch their waste on-site and feed their beds.
- The problem of too much or too little water? Solved: Hundreds of thousands of gallons would be captured and

stored during storms or else fed into the ground to recharge reservoirs and aquifers.

- The problem of polluted water? Solved: Driveways and parking lots would be designed to filter out toxins.
- The problem of high energy demands? Solved: Trees and grass would shade homes and schools, reducing the demand for air conditioning.
- The problem of poor air quality? Solved: The new urban forest would filter out particulates and CO_2.

Even the perennial problem of creating jobs in urban areas had been addressed. This was the truly masterful part of Andy's plan. A retrofit of this size—2,700 acres encompassing eight thousand homes—would require the employment of tons of people of different skill levels, from trained engineers and technicians to competent landscapers and day laborers. In the years to come, trees would need to be tended, cisterns maintained, filtering systems installed or repaired, grass mown, and green waste mulched. There was an endless supply of good, honest work awaiting hundreds of people in Sun Valley alone.

Today, thanks to Andy's urging, Los Angeles's county water and flood control boards are doing a better job of talking to each other and integrating their policies. At the moment Los Angeles's "watershed" extends as far east as Utah and as far north as Montana. That means that rain or snow

that falls within that huge swath of land can and does end up in Los Angeles's water system.

But imagine if you scaled up Andy's idea and brought it to the rest of the 9.5 million people living in Los Angeles County. Or shared the idea with the greater Los Angeles region—with Orange, San Bernardino, Riverside, and Ventura counties. You could effectively address the massive green space problem that plagues Los Angeles. You could worry a little less about finding vacant land for parks because the city itself would become a vast garden, protecting and replenishing the watershed upon which it sits. And the current multistate watershed could shrink closer to the size of Los Angeles's own footprint.

Imagine what an example that would set for other cities that face similar issues of sprawl, such as Las Vegas, Denver, San Diego, and a host of others.

"If I had to look at how we're doing with sustainability overall as a nation," says Andy, "and asked the question, 'Are we doing enough?' the answer is no. In fact, I think we're rapidly approaching the red zone. But my hope lies in people being able to turn on a dime, just like that guy in public works did. I would hate for people to look at me and think, 'Oh, thank goodness someone else is going to fix the problem.' No. It's not going to work unless we all do something. We all have a job to do as stewards of God's creation."

AT PLAY ON THE RIVER OF GLEE

The river of concrete slices into the earth and runs through the City of Angels for fifty miles or so, from the San Fernando Valley to Long Beach Harbor, where tourists catch the boats to Catalina Island. Looking at these two-story walls of cement, it's hard to imagine that this thing, this trickle, this wash, is actually a river—or once was. At one point along the river's journey, the Sepulveda Basin, the concrete disappears and trees take over. Standing at this point, a visitor can almost imagine what Serra, Portola, and Crespi saw more than two hundred years ago. As for the rest, it's more of an engineering marvel than anything else. A terribly efficient conduit for conducting water out of harm's way and out to sea.

You might even be impressed, until you learn it was a river. Then it's hard to see it as anything other than a disheartening sight, a public disgrace, but thanks to the efforts of many people who are talking about saving the river, it has also become a place of hope.

Mike Mullin is one of these people. One morning he walks along the concrete channel that runs through downtown Los Angeles, talking about history, the city's plans for this place, and his own hopes to see the river a vital natural place again. Mike works for the city's watershed protection division, and it's his job to develop the science and the public education campaigns that make a difference in getting the pollution out of the water.

He explains that the city is chronically tortured with the subject of the river. They know they'd like to bring it back to what it once was, but because Los Angeles has grown so large, there is always the fear that a major storm event—a one-hundred-year flood, for example—could cause widespread devastation. How much river restoration is too much? Is there a way to make it totally safe, as some activists insist?

"The way I see the river in the future is not without concrete," Mullin says, "but I see it much better, with parks and wetlands and resources for people, things that bring people to the river. It's the longest open watercourse in Southern California, and every freeway in Los Angeles crosses Los Angeles River, yet most people don't know it's here. With a hundred million gallons of water a day running to the ocean, it's one of the West Coast's largest rivers, and yet it's invisible to people."

One hundred million gallons. That's nearly five thousand swimming pools a day being whisked away. The river does its job so well that people take it for granted. It's been fighting for respect since the beginning

Mike Mullin, who works in the city's watershed protection division, is committed to restoring the natural infrastructure of the Los Angeles River for scientific as well as aesthetic reasons.

Returning the Los Angeles River to its original state is a formidable and expensive task, but one that many planners, citizens, and environmentalists agree should be done.

of the twentieth century, when it was viewed as providing either too little or too much water. When Los Angeles started to grow and the river had trouble meeting demands for water. By the time Mulholland started looking for water elsewhere, the Los Angeles River was no longer considered a valuable commodity. When one hundred people died in the 1930s during flood events, no one dared stick up for the river. It was a menace. The feds moved it and tamed it.

Now the leadership of the city wants to make it valuable again. It won't be done overnight, but it will start with recognizing natural infrastructure as an asset, something to be protected. This is part of a new concept in city planning called "best practices." Best practices entails comparing and employing the most effective, efficient, and beneficial methods for tackling a problem. In the case of the Los Angeles River, it means not letting that river water rush away. It means figuring out ways to slow it down so more of it seeps into the riverbed. Planners and activists are talking these days about doing everything from ripping out portions of the river bottom to installing inflatable dams that would be activated or deflated at will. They dream of building water fountains to attract birds and visitors along the river's path. They envision terraces along the riverbanks, where wetland plants purify the water before it washes out to sea. Already, up and down the waterway, different communities are establishing new bike paths and new parks. In the future there will be overlooks from which to enjoy the view and spot some of the four hundred species of birds that make the river their home. Other people dream of soccer fields where kids could play, restaurants with a glorious view, hotels, and of course, even more development. Others say no, let's stick with nature. Let's bring back the trees so the city can be cooled day and night by a wide swath of trees that runs like a green ribbon through the heart of the city. In either case, that people are paying attention to the river constitutes progress.

Mike gestures to the land below his feet. "Hundreds of years ago, the Spanish came to pretty much this exact spot and they said this was a really nice place. It was sycamores and oak trees, and those trees aren't here now. But if we could bring back some of that, that would be part of what makes this place so incredible. I never found the river as dramatic as the Spanish did because I've always been looking at it from when I was a kid as we drove by and I wondered what that was. When I started with the city, I got involved with water quality along the river, and for me, if the water quality is right, then all the other issues fall into place. The habitat is better, the recreational component is better, people want to be there, and it becomes a resource. In the long run, you know, nature by itself is sustainable. It runs itself. It finds its own way and finds a balance, and urban areas tend to not have that."

Los Angeles is portrayed as such a modern city that it's difficult sometimes to envision a time when nature was just down the block, when the view of unspoiled mountains and valleys was just at the end of town. Mike remembers seeing old aerial pictures of Los Angeles showing wild open spaces just beyond the spot where he's now standing. But that's all gone now. Long gone. Replacing it will take work and an understanding of what a river environment is supposed to be like.

"For my kids, who are both teenagers now, it's obvious that our sustainability and our parks and our water should be better," adds Mike, "and maybe it's because they have a younger perspective on it. If you had to choose between concrete and green, kids choose green. So I'm hoping that there'll be places that I can take them and I can say, 'Look, this is what we did,' and I'm going to be there with all my friends who helped me do it."

He is not alone in wanting to share this with his children. Los Angeles's Hispanic communities regard the river as a special place since so many of their neighborhoods run close to the river's path. Vintage photos show young Hispanic teenagers and small children bathing in the gentler passages of the river. Today, for groups like Amigos de Los Rios, the river may be the only piece of nature their children get to see. Underserved communities in the Los Angeles area made up of recent immigrants—Taiwanese, Mexicans, Ecuadoreans, Koreans, Filipinos—have gathered along the river to help pick its banks clean during various cleanup-day events. These assemblies are beneficial for the environment but are marked by a certain poignancy. For many, it is the closest thing they have to a park.

Activist Melanie Winter was born in Los Angeles, born on the banks of the river, in fact, at Burbank Hospital. She lived in New York for fifteen years, working in the theater, but eventually returned to her hometown to care for her parents. Back in Los Angeles, she witnessed the riots following the Rodney King verdict and was struck by how alienated people felt from others in their own city. Now founder and director of an organization called the River Project, she describes Los Angeles as "Balkanized"—each little neighborhood and community splintered off into its own space without any real opportunity to interact with other demographics.

"It seemed to me that an underlying cause of the riots was the fact that we didn't have the kind of social and public infrastructure that they have in cities like New York. We don't have connective parks, we don't have communal areas where people can get together. When a new set of immigration comes in, you're able to understand who they are because you go to the park and see who they are, or you get on a subway or the bus and you're face to face with them every day. You walk places, and you have a dif-

Melanie Winter conducts six-week programs in local schools to educate and involve students in river restoration.

ferent kind of community setup. It seems to me that we are very fractured, and that leads to misunderstanding and social inequity. I changed everything I'd done in my life up to that point after the riots. I figured if I had to be in Los Angeles, then I had to try to make a difference somehow. I had to make Los Angeles better. I engaged in a lot of social justice work and activism, and that led me by chance to a group that was working on the Los Angeles River."

She remembers seeing bulldozers plowing the sides of the river when she was a kid. Back then, there was hardly anything living in the river. Now, though, she was astonished to see that years of protection under the Clean Water Act had worked wonders for the Los Angeles River. Fish darted in the water again, and birds roosted in trees along the water's edge. It didn't matter that some of those trees were exotic invasive species; the point was that there was life in the old

Melanie Winter with a group of students at Taylor Yard, a 200-acre site along the Los Angeles River upon which Southern Pacific built a freight-switching facility in the 1920s.

river still. Nature was reasserting itself. That meant there was hope.

Melanie sensed that the river was the perfect vehicle for building that sense of community she felt the city lacked.

"I realized the river brings all that together," she explains. "It does provide the means to connect communities. It gives us really the only way to bring balance back to our environment. It's not subways or a light rail, but it does give us an opportunity to have a network of community bikeways and really give Los Angeles a sense of identity again."

Science had always been her least favorite subject in school, but she set out to learn what she could from area naturalists. Today she works to restore certain sections of the river with the help of local schoolkids. She conducts a six-week course at a particular school and teaches kids what she has learned about ecosystems and river restoration. Kids assist her in designing new parks and choosing the plant palette with the help of botanists, and then they go out into the field to pick up trash on the banks, erect interpretive signage, or remove invasive species. Her efforts to restore the river's natural watershed in Sun Valley dovetail with those of Andy Lipkis.

Her biggest challenge, she says, is counteracting the almost daily question she gets from lifelong Los Angelenos: "What river?"

More and more often, the kids she has worked with can answer that question. Mostly second through fourth graders, they take what they learn back home and end up involving their parents. "Man, I love fourth graders," she says. "They're just at that age where they get it, and they can give you incredible ideas."

Once, she remembers, a local reporter asked to meet and interview some of her students about the work they'd done on the river. Melanie rounded up some kids for the last class she'd taught, but she was worried. The class had been months ago, and now the kids had been on summer break. How were they ever going to remember anything Melanie had taught them? But she needn't have worried. When the kids sat down with the reporter, who asked why it was so important to save the Los Angeles River, "I couldn't believe what came out of these kids' mouths," says Melanie. "They were brilliant, absolutely brilliant. I couldn't have explained it better myself."

A good example is the poem third-grader Emilia Hagen, age nine, wrote about the river. It goes like this:

The River of Happiness
by Emilia Hagen

The river was sad and cold one day. A man walked by. He laid the blanket of love on it. He planted trees and took off the river's cement jacket. The love made it clean again. The river laughed, laughed with glee. While fish dance a tango beneath the happy river, the sun shone over the happiness and birds came back and said to me, "I love it here because of the river, the river, the river of glee."

A student enjoying the Los Angeles River on a field trip with Melanie Winter.

IN SEARCH OF LOS ANGELES'S NEW WAY TO TRAVEL

"The freeway experience . . . is the only secular communion Los Angeles has. . . . Actual participation requires a total surrender, a concentration so intense as to seem a kind of narcosis, a rapture-of-the-freeway. The mind goes clean. The rhythm takes over."
— JOAN DIDION

When cars were still newfangled toys, a drive in the country was considered a fun form of recreation. The Sunday drive was seen as a delightful escape; you drove from the city to the country to have fun.

With this fantasy of the footloose life in their heads, Los Angeles's early builders proceeded to create a place that was unlike any other American city. Where other cities were paeans to verticality, Los Angeles grew horizontally. Open space and wide boulevards were seen as a refreshing antidote to the teeming, narrow streets of cities back East. No one anticipated that the paradise they envisioned would be attractive to millions more people—nor did they foresee how auto dependence would affect the city's quality of life decades later.

In the 1920s, for example, people couldn't imagine a time when one would have to drive to go shopping, visit family and friends, or go to work. No one could imagine a time when driving would be a stressful, even dangerous activity. Or that one would be doing it every single day for every single activity among 16.4 million other people. No one could imagine a time when the by-products of automobiles would be not only undesirable but harmful as well: congestion, traffic, danger, smog, and so on.

Ironically, by the 1920s Los Angeles had the largest transit system in the nation—1,152 miles of subway, light rail, and trains. This system made possible the development of a network of early communities and a decentralized urban structure. Eventually, freeways were built that connected these communities, and cars became the preferred method of transportation, thus causing the transit system to become defunct. Darrell Clarke grew up in Los Angeles hearing his parents speak wistfully of the old Red Line trolley cars that used to ply the streets of Los Angeles. The trolleys were discontinued in the 1960s in another example of the city's civic shortsightedness. Since then mass transit in Los Angeles has consisted of buses that have unfortunately become synonymous with transportation for the city's poor.

Some feel that light rail is a major part of the solution to Los Angeles's traffic woes. Light rail has become popular in cities in the past decade, and it all comes down to money. Anyone who's ever been stuck in traffic will concede that train travel is a markedly better way to get around a city than a lurching, diesel-exhaust-spewing bus. But what *kind* of train travel is best? A subway line—like the immaculate Metro in Washington DC—is virtually invisible since it travels underground, unaffected by traffic. But subways are difficult and expensive to build, costing roughly $300 million *per mile*. A light rail line, on the other hand, is the modern descendant of the trolley car. It travels on dedicated track, so even though it runs aboveground, it is not subject to the vagaries of traffic. Light rail is clean, electric, and efficient and costs cities about $30 to $70 million per mile to install. No wonder more cities are considering light rail lines.

After a stint in San Francisco, Darrell returned to Los Angeles in the late 1980s and worked in sales for IBM. One day he read with interest a newspaper article that said the old right-of-way from an extinct railroad line was up for sale, and the agency that would later become the Metropolitan Transit Authority was considering buying it to build a light rail line to the west side of Los Angeles, namely to Santa Monica, the beachfront community where he lived.

The idea that he could leave his car at a parking lot, hop on a train, and be in downtown Los Angeles in a matter of minutes sounded like a dream come true. Darrell was born and bred in Los Angeles, but with each passing year, he'd been getting more and more fed up with commuting by car. "If I got in my car at rush hour, it would take me forty-five minutes to travel seventeen miles to downtown," he says. "Sometimes I'd go on vacation somewhere else and enjoy being able to drive around easily. I'd get numb to it

In the 1920s, cars shared the Los Angeles streets with trolleys. Since then, however, most of Los Angeles's public transportation has been jettisoned in favor of freeways. Top photo courtesy of LAPL, bottom photo by Ricardo Aguero

and forget about it. Then I'd come back home, go to work, and think, 'Oh no. This is not good for my health, breathing exhaust every day of the week, and the chances of being in an accident increasing the longer I spend on roads every day.'"

Darrell, now fifty, was hardly the first Los Angeleno to have this kind of reaction. Los Angeles is legendary for its traffic snarls, which worsen with every tick in population rise. More than commuters are complaining. Public health officials and sociologists have long noted the health risks and psychological effects of such a debilitating daily travel experience.

The social cost of sprawl, and the newsworthiness of the problem, has even filtered down to local politicians. "One of the biggest social problems in our region is in the Antelope Valley," says Zev Yaroslavsky, the Los Angeles County supervisor. "People commute quite often two hours one way to work. They don't get home 'til seven, eight o'clock at night. Parents don't get to spend much time with their kids. As a result, that's where we have some of our biggest teen problems, skinhead problems, methamphetamine problems. It is a lose-lose situation, so sprawl is one thing we have to come to control."

Some argue persuasively that the traffic issue has begun to impact Los Angeles's status as a world-class city and destination. Those who venture downtown via the city's one new subway (the Red Line) and two light rail lines (the Blue and Gold lines) still find the system curiously lacking. The

minute you leave the train, you're stuck walking or taking a bus. Unlike the situation in cities like Washington DC, Boston, and New York, there are still not enough train lines in Los Angeles to offer seamless transfers from one line to the next.

When large numbers of people come together, the traffic problem must be addressed or it will eventually limit a city's talent and creativity pool. If people need to leave their home two hours ahead of time for an appointment or an event at the Music Center downtown, how long before they stop coming altogether? If people cannot commute efficiently to their jobs, how long before they consider moving to another city or job?

Darrell felt the same way. "I'm concerned about the future of Los Angeles," he says, "because people are saying they can't afford to live here. Commutes are terrible. 'Nice climate, but I'm going to leave the city and move somewhere else.' Businesses say the same thing. How many businesses are leaving Los Angeles or expanding outside of Los Angeles because employees can't live here? I really fear for the future of Los Angeles. I was born in Los Angeles, I grew up here, I feel a loyalty, a personal calling to make it a better city. I want to make a difference, to feel like I did something, and it was gratifying to see so many other people who feel the same way."

In 1989, Darrell rushed to join an unofficial citizens' group to support construction of a west-side line—later called the Exposition Line—that could feasibly serve eight hundred thousand people who lived along the corridor from Santa Monica through Culver City to downtown Los Angeles. Darrell's eagerness was not, shall we say, typical. If anything, most of his neighbors were against the idea. When city officials talked about bringing a rail line to a specific neighborhood, residents there responded, "Not in my backyard."

Darrell and his group were like a pack of wandering Don Quixotes, tilting at windmills, garnering respect from neither neighbors nor politicians. "For a while we were afraid to say that light rail is a good thing in mixed company. But we developed the courage to go out and speak for it and not be afraid. It started very small."

The group started showing up at every MTA and local community meeting, trying to speak their minds. They quickly learned that elected officials would never take action unless they knew they had the public's support. "We were gnats, something to be swatted away," Darrell recalls. One official, a state senator, gave them some insight into the way things really work when he said, half jokingly, "You start the parade and I'll march out in front of it."

The parade would have to wait. The MTA started with big plans, but when funding ran out, it decided to put all its eggs in one basket and fund the subway line from downtown to La Brea. This was fine, but slow going. Five years later, the press was calling the subway construction a fiasco. Would it

ever be a reality? The MTA was going broke building the thing, and promised federal funds rarely materialized. In desperation, the agency decided to build a shorter subway line and regroup. The whole enterprise had the feel of a disaster, but when the subway debuted, ridership doubled and the line quickly gained a great reputation. Complaints about the alleged boondoggle quickly disappeared; suddenly everyone griped about the need for more parking at the subway station—a sure sign of success.

Watching all this from the sidelines, Darrell's group decided to regroup too. They formally created an organization, the Friends for Expo Transit, and worked harder to take their cause to the people. They found that they had to combat the notion that a train line would bring crime, violence, and trouble to the neighborhood. Darrell says, "A lot of people had the fear that inner-city people

Darrell Clarke, a Los Angeles native, has been advocating for the construction of a light rail system that would run from Santa Monica to downtown Los Angeles since 1989.

would be coming into their neighborhood and stealing their TVs. We'd have to say to them, 'Right, and what will they do with it? Carry it back to the train platform and stand there, waiting for a train?'"

Unrealistic fears were defused by common sense and humor, and support began to grow. The group circulated petitions and encouraged those who signed to send an e-mail to administrators at the MTA, describing in their own words why they wanted a west-side line. (They learned that officials tended to ignore form letters and e-mails but absorbed the message when it was expressed in plain, heartfelt language.)

They found that the technology of the age made it particularly easy to get their voices heard. "E-mails and Web sites and inkjet printers don't cost much," Darrell says. "They're very fast, agile, and cheap. That helped to create this steady drumbeat of people writing to MTA board members."

Grassroots organizations are fascinating entities. People join them because they feel strongly about something, and the next thing they know, they are volunteering to take on chores that stretch their time and skills. Darrell watched as each of his new friends found their niches. Some did graphics, did public speaking, or wrote materials, others collected petitions, and still others led meetings or juggled the group's busy calendar of appointments. At one point, they considered hiring professional organizers to help them but decided against it. The strength of the organization came from its volunteer spirit.

When people do something from their heart, with their conscience, they experience a sense of purpose that most paid employees never feel.

"Transit advocates come in two flavors," says Darrell. "People who ride buses and people who drive. Both of those types know there has to be a better way. People come up to me all the time and say, 'I never knew what I could do! I never knew I could make a difference.' We've certainly gotten more respect over time. It's interesting to go from being a person on the outside reading an article in the newspaper to later having stature and contacts with public officials. But like we always say, it's not over until the trains are running."

Well, the trains are still not running, at least not in Darrell's neck of the woods. The year 2001 was especially tough. That's when the MTA finally approved the Expo Line. According to plans, construction will begin sometime in 2007, and by 2010 the trains will be running—but only as far as Culver City because, due to lack of funding, the MTA decided in 2001 to build only *half* a line. The news was devastating to the Friends for Expo Transit, but they are determined to stay out there, raising their voices, pushing the city to complete the work it started and take the line all the way to the shore.

Some days Darrell finds it hard to believe that he's been lobbying for a better way to go to work for sixteen years! "I didn't think this would turn into my life's work," he says, somewhat bemused by the passage of years. When he started, his son was only six; now he's twenty-one. In all that time, Darrell has never seriously considered throwing in the towel. "There were lots of naysayers out there telling us to just give up when we got the bad news in 2001. But you can't. You pick yourself up, dust yourself off, and keep going. Once you get involved in something like this, you can't stop. You worked so hard to get where you are, so you have to wonder, 'Why stop now?'"

"We did it because we had a vision of how cities could be better," he says. "The fantasy of Los Angeles is of this place where the roads are wide open and free. And it's just that, a fantasy, because the roads aren't open anymore. The other night I was watching a special on the Mamas and the Papas, and you know that song, 'California Dreamin''? They kept playing that, and it's this song about the sun, the ocean, the Beach Boys, where you'd drive your woody or convertible to the beach and just hang out and surf. That's what people think the fantasy is. Or Los Angeles is this place where the Rose Bowl takes place every year and it's gorgeous on New Year's Day. Well, the reality is there are too many cars on the roadway, and we've run out of space. We can't build anymore. Real estate is so expensive that it's put a damper on everything. You might dream about moving to the beach, but the question is, 'Well, how many millions of dollars is that going to cost you?' I don't know what happened to the fantasy. I think it was always one. Los Angeles just grew up and there's no room anymore."

THE GRAND AVENUE PROJECT

"People cut themselves off from their ties of the old life when they come to Los Angeles. They are looking for a place where they can be free, where they can do things they couldn't do anywhere else."

—Tom Bradley, former mayor of Los Angeles

All the great cities of the world have a cultural heart, a world-renowned romantic place that is the soul of the city itself. Piazza Navona or Via Veneto in Rome. The Champs d'Elysee in Paris. Las Ramblas in Barcelona. Times Square in New York. Los Angeles is one of the best known, most envied, most admired, most beguiling cities on the planet. But where is its epicenter? Where is the heart of Los Angeles's downtown?

"Los Angeles is a very interesting place," says UCLA psychiatrist Peter Whybrow. "The city isn't really a city. As Gertrude Stein would say, 'There's no there there.' There's no center. But in another sense, it could be a more sustainable city than anywhere else. Each of its neighborhoods is self-contained, and if one had vision, each of those could become the backbone of a sustainable community."

Experts on cities would beg to differ. Los Angeles is what they call a polycentric, or many-centered, city. That die was probably cast back in the 1920s, when the public transportation system made it easy for people to live in smaller neighborhoods outside downtown Los Angeles. But Whybrow argues that those smaller hubs don't necessarily feel like home anymore to many people, because residents are not encouraged to emotionally invest in those areas. (Strongly ethnic neighborhoods may be immune to this feeling, however.) Because of jobs, friends, and families, their loyalties are spread out all over the Los Angeles area. If citizens made more of an effort to, say, shop locally, participate in local affairs, or get to know their neighbors, they might develop that feeling of connectedness more Americans say they crave.

This is only one thoughtful approach to the problem of sprawl. Others says Los Angeles doesn't need a center; they reject the notion that Los Angeles and other cities must become "little New Yorks" to broadcast their identity to the world. Nevertheless,

neither of these reactions has stopped some Los Angelenos from imagining a flashier showcase epicenter, a kind of Times Square of Los Angeles. Builders, architects, and planners who have monitored this renewed interest in downtown Los Angeles have been vying with each other to pinpoint which neighborhood or block will emerge as the city's cultural hub. In addition, other efforts to recapitalize downtown have been mounted. Downtown real estate interests have designed and promoted a subway system in hopes of revalorizing downtown real estate.

This question of Los Angeles's geographical identity has again resurfaced because the city recently offered up four city blocks in the downtown area, in competition, to a number of developers. The neighborhood is known as Bunker Hill. Up for grabs were chunks of prime real estate along Grand Avenue, where a couple of major cultural institutions now stand. The city is currently in negotiations with the Related Companies of New York, which may ultimately fill Grand Avenue with new apartments, a hotel, high-end retail shops, and a sixteen-acre park.

Of course there's controversy about everything in Los Angeles, and the Grand Avenue Project is drawing plenty. Just because you build it, say detractors, doesn't mean that it is the legitimate heart of the city. Indeed, in a city as socially and economically diverse as

Peter Whybrow is a professor of psychiatry at the University of California, Los Angeles, and the author of *American Mania: When More Is Not Enough.*

Los Angeles, where to locate the heart of the city depends greatly on who you ask. For some, the city's true historic core is the plaza of El Pueblo, where the city was founded by the Spanish, a location about one mile northeast of Grand Avenue. The financial center is to the south. The "American" or "Anglo" historic core, which was the city's financial center from 1850 to 1950, is to the east.

And then there is Bunker Hill, which itself has a strange and unsettling history. When the area was first developed in 1875, its builders appropriated the name of the Battle of Bunker Hill, fought outside Boston in June 1775—one hundred years earlier— during the Revolutionary War. No battles have been fought in Los Angeles's Bunker Hill, at least not yet. Originally, Bunker Hill was an undesirable location; the hills were steep and arid, and the young city sprouted up in the river valley to the east. But high-end homes soon were popping on the hill, and the city's affluent flocked to its beautiful Victorian mansions.

By the 1960s, however, the neighborhood had fallen into decline. The city's planners deemed the area a blight zone and sent in bulldozers to level everything to the ground. Photos of that era depict gorgeous old houses with Queen Anne gingerbread and spindles being demolished and hauled away. The old apartment buildings where Raymond Chandler sent his private eye Philip Marlowe trolling for femme fatales

and crime were ground to powder. Even the hills were knocked down, the dirt carted off to Marina del Rey to build a yacht harbor. It was the largest urban renewal project the United States had ever seen.

"I think there are some regrets about simply obliterating the historical, architectural, and urban planning legacy of the city," says Dan Rosenfeld, the architect and founder of Urban Partners, whom we introduced earlier in this book. Urban Partners specializes in urban "infill" housing. Urban Partners seeks out and develops vacant lots, dilapidated buildings, and underdeveloped locations in downtown Los Angeles in an effort fill in these spaces, renew the city, and reduce overall sprawl.

Rosenfeld sounds almost melancholy when he talks about the obliteration of the old Bunker Hill. "This was a neighborhood of small, narrow streets, of beautiful

Architect Dan Rosenfeld founded Urban Partners, a firm that works to restore vitality to downtown Los Angeles through innovative development of vacant lots and abandoned buildings.

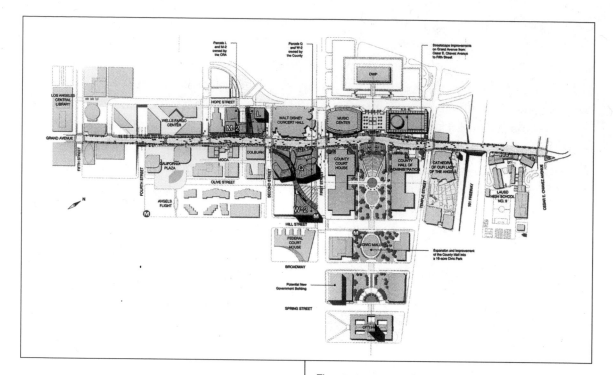

The city is negotiating with the Related Companies of New York to build on Bunker Hill. Their plan calls for a park, residential housing, and retail shops. Courtesy of Grand Avenue Committee, Inc.

Victorian buildings and apartments. There were stairs and tramways going up and down the hill. It had a complicated urban character that you might see in, let's say, Edinburgh, Scotland. And again, that was just wiped off the map."

And then, for a long time, Bunker Hill just sat waiting for an architectural incarnation that never came to pass. The city dreamed of building a gleaming glass and steel canyon of office buildings and homes. The word went out to developers: anyone want Bunker Hill? But there were no takers. This was the era of the suburbs. The city was racing outward in a mad dash to colonize every last parcel of untouched land and make it safe for subdivisions, the barbecue grill, and the two-car garage.

Finally, in the 1970s, Bunker Hill got a few office buildings and housing. In 1979, five whole blocks were offered in a master-plan-type offer to area developers, and the area finally assumed its long-vaunted reputation as a good place for public structures. Today it's home to the Museum of Contemporary Art, the Colburn School for the Performing Arts, the Music Center, and the Walt Disney Concert Hall. What remains are four prime blocks—labeled on city maps as Blocks L, M, Q, and W—and their development is occasioning a general discussion about what the city has learned from its past experiences, what's missing at this loca-

The new Grand Avenue Project features a park that runs from City Hall to a planned music center. Courtesy of Grand Avenue Committee, Inc.

tion, and what Bunker Hill should ultimately be like.

Eli Broad thinks he knows the answer to all these questions. He is arguably the last of Los Angeles's old-time visionary builders. His company, K. B. Homes (formerly Kauffman and Broad Homes), was one of the biggest builders of exurban housing of the 1960s and 1970s. Now Broad, who devotes himself to philanthropic endeavors, is looking inward, to the core of Los Angeles. He is head of the committee to figure out what to do with Grand Avenue.

"We've learned a great deal in the past fifty years," he says, "especially here in Los Angeles. Remember, Los Angeles started, as someone said, as fifty suburbs looking for a city because it did not have a vibrant center, and we're developing that today."

What Broad envisions is the second of two major projects that will revitalize the downtown area. The first is already in place: the sports, convention, and entertainment center that is less than two miles away from Grand Avenue. The second is the Grand Avenue Project, which will create a park from City Hall to the Music Center that will host, among other things, free concerts and movies at night. Such an outdoor venue would be a first in Los Angeles.

In addition, the Grand Avenue Project will add several thousand rental and condominium housing units, as well as interesting retail shops such as a massive destination bookstore. "This," asserts the master builder unequivocally, "will become the civil and cultural district of Los Angeles."

"We're going to link all of that," says Broad, "and we're going to have a center where people are going to want to spend an entire day, not simply drive down to see a game or drive down to see a concert and leave."

"More and more people want to live downtown," he adds. "There are more and more things going on downtown. And I think if you'll look at the history of cities, you will not find a city that's been great that

does not have a vibrant center where all people from all communities could gather, whether it's for sports, entertainment, to celebrate events, or what have you. We're creating that now."

Admittedly, though, at sixteen acres the Grand Avenue park is not nearly the size it should be for a city of Los Angeles's size. The city already has its famous Griffith Park, numbering some three thousand acres, but much of that acreage is inaccessible to foot traffic. This is what everyone always comes back to. Yes, the Los Angeles region abounds with nature trails and hiking spaces

Designers of the Grand Avenue Project hope that, when completed, Grand Avenue will function as a city center, an element that has been historically neglected in Los Angeles's urban planning. Courtesy of Grand Avenue Committee, Inc.

well outside the city, but those places have two shortcomings: they are accessible only by car, and thus by design they deny the right of open space to some of the city's less fortunate residents. What the city needs most is a green open space—a traditional park space—where people can come together and enjoy an afternoon, meet friends and family, relax, and hang out. It needs, in short, its own incarnation of a Millennium Park, a Central Park, a Golden Gate Park.

"You know," says Broad, "fifty years ago, with the benefit of hindsight, we can see now that we did not do the city regional planning that should have been done. We didn't give thought to our transportation needs. That's all changed now."

LESS THAN PERFECT DESIGN?

Dan Rosenfeld, an architect and self-described romantic, begs to differ. He is critical of the way Bunker Hill was rehabbed long ago, and the way it's being planned today. His objections are a mix of thoughtful criticism and object lessons lifted from history. What needs to be understood, he says, is that infrastructure is remarkably durable, that its design can affect human behavior. One day while walking along Grand Avenue, he points to the wide streets with a gesture of admonishment.

"For the past fifty years or so the primary urban planning policy in this city, as far as I can tell, has been to increase the speed of automobile traffic," he says. "Look. This is about an eight- or ten-lane road, effectively a mini-superhighway cutting through the middle of downtown, and the width of this street itself is a difficult challenge. The king of Spain, Philip II, when he sent settlers to found the many communities of Spain that he was creating in the New World in the fifteenth and sixteenth centuries, sent a group of common-sense design principles with them. One of those was that the warmer the climate, the narrower the streets, to create shade. The colder the climate, the wider the streets, to let sun in."

He stops on the sidewalk and waves his arms again.

"Well, here we are, in a warm climate on a street that's several hundred feet wide. There are no shade trees, and it's very hard to walk out here, even on a nice mild day like this. People aren't going to want to linger on the sidewalks to eat and talk and do the social things that public spaces create, so the width of the street in and of itself is problematic. But the biggest challenge I think that we face here on Bunker Hill is the topography itself. In no major city in the world is the center of human activity, of the social and cultural and recreational retail center, on top of the hill. There are religious buildings on top of hills, there are castles, there are homes of affluent people, but human activity—like water—seems to flow down to a valley."

He mentions a couple of famous examples: In Athens, the Temple of Athena on the

Acropolis is on a hill, but the center of democracy was in the valley. In Rome, the Temple of Zeus was on the Capitoline Hill; the Forum, where the public gathered, was in the valley below.

"This is true again and again for logistical and physical reasons," he insists, and explains his reasoning: "People don't like walking up hills, and they tend to avoid building important places on them. It's fine to walk uphill once a day—when you're going home at night, perhaps—but no one wants to hoof it up a hill to shop, run errands, or meet friends. It's just too annoying. The fact that Los Angeles is planning to build a massive public gathering space on a hill shows that the city is still thinking like an automobile-dependent town. That's not the way to go if you want to build public spaces. People walk when they want to have fun, relax, or hang out.

"Human activity tends to want places that are easily accessible at lower elevations," says Rosenfeld. "Fighting the topography is going to be one of the great challenges of a mixed-use project at this location. Bunker Hill seems to want to be what it was historically, before planners started to interfere with it. It's a very attractive residential neighborhood. People like to live up here and then go down to Main Street to do business and go to the theatres. That's what you see in other cities. In San Francisco, it's Nob Hill. In Portland, Oregon, it's Council Crest in the West Hills. In Seattle, it's Queen Anne

and Capital Hill. People live on the hill and want to do things with other people down below."

Can the project succeed, given the amount of money and effort that is being pumped into it and given the fact that so many important Los Angeles buildings are already there, on the site? Rosenfeld doesn't know. "These ambitious plans for Grand Avenue were rolled out, fighting human nature and gravity. And we've done great things in Los Angeles fighting with nature. We've built dams and aqueducts and maybe this one will prevail also, but I think the vision that's developing here is a little different. I think that organically or naturally this wants to be an attractive residential neighborhood."

Broad shrugs off these criticisms. His mantra? If you build it, they will come. Of course he concedes that there is more work to be done throughout the entire city. For example, there is also a recognized need for more space for the city's exploding biotech industry. The region's three main schools—CalTech, the University of Southern California, and UCLA—all groom bright students and professors who end up taking their ideas and investment capital out of Los Angeles because they can't find affordable lab and office space. Downtown, the city is encouraging the development and building of a *Fame*-like high school for the performing arts. The Los Angeles County Museum is undergoing a major renovation and expansion, thanks to Broad himself. The new

Broad Building at the County Museum will have twice the gallery space of New York's Whitney Museum.

"I think Los Angeles will be viewed as one of the four great cultural cities of the world," says Broad, "together with Paris, London, and New York, because it has all the things they have, and in some cases more. I see this city as being a mecca for cultural tourism. I see people viewing our city differently. Right now they think of the film industry and the Grammies and the Academy Awards and that's all nice, but I think the culture that we have is far more important than those events."

Rosenfeld agrees that the city is different than many others, but he nails it down differently. "We used to think that we were somehow biologically different in Los Angeles," he says, somewhat jokingly. "We lived in cars, we couldn't walk, we lived in suburbs, we didn't believe in a downtown, and the physical characteristic of this city as a ten-thousand-mile sprawling mass was somehow its inevitable fate. I don't think people in Los Angeles are physically different, but I think to some degree they are in attitude. The attitude here is one of extreme individualism. People come to Los Angeles, myself included, to pursue their dreams."

For this reason, he argues, Los Angeles is home to the greatest collection of human talent in the history of the world. "And yet for all that talent we can't seem to do the simplest collaborative things," he adds. "We

can't run a subway down Wilshire Boulevard to the beach. We can't run a light rail to the airport. We can't seem to protect the beaches or the mountains or the river the way much smaller cities have been able to revitalize their waterfronts. In Los Angeles you get the best houses in the world, but you get mediocre public buildings. You have great private art collections and mediocre museums. You have great private gardens and mediocre public parks. Why isn't there great urban planning if there's great everything else? We're still a very young city. We're evolving, and I think in a sense coming back to our downtown is a very positive step in the evolution, and perhaps the most positive."

In the end, it all comes down to the strong force that has shaped the renaissance in all the other cities in this book: community.

"I am optimistic for a couple of reasons," says Rosenfeld. "I think that people really are rediscovering the importance of being around other people. There was an attraction to living in a gated community, to having an eighth of an acre with a little aboveground swimming pool and a Los Angeles bungalow. But I truly believe that most people like to be around other people. And I think that when they get to know the strengths and talents of diverse populations, they appreciate the benefits of it."

ANGELS IN THE CITY OF DREAMS

"There are so many things I want to do: hold public office, be a congress-woman, . . . be an astronaut. It won't be hard 'cause I will have people around me supporting me."

—YOBANA CORDERO, RESIDENT, BOYLE HEIGHTS, LOS ANGELES

The city is evolving. The city is growing up. The city is kissed by the sun, and drawing more and more people to its land of promise every year. But what few people appreciate is the debt the city owes to its population of immigrants, specifically Hispanics. Today Los Angeles is nearly 50 percent Latino, which means that the language of Fathers Crespi and Serra is functionally Los Angeles's second language.

The city is basking in the rise of Mexican-American leadership. It elected Antonio Villaraigosa as its first mayor of Mexican descent. The same kids who struggled to get ahead on the hot asphalt streets are slowly gaining a foothold in the city's government. These citizens have a strong appreciation for urban form, for the look, feel, and hum of the city's streets. They shopped at the Grand Central Market, they walked these streets in their heyday, and they watched them deterio-rate as well. They care about the city and are working to restore it.

That population is only as strong as its youth. And therein lies a reason to hope.

Michele Deane is the program director of Girls Today, Women Tomorrow (GTWT), a weekly volunteer program whose activities include sports, gardening, classes, and poetry nights.

In East Los Angeles, the city's Latino hub, a community garden called Proyecto Jardin sits nestled between Bridge Street Elementary School and White Memorial Medical Center. The lot, once home to two dilapidated homes and a heap of trash, caught the eye of a young medical intern who was interested in turning the place into a garden. A little investigation revealed that the hospital owned the place, and administrators were happy to let local residents transform it.

The most visible gardeners are a group of young girls—first-generation Mexican- and Latin-American teens—who show up on weekends in a brigade of thirty or so to tend the plants. They're members of a local youth organization called Girls Today, Women Tomorrow (GTWT), which began in 1996. At the time program director Michele Deane had observed that a number of neighbor-hood girls had nothing to do after school. She proposed forming a basketball team,

which lured a number of girls. "It started with a group of friends," says Deane, whose family has had ties to Boyle Heights since the 1940s, "just hanging out with the girls in the community doing garden projects, basketball, getting them to think about self-esteem, building up their confidence. And it was all voluntary."

Of course, those simple projects engendered deeper feelings when the kids started coming together. "It's a state of consciousness of thinking bigger," says Deane. "'How do I face these challenges?' 'What do I want to do?' 'Who can I become with the support of everyone around me?' It's a state of consciousness coming from the world around you instead of seeing only the obstacles. Once they saw other people doing it, they started doing it for their friends, for the younger kids growing up. Something in the neighborhood's consciousness shifted."

GTWT has since blossomed into a weekly volunteer program that stretches well beyond sports. Girls can drop by the local youth and family center nearly every day of the week for some kind of activity or class: yoga, kickboxing, computer lab, Web site development classes, and video shooting and editing classes. There are chat nights and poetry nights and weekend retreats where girls get to hang out with adult women from the neighborhood: teachers, artists, nurses, businesswomen.

"We really needed something like this in the neighborhood," says Laura Palomares, one of GTWT's leaders. "The reality is that there weren't any safe public places for kids. There have been shootings in this area. There have been lots of budgets cuts at the schools. The libraries aren't what they should be. There are more military recruiters at the high school than college recruiters these days. We wanted to do something about that, and we wanted to bridge the gap between school and parents."

Today the program reaches up to 250 girls in a single year, aged twelve to twenty-two, all by word of mouth. The group gets funding through a variety of organizations and is currently working on buying a house in the area to use as its base of operations.

GTWT offers kids in the neighborhood a wide range of fun, productive activities in a context that promotes community building, relationship, and responsibility.

The community garden was just another way to help empower these young women. As they help green Proyecto Jardin, the girls are exposed to a bit of nature in their urban environment, they think more about the kind of food they are putting in their bodies, and they find another way to rekindle an interest in their ancestry. Many of their grandparents, for example, can recall growing medicinal plants to use in herbal remedies.

"Born and raised in South Central, and coming from immigrant parents, we always have plants in the backyard," says Palomares. "Whatever bit of land we had, we grew something. Because we live in cities, gardens have been growing smaller in people's minds. Gardening helps the girls be in tune with Mother Nature, and the time away from school, away from their parents, really helps them grow."

GTWT hopes to use produce from the garden in home cooking classes to further reinforce the students' understanding of where food really comes from. "I think it has to do with the economy," says Palomares. "People's eating habits are getting worse and worse. A thirty-nine-cent burger is cheap, so people buy it. Also the food in the schools is bad. They're claiming that so many kids have attention deficit disorder. They have too much sugar in their diets. Once we get the good home cooking classes, it will help what's going on and will help the obesity situation that we're facing. The girls here are getting in touch with the land. That will help them learn more about themselves, which will help them understand and reach their goals. It's cyclical, really. I think it starts with Mother Earth and nature."

There is also significant research showing that gardening, like sports, benefits young women in other ways. A study conducted by the University of Illinois at Urbana-Champaign found that inner-city girls who are exposed to nature tend to exhibit higher self-discipline and avoid risky behavior. The researchers found that these girls were better able to handle peer pressure, sexual pressure, and challenging situations. They made better choices and performed better in school.

You don't have to read the pages of a scientific journal to know that there seems to be some truth in those findings. You just have to meet some of the girls who have been through GTWT's program. Outside at the Jardin one day, a college-age woman named Elizabeth Vasquez is busy working away and stops to talk about the program. "I've been part of it for five years already," she says, "and one of the things that we do is just experience different things. We go to events that we wouldn't have the opportunity to do,

Laura Palomares and a member of GTWT.

like snowboarding, skiing, going to the mountains, stuff that we would normally not be able to afford. This is one of the things we also do: just come to the garden and help out our community and also benefit from all the fruits and vegetables here. We can make a salad with what we grow."

Elizabeth, who is a sophomore at the University of Wisconsin–Madison, credits GTWT with inspiring her to go to college. Her grades were so good and consistent through high school that she landed a four-year scholarship to Madison. "They got me where I am now," she says of GTWT and its strong mentoring program, "and they're always encouraging me. They'll call me up and the mentors ask, 'How have you been? Do you need anything?' My mentor's gone to college too, and I ask her about her experience and I'll tell her about mine, and then we complain about the same things and stuff like that. It's good for the community to have a program like this because in Boyle Heights we have a high percentage of dropout rates in high school, so not a lot of young Latin women even get a higher education."

Another girl, Ginette Sanchez, has been in the program for two years. "I'm in the fashion world," she says proudly. "I'm studying fashion design. This program has a fashion show annually as a fund-raiser, so they allow me to present one of my designs

Former GTWT members credit the organization with broadening their self-confidence and vision for their future through exposure to new places, ideas, and activities.

and I actually modeled it. I had a great experience and it's been really fun. It's really important because it makes me feel like there's a future for me. When I was small I lived only with my mom, and there wasn't enough money. So I always thought that I wouldn't have a future. Now that I have positive role models, I'm going to college and I'm being positive by thinking that I'm going to be someone in life as well."

She excuses herself because she has more work to do. As she turns back to the plants in her care, you can't help thinking: she's absolutely right.

SEATTLE
The Future Is Now

"Seattle has a history of going against
the accepted conventional wisdom. . . .
Seattle is a place where you can take
on the establishment and win."

—DICK FALKENBURY,
SEATTLE ACTIVIST

Once upon a time, when the world was
young, a race of humans called the
Salmon people lived in a large house at the
bottom of the sea. They had a special kin-
ship with the people who lived on land. Each
year, when the waters of the Pacific turned
warm, the Salmon people dressed up their
sons and daughters as fish and sent them off
to feed themselves to the humans who lived
on the land.

The land people did not catch these beautiful fish by their own skill. Each fish had the
power of choice. He or she *chose* to give
himself to a fisher. But if a fisher had dishon-
ored the spirits of the salmon in the past, the
young salmon did not give themselves to
him. To be worthy of such a sacrifice, the
fisher had to follow the rules. When a land
person finished eating a salmon, he or she
had to return the fish's bones to the water. If
a land person could not eat all his salmon,
he had to return the uneaten portion to the
sea. In this way, the land people learned
never to take more salmon than they could

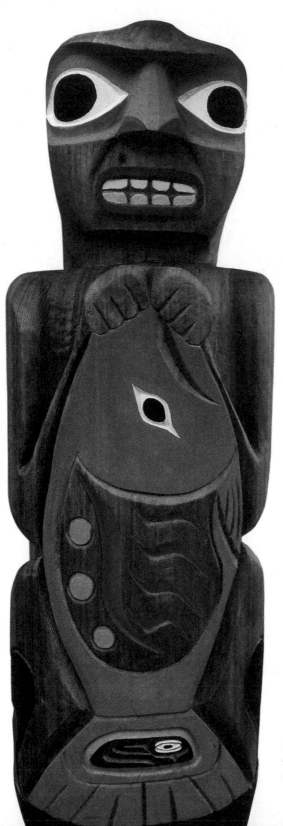

rightfully eat. If they did this, the spirits of the salmon would be honored, the fish would always return to the rivers and streams in great numbers, and this supply of delicious food would last forever.

Animals figured prominently in the spiritual cosmology of the Native Americans who lived along the coastal waters of the Pacific Northwest. Tribal folklore and artwork pay homage to Raven, Bear, Eagle, Beaver, Hawk, and many others. Totem poles, tattoos, and food bowls were decorated with images of these creatures. Salmon was a major food source and regarded as a symbol of abundance, prosperity, persistence, instinct, and determination. The Native Americans understood that for all their abundance, salmon were fragile. They could easily be overfished and their numbers greatly reduced. That's why a staunchly ecological message seeped into their early rituals, one that survives among residents of the Pacific Northwest today—Native Americans and newcomers alike.

You can hardly miss the role salmon plays in the economy of Seattle, our fourth and final city. Salmon imagery abounds in the region, as does a zealous environmental ethic. With its flurry of grassroots organizations, glorious Space Needle, Experience Music Project Museum, monorail, endless coffeehouses, and gorgeous mountains, islands, and bay, Seattle has earned a reputation for being one of the most attractive, livable cities in America—and arguably the "greenest."

Native American tribal artwork often features animals indigenous to the region, an indication of their importance to the culture. Photo courtesy of the Northwest Indian Fisheries Commission

Green roofs, like this one on top of the Justice Department building in Seattle, have helped reduce the city's greenhouse gas emissions by as much as 60 percent. Photo courtesy of Mithun

To be sure, there are numerous laudable highlights. Seattle's public electric company, Seattle City Light, promised in 2004 to conserve energy through the use of alternative resources to run the whole city without emitting greenhouse gases; it's the most ambitious program in the United States. The Green Seattle Project is committed to rescuing 2,500 acres of urban forest from invasive plant species. Like Chicago, the city is mounting a massive landscaping effort around town to help retain all or most of its renowned drizzle. More than two thousand community garden plots grow throughout the city, providing nourishing food for city dwellers, many of them people on low incomes. Green roofs grow atop the Department of Justice building and City Hall, and city administrative offices and operations reduced their greenhouse gas emissions by 60 percent in the decade ending in 2000. Indeed, Seattle Mayor Greg Nickels made national news in 2005 when he challenged the Bush administration's stance on global warming. Nickels signed up more than 200 American cities to voluntarily meet the Kyoto Protocol to reduce greenhouse

Seattle's green open space and varied terrain have long attracted people who appreciate an unspoiled environment. Photo courtesy of Mountains to Sound Greenway Trust

emissions; his Web site (www.ci.seattle .wa.us/mayor/climate) keeps a running tally of all cities that join the movement.

In recent decades, the city has been the victim of its own great press. Each time another lifestyle magazine proclaims it a top destination, more and more Americans relocate here, straining the area's housing, roads, and resources. This has presented new challenges for the city, demanding intelligent planning. Seattle's government has tried to do its part to hold the line on reckless suburban growth, encourage the work of infill developers, and empower its neighborhoods to develop appropriate growth plans. On the mass transit front alone, Seattle is home to a generous system of bike lanes and trails and an excellent system of buses and ferries, and it is currently in the process of building a light rail system.

"The best thing about Seattle is that there is total access to government," says Cary

Moon, an activist we'll meet later. "Most of the truly great things in Seattle happen because the citizens want it." A few classic examples: The state once wanted to build a highway through the Arboretum on Seattle's east side; residents fought back and the green space stayed. In 1965 the city wanted to raze the famous Pike Place Market, arguably the city's top destination after the Space Needle. Citizens said no; the market stayed. More recently, a grassroots petition drive led to a plan—now dead in the water—to build a new monorail line downtown.

From 1990 to 2000, the population of King County—the one including Seattle—leaped 15.2 percent to more than 1.7 million people. That is small by New York or Los Angeles standards, but the traffic situation in downtown Seattle would shock most Los Angelenos. The city's exquisite-looking Elliott Bay and nearby Puget Sound are sadly polluted. Rents and home prices keep rising as the area attracts more and more professionals eager to work among the area's software and high-tech firms and its world-renowned companies Microsoft, Starbucks, and Amazon.com.

Technology was supposed to be Seattle's salvation, but that progress has brought endless challenges, which Seattleites are combating with their signature brand of community action and "green smarts." They are discovering and proposing new methods of mass transportation. They are leading the nation with innovative, environmentally friendly architecture, and they are taking steps to rethink and redesign their city so that the salmon will run free and abundantly once more.

A CITY OF BOOM AND BUST

Like Los Angeles, Seattle is another relatively young American city. Its history is full of stories of earth moving and land shifting. Its first inhabitants were members of the Duwamish and Suquamish tribes, who fished the bay for salmon. Then came the Denny Party, a group of non-Native settlers who arrived on the scene in 1851. They came, they saw, they harvested trees.

A few years later, the city got its first sawmill, which got to work leveling whatever lay in its path. Logging and fishing would become the chief industries here, but before settlers could even build a city, they needed to clear the hilly land of trees, which reached right to the water's edge. Trees were valuable for timber, but hills were not. By 1876—the year Los Angeles got the railroad, the year General Custer met his end at Little Big

Horn—young Seattle was busy chopping away at its hills with steam shovels and high-pressure water guns to make the land flat and conducive to development. The dirt was carried or washed downhill and dumped into the bay to build the city's now-famous waterfront. The salmon beheld this mountain of earth colliding into their territory—their cool, clear waters turning warm and muddy—and fled for hospitable climes, and Elliott Bay became Seattle's portal to the world.

Timber stayed the area's chief export for decades. The technology got so good that by 1884 loggers throughout the state cut 1 million board feet of lumber for the first time. Near the end of the century—in 1897—prospectors found gold in Canada's Yukon River, and dreamers and opportunity seekers flocked north to strike it rich. Seattle was the jumping-off point for most people bound for the Klondike. Seattle was where you went to load up on supplies, get a good meal, spend a few hours with a member of the opposite

The Columbia Mill, built in 1890, at what is now the intersection of Rainier Avenue and Brandon Street. Photo courtesy of Rainier Valley Historical Society

sex, and book a passage north. The lucky miners passed through the town on the way back, spent their money, and decided to stay. Seattle's population tripled between 1900 and 1910, from 80,000 to 237,000 people.

Seattle's world was an extractive one. That is, it earned its living largely by harvesting natural resources, such as fish, timber, coal, and so on. That changed with World War I, when the young aircraft maker Boeing landed a contract for one hundred planes from the federal government. Seattle retooled itself as a city of industry. It became a city of cutting-edge ships, planes, and factory goods. The city was hard hit by the Depression but rebounded again with World War II. Ships and planes rolled off assembly lines as smokestacks billowed blackness into the Seattle skyline.

But that could not last either. The cycle of boom and bust—so common to industry-dependent cities—became an all-too-common story for Seattle. After the war, the factories fell silent again. Uncle Sam didn't need weapons of war again just yet, so industry had to cast about for its new customer. It found it—just as Detroit did—in the burgeoning middle class. Orders began to mount for passenger airplanes; the world of air travel for the common man had just begun. In 1962, when Seattle hosted the World's Fair—"the Century 21 Exposition"—organizers played up the angle of Seattle as a city of technological marvels. A city of industry. A city for the modern era. Nearly 10 million people poured into Seattle for the World's Fair and found themselves dazzled at the sight of the 605-foot-tall Space Needle looming over downtown

The Boeing plant in 1943. Photo courtesy of the Museum of History and Industry, Seattle

A tourist attending the Seattle World's Fair in 1962 photographs the Space Needle. Inset, the official poster of the fair. Photos courtesy of the Museum of History and Industry, Seattle

SEATTLE WORLD'S FAIR

SEATTLE, WASH., U.S.A.
April 21-October 21
1962

Seattle. The Needle signified the city's view of itself. Seattle felt flush and happy.

But how could it last? After the boom, again came bust. Inflation and the high cost of oil kicked the stool out from under Boeing, and thousands in the area found themselves out of work—and not just in the high-tech industries. The nation was waking up to the reality that its natural resources would not last forever. A series of court decisions began limiting logging and fishing industries. A new generation of Native Americans asserted their ancestral rights to fish wild salmon, and the courts agreed, awarding them 50 percent of the wild catch, sending the non-Native fishing industry into a downward spiral. A famous billboard of the time read, "Will the last person leaving Seattle turn out the lights?"

The age of extraction had been dealt a serious blow, and the world of technology was revealed as entirely too dependent upon the winning of large contracts. New industries would have to blossom if Seattle was going to make it, and thankfully they did. The city found its salvation—its new salvation—in computers. Today, nearly every computer in the world runs on software developed in this region of the world. The city today attracts highly educated professionals who want two things in life: a challenging career and a close connection to natural surroundings. Where previous generations focused on what Seattle's natural resources could do for them, today's generation wonders how they can benefit the environment.

THE CONSCIENCES OF SEATTLE

Depending on your perspective, Seattle's conscience is wrapped up in the spirit of a man or the spirit of a fish.

Born in the chilly, freshwater streams and rivers of the Pacific Coast, salmon migrate downstream to the open sea. There they transform themselves into saltwater creatures and gorge happily on copious food from the sea. (Such bountiful meals are scarcer in the salmon's birthplace, given its size and calorie needs.) Meanwhile, deep in the salmon's brain, a homing device more accurate than any GPS tracker is counting down its host's time on the earth.

When the salmon's days are numbered, its brain gives the signal and the fish bids the sea farewell and heads back to precisely the same freshwater stream where it was born. Some salmon have swum three thousand miles to return home, mate, and die. On the way home, the fish fights both gravity and the force of water rushing against it; and yet, it fights. In the course of this journey, its body changes shape. Its lip becomes hooked, and its back hunched like a prizefighter marshalling his muscles for a brawl.

The salmon fights its way up fish ladders, up man-made dams, to its ancestral waters. For thousands of generations, the same families have spawned in the same spot. The males and females make their nests, spawn, and expire. Their battered bodies feed the river scavengers and insects that will in turn feed their progeny. If all

Once-abundant salmon populations have suffered from the dramatic rise in pollution, mostly from residential sources. City government is working to reverse the damage and restore water quality in Seattle's many streams. Photo courtesy of Mithun

goes well, the story will repeat itself again and again.

But now, more than ever before, it does not go well.

The decline in salmon populations has wreaked havoc with the foodways of Native Americans in this region, but they're not the only ones who should be concerned. Today, Seattle's city planners and citizen activists are very aware of the threats posed to salmon by rampant development, and they are trying to undo the damage done unknowingly by previous generations.

As we've said, Puget Sound looks beautiful but masks terrible problems under the surface. Toxins in the soil at the bottom of the sound give fish lesions. Some orca whale females that inhabit these waters lose their firstborn because their mother's milk is so contaminated. And spawning populations of salmon have dropped to twenty-two independent groups from historic levels of well over thirty.

It would be easy if we could point the finger at industrial polluters, but the federal sanctions have gotten so strict that most of those problems have been cleaned up. No, the real problem these days is pollution from residential sources, the same toxic stuff we have described throughout this book.

Fish ladders facilitate the upstream journey of salmon, providing them with a means to bypass dams. Photo courtesy of U.S. Army Corps of Engineers

Because salmon require pristine conditions in both freshwater and saltwater habitats, they are a good barometer species for the health of both. Declining salmon populations tell us that ceaseless building—new subdivisions, roads, and development—has impacted the land around rivers, contaminating the waters and eroding the soil. Logging and farming loosen the soil and leave it vulnerable to heavy rains that wash it into freshwater streams, which in turn rise high with silt. Particles from auto exhaust, worn brake pads, fertilizers, gas, oil, transmission fluid, herbicides, and pesticides—the toxic soup of urban and suburban life—all wash into waterways with every rain. Some of the old suburbs leach raw sewage from antiquated septic tanks into the water tables.

All this stuff accumulates and turns parts of the sound into dead zones that cannot support life. They take their toll on the salmon's habitat, polluting the water and raising its temperature, creating an inhospitable environment for a creature that requires pure, bone-chilling-cold water to stay alive.

That's why each community that lives on a major watershed that ultimately feeds into Puget Sound has now created a planning committee to develop locally acceptable strategies to restore salmon to this important waterway. This collaborative effort, known as Shared Strategy for Puget Sound (www.sharedsalmonstrategy.org), is a massive undertaking. It requires that local communities track down the sources of pollution—overt or otherwise—that feed into every river, stream, or creek that ultimately runs into Puget Sound. The collaborative is tapping into local, state, and federal grants to help restore the habitat along those waterways.

Today, thousands of years after the first Native American plucked a salmon from the waters, the salmon is still the thread that runs through much of Seattle's life. Since the 1980s, the city, state, and federal governments have taken the following steps to ensure that this precious creature survives:

- Building more fish ladders to make it easier for salmon to "hop" upstream and bypass dams (at least twenty-nine salmon "runs" exist in Seattle alone)
- Barging, ferrying, or trucking salmon around dams

- Limiting how much water factories and farm businesses suck out of riverways
- Ceasing or limiting how much logging and timber business is conducted near waterways
- Limiting salmon fishing permits and seasons
- Restoring habitats along rivers, and dredging to remove contaminated silt
- Upping the amount of water that flows through big dams

The salmon, the icon of the Pacific Northwest, has become a different sort of symbol, rather like the canary in the coal mine. If the salmon goes, then everything up the food chain suffers—including six hundred thousand jobs and $1 billion a year in the fishing industry.

MAN VS. MYTH

"In every deliberation, we must consider the impact of our decisions on the next seven generations."
—THE IROQUOIS CONFEDERACY

A sculpture in Pioneer Square, Seattle's historic district, depicts the city's other conscience: Chief Seattle, a Native American and leader of the Duwamish and Suquamish tribes. Seattle—his true Indian name sounded like "See-yahtlh"—had the privilege or misfortune of watching his entire world change

before his eyes. When he was a boy, growing up on what is now Bainbridge Island, he saw his first white man—the English explorer Captain George Vancouver, who arrived in two ships in 1792. Seattle was renowned in his day for his daring wars with other tribes, his gift for bold military tactics, and his shrewd relations with European-Americans. He embraced the white man's firearms, his Christian religion, and his trade goods. He protected some of the early white settlers and even halted an assassination attempt on the life of an early white trader, Dr. David Maynard. For all this, the white settlers named their city in honor of Chief Seattle.

Chief Seattle, leader of the Suquamish and Duwamish people, in the only known photograph of him, taken in 1864. Photo courtesy of the Museum of History and Industry, Seattle.

But when people speak of the chief these days, it's usually in a hushed, reverent tone. That's because Seattle, we're told, practically predicted the environmental movement. The story goes that in 1854, when the United States government tried to persuade the Puget Sound Indians to move to a reservation, Seattle stood before the territorial governor and gave a speech that included these lines, quoted often in environmental circles:

> *All things are connected.*
> *Whatever befalls the earth,*
> *befalls the sons and daughters of the*
>   *earth.*
> *Man did not weave the web of life;*
> *he is merely a strand in it.*
> *Whatever he does to the web,*
> *he does to himself.*

The words are beautiful and have been reproduced on everything from T-shirts to backpacks to "green" tea-bag cartons. Over the years, even officials from the United Nations and NASA have quoted them.

The trouble is, Seattle never said them. In fact, historians are still unclear what he did say in his 1854 speech. Seattle didn't speak English, and the only man taking notes at the speech didn't speak the chief's tongue. Much of the famous Seattle speech was written in the early 1970s by a TV scriptwriter for an environmental film documentary. Somehow, the false "ecological" version of the speech was confused with the real thing and more

recently ended up on the Internet, where it took on a life of its own.

The extrapolation has probably lasted this long because so many of us want to believe that it is true. Regardless of who said it, the sentiments in the speech are real for many people. In our collective unconscious, we seem to be longing for a "conscience of the environment," an authority figure who is authentic and above reproach. That's fine, but doesn't our own authenticity count? Isn't it enough to answer the call of our own consciences?

Luckily, the Seattle area is home to so many Native Americans that one doesn't really need to look to imperfect history lessons to know how to do right by the environment. All you have to do is take a walk with one of the elders.

One drizzly morning, Billy Frank, chairman of the Northwest Indian Fisheries Commission, walks along the river where his people have lived for thousands of years. The Nisqually tribe, one of twenty different tribes along the Pacific Coast, has been working to clean and protect the waters of the Nisqually River.

"Well, I love this river," Frank says. "This is the salmon's home. When the salmon goes out in the ocean for seven years and comes back, we want to make sure that this home is here. That means all of the trees, that means the environment, that means the quantity and quality of the water, that means everything has to be intact, and we're trying to protect that. How we do that is by

Billy Frank, chairman of the Northwest Indian Fisheries Commission, at the Nisqually River.

working with people, working with a coalition, with the utility companies. There are three dams on this river alone."

Frank knows the history of his people well. The way he sees it, the blood of the salmon runs not only in his veins but in those of European-Americans as well. "The salmon sustained all of us," he says. "When the Europeans came here, the salmon sustained them as well. It's sustained us all of our lives, and it's part of the blood that flows through us. We talk about salmon like they're a part of our family. We have ceremonies for our salmon when they come back. We talk to them and we have our drums and we have our ceremonies. Everything is about the salmon ceremonies. The salmon is so powerful; he goes way up in the ocean, up to Alaska in the cold weather, and when he comes back home he comes back to this exact river. It's a wonder of the world, the salmon is, and we got to make sure that that salmon's going to be here from now on."

Frank's father lived to be 104, and his mother 96. Frank himself is 73 years old. All of them have spent their lives atop the Nisqually watershed. He remembers when the water was more polluted than it is now, but a public outcry in recent years has focused attention on what people were knowingly or unknowingly dumping into the river.

"It takes all of the tribes to put this coalition together," he says. "Forty years ago we didn't have an infrastructure to put things together and bring people together. Today we have a human infrastructure as well as sewer systems. So the tribes have come a long way in the last forty years, and today we stand ready to bring people together. The leadership is there, the Indian leadership, as well as our technical crew, our science people. We have a public relations department. We write regulations for ourselves now; we don't depend upon the state of Washington. We work with the state of Washington, we work with the federal government, we're partners with them to make the environment whole."

For thirty years the tribes have elected Frank to manage their fishing operations. He's charged with improving water quality not just for salmon but for clams, oysters, and other seafood plucked from coastal waters. He meets regularly with leaders in the timber industry, the U.S. government, local utilities, big ports, small and large businesses, environmentalists, and of course, leaders of each of the tribes themselves. Education, he says, is the key to everything they do. "They have leaders now in our tribes that are unbelievable," he says. "They take it another step, trying to make people aware of how important the environment is to us, how important the water is to us, how important the ocean is to us, how important our environment around us in our own backyard is."

He takes a few more steps along the water and stops, his hands held out to feel the droplets of rain.

"It's raining today, as you see, and we love the rain," he says. "The rain is part of our country. All of our green trees and all of the flowers are blooming, and it is just a wonderful place to live. Don't decide to move here or anything," he says with a laugh, "but this is a great place. It takes good people to do good things."

He pauses and watches two young men go by in their boat. He smiles.

"This river is nothing but life to us Indian people," he says. "Water is life, as you see in these two boys just going by on their boat. They're pulling their nets out today and they got a lot of salmon in their nets, and so they're enjoying life right now, and that's what it's all about."

Frank himself moves like a young man. Compared to the age his father reached, he is still a boy. Now and then he remembers

A great blue heron in flight near Seattle.
Photo by Kevin Ebi / LivingWilderness.com

what his father used to say about their country.

"My father, when he was a little boy, he said we had everything here," he says. "Our Indian people, before the European people, we had everything. Everything was pure. Our medicines were here and all of our cedar trees were big giant cedar trees that we could make canoes out of. All of that was here at that time. We never had sugar diabetes. We weren't dying of diseases. So today we're still here and we still have those principles walking with us every day. We have the old people dreaming and we hear the drums, we hear our Indian music, we hear our language, and we hear everything about what we're all about as Indian people."

"So if we can take that and bring it to the society that we're in today and try to find a balance," he continues, "we can all work together and live together and protect our environment and protect our water from now on. This water is life, and if we don't have water, we don't have life. So life and salmon are together, and all of our medicines and all of our trees and all of our environment—our rain, our sun, our moon that guides all of the salmon back to us—this is what it's all about. Our Indian people are leading the way to make sure that that's coming about."

In the past one hundred years, Native Americans have seen the degradation of their natural environment, Frank says. But things are different now and will continue to be different for the next one hundred years because so many tribesmen are sitting at the table in local and federal governments, guiding the process and drawing upon their collective ancestral memories of how things used to be. In the mid-1970s, the tribes acted to restore the bald eagle to the region, and today eagles are plentiful again.

"They're all over here now, they're flying up and down our rivers," Frank says. "They're up in our bays and everywhere. They have nests, and we protect the nests now. Eagle is so important, and he's a barometer for all of us. If he's here, if our birds are here, they're all flying and they're all happy, water's flowing, our trees are green, and the birds come back every year and our salmon come back every year, we're happy. The whales come here every year and visit us— right here in front of us—and on their journey back north and their journey back south, they visit us in the springtime. This is part of their journey, and it's our journey to stay here and work hard for the environment."

As he stands there, a blue heron flies over the water. Frank starts moving again, heading back to his truck.

OUT ON THE WATER WITH A SUSTAINABLE FISHERMAN

It's insanely early on a summer morning when our film crew boards the fishing boat *Howard H.* in the town of Westport, just due west of Seattle. We're here to watch Doug Frecke at work, plying the waters off the Pacific Coast for albacore tuna, crab, and salmon. He's been doing this work for twenty-five years, ever since he was a kid and went out on the water with his father. Frecke interests us because he's diligent about fishing sustainably, strictly following catch limits and working with agencies and fish supply houses that encourage such practices.

The day is dawning overcast and gray, but not foreboding. It takes a few hours to reach Frecke's fishing grounds, and along the way we discover he's something of an environmental philosopher.

"Oh, I get a thrill out of landing fish, particularly salmon," he says. "I like salmon the best because when you get a salmon on the end of your line, it's just you against the salmon."

As he talks, he and his first mate Josh Laudenglos work to get their lines ready. They always want to make sure their gear is in good condition. If they lose a line, out-

The *Howard H.* at sunrise. Its captain, Doug Frecke, is a passionate advocate of fishing sustainably.

fitted with various lures, they're basically losing about $100 of equipment. It takes several salmon to make up for that.

A conversation with Frecke is eye-opening because he makes us realize how much impacts the tasty morsel of fish on the end of our forks.

"I think the salmon population's grown a little bit," he says. "It's so dependent on the ocean conditions. When ocean conditions are right, they really flourish. Now that we've got the logging regulations in place, the burning areas have to be protected, and in cities there's a lot more recognition that we have to be careful around the streams. A lot of recognition. We can't keep throwing all that nitrogen on our lawns and have it run right into the streams and expect the salmon to survive. There's two or three hatcheries right there in the Seattle metropolitan area that are growing. It's looking good."

He isn't fishing very long when his first fish strikes. He hauls it in, measures it, and passes it to Josh to process it. He needs to catch about twenty salmon a day to make his daily excursion worthwhile. Back on shore, each of those fish will fetch $40 to $60, and together they'll pay for his day on the water.

"Sustainable fishing is real important to us because we want to have these fish around for our kids and their grandkids," he says after a while. "In all these salmon stocks, up and down the Washington-Oregon coast, scientists estimate how many fish are coming back to the river every year. They have models that they crank into their computers and give an estimate. First, we deduct all the fish that are needed for spawning in both our natural systems and our artery systems. Then they take out the fish that are intercepted by the Canadians and the Alaskans. Then what's left over is available for harvest. There are some years where we don't get to fish at all. Then some years we get to take a few thousand fish."

It's critical that a number of salmon reach the spawning grounds each year to reproduce and begin the cycle anew. Every spring there's a coast-wide meeting of the federal and state fish managers. They calculate what's required for perpetuating the stock, and everything follows from that number. They have to build enough excess salmon into the system to feed wildlife too.

"Salmon is one of the foods of nature," says Frecke. "Look at the bears and all the other animals that eat salmon when they come back to spawn. They even eat them when they come out of the rivers when they're small. They're prey for the bigger fish in the sea when they first come out into the sea. We had a situation off Vancouver Island where the mackerel were right in front of the streams and they almost wiped out the salmon stock. It was up by Barclay Sound. Situations like that are hard to document, but we know they happen and we do the best we can to take account of it."

The way he sees it, though, there's an internal logic to the system, if we can learn to respect it. "It's a delicate balance, but nature has her ways to make up for deficiencies in

Today, salmon populations are carefully monitored by state and federal agencies that take into account the number of salmon to reach the spawning ground each year and how many salmon will be consumed by other wildlife. Photo by Jonathan Bell

sidered critical or endangered, then the most that we can take is one hundred of those fish. The other nine hundred have to get back to the river."

The guys have a few maxims that keep them upbeat when the fishing is slow. Frecke likes to say, "You got to get two before you get four." His buddy Josh is more blunt: "To be a good fisherman you have to be an eternal optimist 'cause everything else sucks."

Frecke frowns a bit and shakes his head. "Our goal is to get twenty fish, minimum, a day. I don't think we're going to make it today."

It doesn't pay to return to land every day if you haven't caught fish. So the guys will sometimes stay out for four days at a time, poking around in time-honored spots where the fish like to hang out. "Salmon usually like rock piles," he tells us. "There are various rock piles around that we go check, and it sort of depends on the tides. Sometimes you find them in the beach. Sometimes you find them offshore. One of the fallacies that people believe is that there's this homogenous blend of fish all through the ocean, which couldn't be further from the truth. They go where the temperature's right and where there's food. A lot of places in the ocean are barren."

For the past three years, Frecke and others have noticed some unusual warm water conditions. They chalk it up to global warming, but they aren't climatologists. All they know is that the temperature of the water close to

one area while they overlap in others," he says. Contrary to popular belief, Frecke says, the federal and the state fishery managers work well with fishermen—at least the ones he knows—and they aren't about to let any fishermen knowingly overharvest any of these stocks. "In the past we've made some mistakes, but in the last ten years they realized the mistakes and they've made corrections. What we're allowed to harvest, in my view, is almost miniscule compared to the total amount of biomass that is out here. Our state policy is that the maximum we can take on any of these critical stocks is 10 percent. So, if we get a thousand fish forecast for the Squagit River and that particular run's conthe beach is significantly warmer than it has been in their lifetimes. "Very seldom in this time of the year you'll see sixty-three- or sixty-four-degree water here," he says. "We're not up there yet, but I noticed today we're at sixty-two and a half. The tuna run in warm water fifty to one hundred, or two hundred miles offshore. I think that's one reason salmon fishing is not good. They don't like warm water. They are probably up in British Columbia, where the water's cooler. Last week we were fishing down off Oregon, and we found cooler water down there and quite a bit better fishing."

He mentions that the number of fish coming out of the Klamath River in Oregon has been low, effectively shutting down that fishery for the rest of the summer. We ask him why. "The fish have to have water," he replies, "and they're taking too much water out of the river for irrigating crops and diverting it to northern California for power. You can't blame that on the fishermen."

From the way he says it, we understand instantly that probably every fisherman resents the implication that he is greedily emptying the sea of fish. No wonder he says it a couple of times: you can't blame the fishermen. And he's right. Who's eating all that crab, shrimp, lobster, and salmon? Who's lining up at the sushi bars? Who's grilling tuna burgers on the barbecue? But also, who's watering their lawns and washing their cars?

"It's all interconnected," says Frecke. "You can summarize it that way. You know,

we can't use all the water for irrigation and expect to have salmon. Even the rivers in the metropolitan areas, the bulk of them are diverted, and you have to be cognizant of nature's needs as well, as far as what we need for our lawns and our gardens. We have to make sure we have enough water for nature."

The morning warms up and he's on a roll, excited now, talking as he fishes. One thing is certain: it's odd to be surrounded by all this blueness and to understand for the first time that what happens to your lawn back home somehow impinges upon this aquatic world. Spend a day with a fisherman and you'll probably never look at water the same way ever again. As for Frecke, it's still too early to know whether this will be a good day or a bad day, but it's definitely a slow day. You have to catch two before you catch four.

"We thought we were going have a real shortage this summer in the Seattle area," says Frecke, "but we've got enough spring rains where it looks like we're going be okay. We have to have enough in those reservoirs to release water for the fish and to have water for watering our lawns."

A CITY OF GREEN BUILDERS

The great irony of Seattle's popularity is that so many people are flocking here that they are, literally, loving the place to death. As we saw earlier, each time you disturb the soil with large building projects, the land erodes

The Seattle skyline, from the south. Photo by Jo Ann Snover, ShutterStock

and washes into the area's waterways, eventually polluting and clogging those arteries and making it difficult for the wildlife to survive. If a city is to grow in a sustainable manner, people have to find new ways of building homes and businesses that do not impact or destroy so much of the natural world. The desire to do this has led to a movement in environmentally friendly construction and architecture, called green building. Seattle has gained a reputation as a hotbed for this kind of work.

For Martha Rose, the philosophy of green building is the culmination of a lifetime of strong ideas about sustainable shelter. When

she was only nineteen years old, Chicago-born Rose took a job as a carpenter on a construction site in the Washington DC area. "The work was hard," she remembers, "but I liked it."

The granddaughter of a Chicago builder, Rose had always had a strong reaction whenever she saw new houses going up on what was once farmland outside Chicago. "Every time I saw new development in rural areas, I didn't like it," she says. "And that was when I was young. Every place else that I went, I'd see the same thing. In DC and in

Portland, Oregon. My feeling was the same: I just didn't like it." There had to be a better way to make new homes for people than to keep gobbling up precious swaths of green, untouched land, she thought.

There could be better ways to build, too. On her first job as a young carpenter, she was appalled when her boss had her install shoddy doorknobs on a door. "I think the only thing that was metal in those knobs were the screws holding them to the door," she remembers. "The rest of it was plastic. It was so cheap it made me sick. I would rather have a smaller house better built than a big house done cheaply."

Eventually, she would have her chance. In 1982 she took a job as a building inspector in Seattle, a job that allowed her to travel throughout the city, where she saw countless vacant, near-vacant, or dilapidated parcels of land within the city limits that were crying out for intelligent repurposing. If you were going to build homes, she thought, this was the place to do it: inside the city, where you didn't have to impact farmland or, worse, raw nature. This type of construction has a name—urban infill housing—and refers to the filling in of city lots. Such construction is usually speculative; the builder buys a piece of property, erects a townhouse, and then puts the new structure on the market. The practice is controversial because longtime residents often don't like the way the new structures alter the character of the neighborhood. But

Seattle was a city on the move. Its population was growing, and newcomers especially liked the idea of moving into a vibrant city center.

Rose began building homes in downtown Seattle, always looking for ways to improve her methods and build safer, more efficient, more ecologically sound structures. For example, the start of any construction job is usually a messy endeavor. The demolition crew sweeps in, levels everything to the ground, and hauls away the debris of the older structure to a landfill site. Rose and other green builders were beginning to see that that process was highly detrimental to the environment. Much of the stuff they were hauling away to the landfills could be reused or recycled, and the big machines ended up tearing up the adjacent land, ruining the topsoil and local vegetation, and sending tons of loosened soil down storm drains.

Martha Rose, the granddaughter of a Chicago builder, began working in construction as a carpenter. Her Seattle company leads in sustainable building.

Martha Rose Construction used many green techniques to build these townhomes. Photo by Northwest Property Imaging

Today Rose has adopted an earth-friendly approach to site management. Before the job starts, she calls in a salvage company that picks through the existing structure for usable items, such as hardwood floors, cabinets, and mantelpieces. Each of these items is carefully pried out and donated to shelter organizations or sold to people looking to restore old homes. Next, the empty shell is demolished, and the resulting concrete, wood, and bricks are sent to a special recycling site that sorts "commingled debris." The wood is ground up for composting, the metal is recycled as scrap, and anything unusable is ground up and used to layer landfills. Thanks to this novel method, only 5 percent of structures—instead of 100 percent of them—ever makes it to a landfill!

Recently, Rose has started using demolition crews that use only biodiesel equipment to knock down buildings. "Believe it or not," Rose says, "the inventor of the diesel engine, Rudolf Diesel, actually designed his original engine to run on peanut oil. Later, people came along and started using petroleum fuels." Today's biodiesel fuels, made from various vegetable products, are gentler on the environment and burn cleaner.

Next, the crew tries to save as many trees on the site as possible. They erect fences and filters to halt further erosion and place a layer of wood chips on the ground to give the machines a slightly firmer footing and traction, so they don't spin and tear up the earth. When they start building basements, they take pains to mimic the natural process forests use to capture and retain water. They do it by establishing infiltration pits filled with crushed rock, which allows local water to seep into the ground and slowly percolate into the earth instead of running away into storm drains. Because Seattle is a fairly mild climate, they are able to use a new type of porous concrete that allows water to wick into sidewalks and eventually drip into the ground.

They try to eliminate the use of toxic pressure-treated lumber. Instead of installing roof shingles with a twenty-year lifespan, they opt for those that last thirty years, to lessen the need for shingles later down the line.

In recent years, the goal among green builders has been to reduce energy loss as much as possible. Most people assume that means using solar technology, but heating a home with solar and using solar panels to run your home's electricity are still quite expensive technologies. (Solar water heating is the most cost-effective solar technology at this time.) So when a green house goes up, carpenters try to build larger spaces in the walls for thicker insulation. They even insulate the underside of the concrete slab on which the house sits. "You can pretty much build a house these days so efficiently that your heating costs go way down," says Rose. "I did the same thing in my office and home. I've been here a year and I cannot believe how comfortable it is."

The Martha Rose Construction Company is still small by most city standards. Rose estimates that she builds three to eight houses a year in Seattle, but each of them has been certified as energy-efficient and environmentally friendly structures by Washington's "Built Green" organization.

"What I do is always risky financially," says Rose. "I'll build a house really well and I'm taking a chance that I will be able to make my money back, plus a profit, and that's tough. Homebuyers are not yet educated about what a green house is all about. You might spend more money up front, but you'll save money every year you live in that house, compared to houses that are not built this way."

"The emphasis right now is on using more durable goods—things that last longer," she adds. "We are installing commercial-grade tile and carpets and cedar siding, which will last forever. We install dual-flush toilets, which have two buttons on them, one for a light flush, another for a heavy flush. Three-quarters of the time, you would use only the small button. That's a toilet that was developed in Australia. It helps homeowners save money in water and sewer costs, but it costs builders three times as much. You can use paints and adhesives that don't have harmful fumes or VOCs [*volatile organic compounds*]. You can use fiberglass that is not made with formaldehyde. You can install an all-natural linoleum and Energy Star appliances and compact fluorescent light bulbs. All these things are available, if you look for them, but if you don't know why you should want them, you're going to think this house is more expensive than others on the market."

It's estimated that only about 5 percent of the population wants this kind of house, but nearly 20 percent of the homes going up in Seattle these days are certified by Built Green, including several low-income housing complexes. Slowly but surely, traditional builders are incorporating some of these energy- and resource-saving strategies in their structures. The cost to build a green house is about 5 percent more than that of conventional construction. But that tiny percent translates to big bucks when you're building something as costly as a house. If it's not done carefully, the green house might price itself out of the neighborhood.

Still, Martha Rose would not consider any other kind of work. "I think this is important," she says. "It's the difference between a teacher who wants to work in private schools versus public schools because he or she feels private schools are more rigorous. Or a lawyer who wants to be a public defender versus working in big law firm. Of the builders who do this work, some are doing it as a selling feature for those homes.

They want to be able to say, 'Look, here's a green house for sale!' But most are doing it because they feel strongly about it. Hey—somebody has to start doing it. Pretty soon it's going to be the norm. We're on the bandwagon before everyone else is on the bandwagon. I'm proud of what we're doing. I want to always be able to go back to a house I did in five years and have it be in good shape. I want to offer something that the masses aren't producing. A notch up in quality means a lot to me."

BUILDING GREEN—AND BIG

What if you could scale up what Martha Rose is doing and apply the same principles she uses on single-family homes to businesses, shopping centers, schools, and larger housing developments? Then you could more effectively steer entire neighborhoods or entire cities on the path to sustainability. You could more efficiently use all the natural resources—water, electricity, natural gas, oil, and building materials—that go into every living space and workplace.

In Seattle, one of the most visible examples of green building is the Recreational Equipment, Inc. (REI), store, the flagship of the famous outdoor retail chain. REI is the kind of store where you can find everything from cutting-edge rock-climbing equipment to a rock-steady canoe for the whole family, from high-end Gore-Tex parkas to a frivolous keychain with a built-in compass.

The redesigned information desk at the REI flagship store in Seattle is part of a complete renovation that emphasized sustainable building materials and energy efficiency in keeping with REI's values and the products it sells. Photo courtesy of Mithun

The store was founded in 1938 to sell ice axes to mountain climbers. Since then, it's become a fixture in Seattle and a destination of sorts for outdoor pilgrims visiting Seattle.

In the 1990s, REI realized it needed a face-lift. Its flagship store in Seattle's Capitol Hill area had grown too small. The place was dimly lit, tight on space, and housed in three different buildings, which customers accessed by stomping up a variety of ramps. REI hired Mithun, a Seattle architecture firm with a knack for moving in step with the natural world. REI's directive was clear: The company wanted a showcase for its wares and ideals; a place where customers could experience the outdoors even as they were browsing for a pair of hiking boots; a place where REI could demonstrate its commitment to natural resources conservation. Above all, the company wanted its building to be as energy-efficient as possible, to use recycled or sustainable materials in the construction, and to reduce the waste stream resulting from the construction of the building itself.

The team at Mithun, headed up by architect Bert Gregory, gulped hard and went to work.

Today, the new REI building—built alongside Seattle's I-5—is one of the coolest buildings in town. It looks like something a kid would design, a kind of souped-up tree house, complete with its own outdoor forest, waterfall, and rock-climbing wall. Gone are the low-light conditions of the previous place. This store is a passive solar structure, which means it's designed to absorb as much natural daylight as possible. A tower of glass encloses the rock-climbing wall in the center atrium. During cooler months, the sun streams in unimpeded; during warmer months, the staff can reduce the sun's harsh glare with sunscreens. At critical locations, the glass is coated with a low-emissivity ("low-e") film, which slows the transfer of heat, so the inside stays warmer in winter and cooler in summer.

Retail is not the only function of the place. There's a 250-seat auditorium, a bike test trail, a boot and stove testing area, a café, an art gallery, a child's play facility, corporate offices, repair shops, and bike racks and showers for all employees. The only thing missing are apartments; you'll want to move into the place.

What you see is not nearly as fascinating as what you don't see. The water running the waterfall, for example, is captured from roof rainfall. The stone used in the building did not come from an active quarry; it was picked off the surface, rescuing and using what would have been considered quarry "waste stone." Much of the wood is engineered lumber, eliminating the need to cut down more trees. The countertops are made of recycled newspaper and soybeans. The rubber walking mats located around the store are fashioned from recycled tires. The grates around the trees outside are recycled plastic.

Seventy-six percent of the demolition waste generated during the construction of the building was diverted from landfills and reused in some way in the new building or on the property. For example, the retaining walls in the landscaping incorporate broken concrete sidewalks originally present at the site. In all, the builders recycled 130 tons of structural steel, 5,800 tons of asphalt and concrete, 1,850 tons of masonry, and 195 tons of wood.

One day, architect Bert Gregory walks around the store, pointing out some of its features. The waterfall cascades in the distance behind him. Back in 1993, he says, when REI approached his company with this project, the team had to bone up on what it really meant to build green. The hard work has paid off. The project has garnered a number of prestigious architecture and design awards, in addition to being named,

Architect Bert Gregory of Mithun, the company REI hired to do its massive renovation, designed an on-site waterfall that uses water captured from roof rainfall. Photo courtesy of Mithun

by the American Institute of Architects, one of the Top 10 Green Projects in the United States.

"I think the sea change is the realization that as part of an urban environment you are actually within an ecosystem," says Gregory, "and that you're connected to nature and the need to protect the external ecosystem outside of the urban environment. The next century will be about trying to understand how we can construct fabulous, livable, delightful cities that everybody wants to live in and that actually help protect the environment. The next century is really all about that activity."

Seattle, he says, pioneered this type of construction back in the 1980s, with the formation of the group Sustainable Seattle, which coalesced the work of certain architects, landscape architects, and leaders in city government who were interested in learning how to create green buildings and make a collection of them be the basis for a truly green city.

"Urban environments are extremely important to our society," says Gregory. "They are the best place to house people because they're the most efficient place for transportation, the most efficient place for energy, and very efficient for water, and infrastructure costs are lower in urban environments. Great urban environments can actually help reduce demand on all these resource issues."

NEIGHBORHOOD PRIDE SWELLS OVER SWALES

"Sheriff, what kind of fantastic trees have you got growing around here?"
—FBI SPECIAL AGENT DALE COOPER,
Twin Peaks

Longfellow Creek in West Seattle is one of the most important links in the salmon world. It's the thoroughfare by which countless coho salmon fight their way upstream from Puget Sound to their spawning grounds. But Longfellow Creek had a problem like so many other creeks. Historically, rainwater that collects in Longfellow's watershed rushes into an underground pipe, which later dumps water and pollutants into the creek, and thus into Puget Sound.

As housing became more and more scarce in Seattle, the Seattle Housing Authority decided to transform an abandoned housing development in West Seattle called High Point, which overlooks Elliott Bay, into a vibrant, mixed-use, mixed-income community. But building a new neighborhood in the twenty-first century is a lot different from building one in the 1950s, when High Point was first built. This time around, the city wanted to correct the errors of the past. High Point makes up 10 percent of Longfellow Creek's watershed. Could the outside architects, Mithun, and Seattle Public Utilities design a neighborhood that would pack 1,600 families—nearly double the orig-

Seattle's famous Puget Sound at twilight. Photo by Tom Iraci, U.S. Forest Service

inal number of High Point residents—into the same 130-acre tract without devastating Longfellow Creek?

The answer, of course, was yes. But the technology they used was nothing more complicated than what already lurks—and works—in the woods.

They used swales.

In the Los Angeles chapter, we saw how swales were proposed as the answer to many of that city's water problems. Simply put, a swale is a slice in the earth filled with crushed rock, straw, sand, and other high-drainage materials that allow rainwater to more easily percolate downward during storms and replenish groundwater resources. As the water drips down to lower layers of the earth, impurities are filtered out of it by the soil itself. If and when the water reaches the creek, it's that much cleaner than if it had simply rushed down from asphalt to drain to creek. Swales are a natural drainage

The High Point development utilizes the country's largest system of swales to manage stormwater and replenish groundwater.

system, and the ones at High Point are being touted as the largest system of its kind in the country.

On a chilly fall day, Miranda Maupin, a senior planner for the city's public utilities, visits the High Point site with Tom Phillips, project manager with the Seattle Housing Authority. The pair hop from foot to foot to stave off the cold, and Maupin's decked out in a yellow rain slicker to beat back the insistent drizzle. The earth is mud-luscious and ready for the builders. Already a salvage team has gently picked apart the forty-year-old High Point structures and recovered all the old wood, which is slated for recycling. The ground has been stripped here and there of its vegetation, except for the trees. About one hundred trees have been enclosed in fences to protect them during this long phase of construction.

"This is definitely a once-in-a-lifetime opportunity," says Maupin. "Longfellow Creek is just down over this hillside here, and it drains out to Puget Sound. This is one of our most productive urban creeks. It has coho salmon that return each year from Puget Sound. What we wanted to do here is not a one-of-a-kind thing but a prototype that could be replicated. If you can do it here in the middle of urban Seattle, you can do it anywhere. The project is dense by Seattle standards, sixteen units per acre, so we're dealing with very narrow streets. If we can accomplish it here, we can accomplish it in our urbanizing cities and counties."

The project calls for three different types of swales: vegetated, shallow, and conveyance. A vegetated swale is a narrow plot of land stretching along the side of a roadway that is planted with trees, perennials, and ground covers. Under the sod, the swale consists of eighteen inches of gravel and can hold about a foot of water when it really comes down heavy. This will help decrease the amount of water running into the creek. A shallow swale is covered with grass and trees only, stretches down about seven inches, and can hold about two inches of excess water. A conveyance swale is ground pitched at an angle in order to transfer water from one type of swale to the other. It can hold about one foot of water, too.

Miranda Maupin, a senior planner for the city's public utilities (left), with Tom Phillips, project manager with the Seattle Housing Authority (right), on-site at High Point.

As you can see, this is pretty simple technology and could even be duplicated by homeowners in their own backyards to help retain moisture during dry spells, reducing the need for watering their land-scaped areas.

The developers of High Point hope that their example will be a dry run for the rest of the city. "There's a way that this can be an ongoing practice by doing the kinds of innovative things we're doing here on lots of different projects in the future," says Phillips. "We're going to get a great place, a spectacular place, for people to live here. But I think we're going to really set some precedents in terms of what could happen in the city with other kinds of projects in the future. It's important not just for what we create, but because it's really high on people's list of where they want to live. We've done some focus groups in terms of who's going to move here, and that's really high on their priority list. They want to move to a green community, and they're willing to pay extra. So this is a good business idea."

Reinforcing the green attitude is the approach the builders are taking toward existing trees on the site. Early on, each of the tall trees was assessed according to its value if you had to buy it at a nursery today, transport it to the site, and plant it by any means necessary. The cost of each tree is emblazoned on the wire fence enclosing it, like so: "Bigleaf maple, *Acer macrophylum*, appraised value: $42,365," "London plane, *Platanus x acerifolia*, appraised value: $35,666," "Douglas fir, *Pseudotsuga menziesii*, appraised value: $19,248," "Lawson cypress, *Chamaecyparis lawsoniana*, appraised value: $24,417."

Each fence carries this stern warning to everyone working on the site:

TREE PROTECTION FENCE
No trespassing on critical root zone of this tree without direct approval of owner's representative. Work within the critical root zone shall result in a fine of $1,500 or the appraised landscape value, whichever is greater.

"That one here is actually $71,000," says Phillips. "That's the highest one. If a contractor messes with the root system at all, he or she is subject to actually paying that amount."

Some of the water captured by these trees and the drainage system will trickle into an on-site pond. Because the system moves so slowly, by the time the water reaches the pond, its temperature will have been regulated according to the ambient temperature of the surrounding earth. That's less of a shock for the fish and other organisms living in the pond.

As for the buildings themselves, the site is planned with low-VOC products to reduce the amount of harmful fumes. Many of the products installed in the houses are designed not to exacerbate asthma, a major problem for urban kids today. The site managers are encouraging the use of electric-battery-charged lawn mowers and leaf blowers over gasoline-powered ones. "We're pushing the envelope," says Phillips. "In the long run this will be a better place for people to live."

High Point provides a model for the strategic use of trees, swales, and plantings to mimic nature's systems for managing and purifying water.

In some neighborhoods, people have nothing in common. In others, they are bound together by common factors of wealth, social status, race, religion, or what have you. At High Point, the common element will be an interest in the green lifestyle. This, says Phillips, will be the way in which people build their community.

"People are starving for what community is," he says. "Community to me means, if it's Sunday afternoon and the guys who maintain the park aren't coming until Monday and somebody knocks over a trash can by mistake, well, somebody picks that up and puts it back. Maybe even kids do that. Community is looking out after your neighbors and looking out after the physical place where you exist, so that there's a care beyond your own household, your own family. You are part of something bigger in the place where you live."

Miranda concurs, but she has another insight: "I think community for people in Seattle is becoming more about connecting with our ecosystem, creating healthy ecosystems in our communities. The street in front of our house that we take for granted becomes a living system, and it's part of that circulatory system of our neighborhood that connects the water we drink to the stream down the block. The idea of a living community is really expanding to embrace other critters and the water and the critters that we depend on."

"In the big picture," she adds, "Seattle hopes to be the kind of place where wildlife can thrive even at the edge of a growing city.

Not Just Swales

The High Point community will employ some of these other green building strategies:

- 25-foot "skinny streets" to create shade
- 20 percent retention of existing old trees
- drought-tolerant landscaping
- reuse of existing concrete and sidewalks in the streets' infrastructure
- recycled vinyl flooring
- use of fly ash, a by-product of power plants, in the concrete
- all structures will exceed the state's energy code by 20 percent
- all structures will exceed standards set for home insulation
- use of compact fluorescent light fixtures
- use of energy-efficient gas-fired heating and hot water systems
- all structures will meet or exceed indoor air quality standards

A place where salmon and orca pods can grow and prosper in Elliot Bay without being stressed or poisoned by what's being dumped into their water. I think we see a different vision," she says, "a greener, healthier vision where we can eat the flounder out of Elliott Bay without worrying about our health and we can show our children salmon coming up Longfellow Creek in twenty-five years."

In a way, High Point is an exercise in density, too. If you can have a good quality of life in a densely populated area, would you choose that if you knew that it meant farmland and wild areas could remained untouched? Could you set aside your dream of living on a one-acre spread of your own

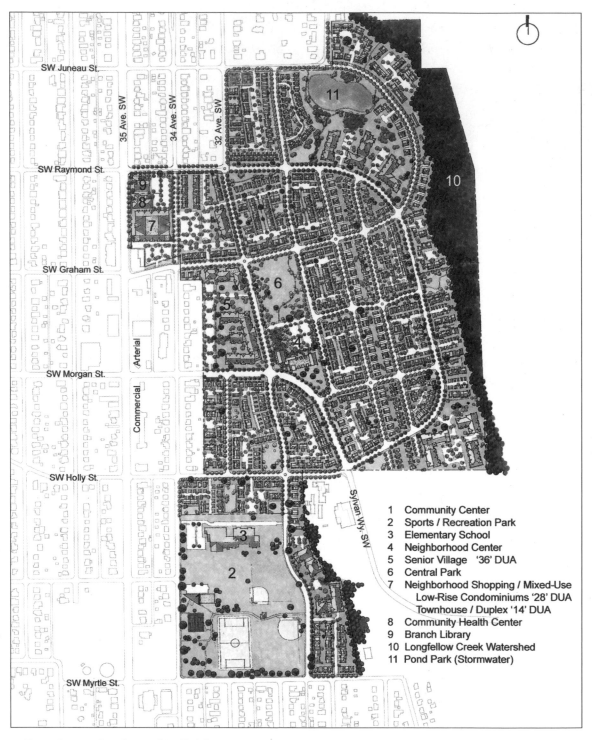

1 Community Center
2 Sports / Recreation Park
3 Elementary School
4 Neighborhood Center
5 Senior Village   '36' DUA
6 Central Park
7 Neighborhood Shopping / Mixed-Use
     Low-Rise Condominiums '28' DUA
     Townhouse / Duplex '14' DUA
8 Community Health Center
9 Branch Library
10 Longfellow Creek Watershed
11 Pond Park (Stormwater)

This architectural rendering of the High Point development project shows mixed-use zoning, including the housing, services, and recreation that planners believe are needed to support a vital community.

in the suburbs? Yes, you would have to live closer to other people, to live more of a city life than the American dream says you will. But you can ditch the hour or two daily commute, and you'll never be bored because an entire city is at your doorstep.

"We get the best of both worlds, and we still have our incredible views," says Phillips. "Mount Baker's out here, Mount Rainier's here, the Olympic Mountains are out that way, and that's all part of the richness of this, sitting having a cappuccino on my front porch over here."

A TALE OF TWO TRAINS

"The sustainability agenda demands transit, especially the development of rail systems that are competitive with the car in passenger appeal and speed."
—PETER NEWMAN AND JEFFREY KENWORTHY, *Sustainability and Cities: Overcoming Automobile Dependence*

Seattle has a history of streetcars and mass transit, just like Los Angeles and other cities in the early twentieth century before the car became dominant. Seattle operated a streetcar network until 1940 and has operated a historic waterfront streetcar line (now run by King County Metro) since 1982.

But Seattle also has an interesting legacy in a form of mass transit we have not seen in any of the other cities in this book.

In 1910 Universal Elevated Railway proposed building a bizarre-looking train on Seattle's Second Avenue, high above the crowds. In the 1950s, Americans would have called the train "futuristic," because that was the heyday of science fiction, Sputnik, and the launch of the great space race. Mid-century Americans knew what the future looked like: it was sleek and shiny and rocket-shaped. Back in 1910, a rocket-shaped train looked downright scary, other-worldly, and freakish. Seattle declined its first offer to build a monorail downtown.

By the time of the World's Fair in 1962, the world had changed. Seattle was ready. A local company built and installed a monorail using plans drawn up by a Swedish designer. The trains and their circuits were elegantly simple: their wheels were thick rubber, their bodies flexible enough to bend with each curve of the sinuous track. The trains were clean, modern, and electric—and crowds flocked to them, riding a mere 1.3 miles from the Westlake Mall in downtown Seattle to the fairgrounds at Seattle Center, site of the Space Needle.

The fair came and went, but the Needle and monorail stayed, relics of an overly optimistic space age. With time, the monorail began to look more goofy than futuristic, a kind of amusement park ride that had seen better days. Seattleites dreamed of a train that did more than shuttle tourists. Why couldn't it go further downtown? Why not to Pioneer Square? Or the university? Or the airport?

There was talk of all of this, but nothing happened. Seattle was a driver's city and was destined to remain that way, or so it seemed. Traffic got worse and worse.

Then one day a couple of ordinary citizens got the crazy idea of breathing life into the monorail again. They started their own mass transit movement, founded their own transit company, and worked hard to bring the dream to the public. It hasn't been an easy trip. In fact, the Seattle Monorail Project was defeated by voters in November 2005. But you cannot help but be fascinated by what is truly a people's movement.

Dick Falkenbury is a local tour-bus driver who decided that something had to be done to make good on the promise of the monorail. Seattle was itching to become a world-class city but was still relying on cars, ferries, and buses to get people around. In the 1990s, when all this started, the local transit company, Sound Transit, was deep into talks on a light rail system, but plans seemed hopelessly bogged down in red tape, budgetary difficulties, and embarrassing political fights.

The light rail wasn't projected to ride along the west side of town. Moreover, Falkenbury didn't think light rail could do what a monorail could. He'd driven both cabs and buses, and he knew that the only thing that matters to riders—the only thing that would make a driver leave his car at home—was timeliness. Monorails have the best on-time record of any form of mass transit because they travel on dedicated tracks, off the ground, unfettered by other forms of traffic going on below.

Grant Cogswell, a local poet and screenwriter, suggested Falkenbury erect folding sandwich signs on high-foot-traffic corners, asking people to sign a petition. It worked beyond their wildest dreams. "We spent $2,500 collecting eighteen thousand signatures, which is something like 7¢ a signature," says Falkenbury. "It was truly miraculous."

Armed with those petitions, they compelled city officials to give citizens a vote on the matter. Since 1997, there have been four votes on the monorail issue, and the first three times Seattle citizens voted yes to a noiseless, electric, nonpolluting way to get around the west side.

With thousands of other citizens, Dick Falkenbury has championed the idea of a mass rapid-transit system for the city.

"I did the monorail not because I love monorails, but because I love the city of Seattle," says Falkenbury. "I'm not in love with the technology. I'm in love with the idea that in order to make rapid transit work you have to get out of the traffic. You also have to get moving. You have to be able to deliver, and until you're out of the traffic flow you're just another vehicle stuck like everybody else."

From the beginning, some citizens and city officials fought the idea, saying it was too expensive. (The initial cost was $1.75 billion for fourteen miles of track.) Downtown developers and businesses also decried the plan, claiming the elevated plat-forms would blight the downtown area.

Nobody likes to walk under tracks, they said. Tracks cast shadows. They cast a pall over otherwise attractive streets, they said. It was a story similar to the building of Millennium Park in Chicago: when someone comes up with a bold plan, the only thing people see at first are the big numbers and all the negatives.

But the project had plenty of positives, too. Imagine what would happen when a city of eco-friendly citizens got together and compiled their wish list for a "green" transit system. What kind of transit would they create? Well, they specified a system that

The original monorail is still in operation today, more than forty years after it was built. Citizens had hoped to extend its length, building the world's longest monorail line. Photo by Natalia Bratslavsky, ShutterStock

would use as much recycled, nontoxic, and salvaged materials as possible during construction. They called for local construction products to reduce the expense and fuel of bringing materials from out of the area. They would employ products, methods, and applications designed to minimize waste and toxicity levels later down the line. They also wanted to hire designers who were committed to creating cost-effective designs that don't become obsolete overnight. They would explore regenerative braking, a technology exploited in modern hybrid-electric cars such as the Toyota Prius. Each time the monorail brakes, the energy of its forward momentum would be captured by the engine and stored in its battery. You could say that the electric train recycles its own energy. Regenerative braking also reduces the need for friction brakes, which pump pollution into the environment as metallic brake shoes wear out.

All this sounded great. The first phase of the project, the fourteen-mile Green Line, was expected to run from the northwest neighborhood of Ballard through the downtown and south to the neighborhood of West Seattle. The project was projected to add 2,100 jobs to the economy and bring more revenue to town, since people would be more likely to venture downtown without their cars. The train would reduce air pollution by lessening auto emissions, reduce water pollution by lessening toxic runoff from cars, and encourage people to walk more or take their bikes to town,

since they would be able to roll them aboard the train.

"It's very a different project," says Kristina Hill, a professor of urban design and landscape architecture at the University of Washington, who was a longtime project board member. "I think it's the only transit project in the world that is created by citizen initiative. In the 'direct democracy' lingo of the West Coast, that means that any citizen can put together any plan, and if he or she gets enough signatures, put that on the ballot, and then people vote on it. People said it couldn't be done, that you can't build infrastructure by a petition. But I think that the monorail is the proof that citizens really can build transit even if their elected officials aren't taking a leadership role. It shows how possible it is for people who care about something to change the city that they live in that way."

But Hill's dream never came to be. Money—or lack of it—threatened to kill the dream. Funding for the project had always been a big issue. When the people went to the polls, they insisted that the monorail be funded without raising new taxes. Until the monorail was up and running, its only revenue would come from an existing motor vehicle excise tax. As Seattle Monorail Project (SMP) officials began hashing out the numbers in closed-door meetings over several months, they saw that the auto tax would not be enough. Indeed, many transit projects have access to more than one revenue stream. So they looked into other ways to raise the money.

In July 2005, Seattleites reeled when the board's report was finally made public, and the press reported that the true cost of the monorail would be close to $11 billion by the time the project was paid off in forty-eight years. (Costs included $2 billion for the actual construction and nearly $9 billion in financing costs, supported in part by a public bond issue.) Why, you could feel the ire all the way to Tacoma. For days the newspapers and TV news shows—some of which had been longtime monorail supporters—ripped the plan to shreds. People felt betrayed, and the I-told-you-soers gloated. This is what happens when you let nonexperts plan mass transit, they said. The resulting hullabaloo brought about the resignation of two top monorail officials and effectively sent the project back to the drawing board. When the dust settled, Kristina Hill found herself the new acting director of the project.

"It was as if a bomb went off and everybody ran away because the headline was so frightening to people that our project cost had escalated to $11 billion," Hill said. "But our project costs are still $1.94 billion in today's dollars."

She and other officials said that the $11 billion figure was blown out of context, not to mention poorly explained to the public. In forty-eight years, they contend, inflation may well have eroded the value of the dollar and a $9 billion "finance charge" may look trivial. Also, they note that many public works projects—at least one hundred currently ongoing in the United States—will

Kristina Hill discusses the Seattle Monorail Project.

cost in this ballpark or more. So there was nothing unusual about the cost of the monorail, except perhaps that no public works projects in Seattle had ever been described this way. It would be like buying a $150,000 house and telling everyone that you'd paid $300,000 for it. Technically, you may well pay that much after the interest is paid off in thirty years. But who describes a house that way?

In the weeks that followed, some officials began hinting that other projects in town were at least this expensive, or more. This had little effect; the damage had already been done. The monorail seemed to have suffered an enormous public relations setback.

The project was back to square one, with supporters having to win over the people all over again. "The challenges going forward," said Hill, "are to focus on reeducating the public, selecting a new director and board, and, ultimately, devising a new finance strategy."

But SMP was unable to win the public's support. In November 2005, voters decided to scrap the whole project. As outsiders watching from a distance, we couldn't help but compare this fiasco to other big projects that citizens and officials griped about, only to make constant use of them once they were up and running. In fact, the light rail system that Seattle is now finally building went through a period of ups and downs that were arguably more embarrassing. This is probably the way it goes with big, exciting, potentially liberating projects that add to a city's sustainability and community.

It's funny: Our nation seems to fear deficit spending only when it's practiced at the local level. It's apparently quite all right for the federal government to spend billions on warplanes that don't ever leave the ground or ships that never leave their harbor. What's wrong with investing in the places where Americans live and work?

Not long after the budget fiasco hit the news, a local newspaper ran an editorial urging citizens to stop dreaming and abandon the monorail. "It's reality time," sniggered the Seattle *Post-Intelligencer*. Try telling that to Marian Byrnes in Chicago or Doris Gwaltney in Philadelphia! Excuse us for saying so, but we think our cities need more dreamers. The most progressive

advancements have always come out of the heads of those who were initially mocked.

Don't get us wrong: We're not sure that a monorail was the only answer to Seattle's traffic problems, but we do believe that there is a need for some kind of west-side line, as was urgently expressed by Seattle voters time and again at the polls. We understand the allure of the monorail: unlike a ground-hugging or underground train, it would offer some of the best views on the West Coast. The "rail" itself—the three-foot-thick ribbon of concrete that the train straddles—can carry eight times as many people as a full lane of traffic.

But truth be told, the species of rolling stock is probably irrelevant; sustainable mobility and the sense of community it conveys upon a city are not. A Seattle activist, Cary Moon, made a provocative point about the project when she wrote in a letter to the editor of the *Post-Intelligencer*, "When gas is $8 a gallon and we're still at war to protect our oil supply, will our children be proud that we were too clever to invest in transit because we found it too expensive?"

A few months before the big vote, we were in Seattle shooting more footage for our documentary. We caught up with Kristina Hill at the old monorail station downtown to find out what SMP's plans were for the future. She reminded us of a wonderful line. "You know that bumper sticker that says 'If the people lead, the leaders will follow'? I think the monorail's a perfect example of that. The people decided we needed more transit faster

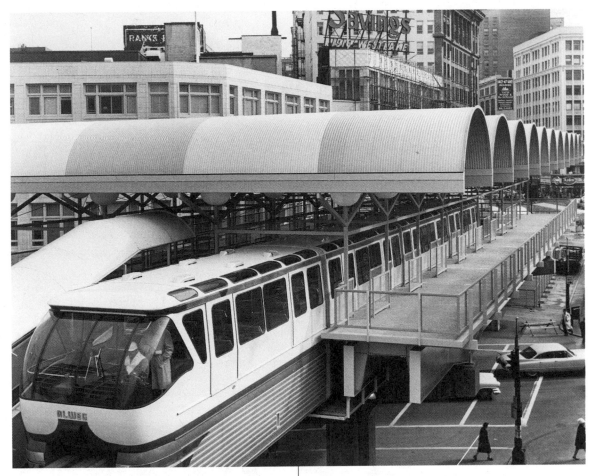

Monorail at Westlake Station, Seattle World's Fair, 1962.
Photo courtesy of the Museum of History and Industry, Seattle

to get off our dependency on oil, to clean up our environment. The leaders weren't ready to ask for that much money, but the *people* were ready to ask themselves for that much money. This is a great example of people leading, and I'm proud to be part of that. It has not helped my career and my work as much, but it's certainly helped my understanding of leadership and democracy."

In general, says Hill, Americans have an ambivalent relationship with transit. Other than complain about buses or trains that don't arrive on time, most of us never con-

sider how we might influence what types of mass transit options are provided to us. We accept what's in place, complain about what's not there, or passively let others pull the strings to effect change.

"We need to invest in that relationship with transit in a more personal way," says Hill. "Having direct democracy or citizen movements helped us to create transit from a grassroots level. It will help us invest in it and see it not as something that government does for us, but rather as something that we do for ourselves to make our own choices and changes."

It surprises people that Seattle could have grown as big as it has *without* high-capacity mass transit, using just its buses, cars, and ferries. Even before people were agitating for the monorail, Seattle's existing mass transit agency, Sound Transit, was touting a light rail system as the answer to the city's woes. Citizens voted for light rail as part of a regional transit plan in 1996 and funded the light rail line now under construction. The first line will run from Seattle's airport through southeast Seattle, under Beacon Hill, and onward to the University District and Northgate.

Light rail, as we saw in Los Angeles, has become the darling of mass transit buffs and sustainability gurus all over the nation. At least twelve major cities have new light rail systems in place. In Portland, Oregon, the light rail has made the downtown area a livable and vibrant place. In San Francisco, light rail runs past new homes facing the Bay on its way to the Giant's baseball stadium. Light rail clatters past California's state capitol in Sacramento, to Netscape and Cisco offices in San Jose, to Qualcomm Stadium in San Diego, and to a new town center in Denver, Colorado. We have light rail systems sprouting up in other cities too: Minneapolis, St. Louis, Houston, Phoenix, and *Hoboken!*

Pike Place Market, "The Soul of Seattle," has been in continuous operation since its founding in 1907. Its nine acres and one hundred years of operation encompass thousands of unique stories—stories of immigration, internment, gentrification, and urban renewal. Photo by Mark B. Bauschke, Shutterstock

Light rail, supported by bus service and good pedestrian and bicycle routes, will be part of an intricate transit system that people have dreamed about for years. Already, realtors report a boomlet in areas that would be graced by the various train stops. "We've been watching that very closely," says Matt Galvin, a young entrepreneur who, with his partners, runs twenty Pagliacci Pizza restaurants and delivery businesses throughout the city. "If we're thinking of opening a new store, we want to know where the stops are going to be."

Good transit will propel Seattle into the ranks of truly world-class cities. That's why it's a shame that the monorail won't be built. SMP predicted that the train would have run about 20 million trips a year, shuttling people to the Space Needle, Pike Place, and Pioneer Square, not to mention Mariners, Sonics, and Seahawks games—all without the use of cars. The key is capturing two types of riders: tourists *and* Seattleites. No one wants a train that only tourists ride. That's what the original monorail was.

These days the space-age promise of the old monorail seems a little hokey. We're not looking to go to the moon anymore. Getting to our jobs and back home again is tough enough. The notion of a "futuristic" city has changed.

"I don't think of cities as utopias," says Professor Hill. "I think of cities as new. When you think in terms of urban design history or human history, cities are like a five- or six-thousand-year-old phenomenon,

and I think there's still so much about cities that we're still learning to get right. I think the city is just emerging now. It's really in a period of flowering. I think this is the time when we can prove whether cities will be a celebration of human culture or whether we're not going live up to our potential, when all of us live in such close contact with each other and can share dreams and acknowledge each other."

FAMILIES FIND ONE LESS CAR IS A CINCH

He: What took you so long?
She: I got stuck in traffic.
—Kyra Segwick and Campbell Scott as Seattle residents in Cameron Crowe's 1992 film, *Singles*

Automobiles are the biggest single contributor of CO_2 in the world. Cars and small trucks gobble up 40 percent of all the oil-based fuels used in the United States and spew 20 percent of the nation's CO_2. They contribute 60 percent of the CO_2 emissions in the Northwest. In its lifetime, the average car will cough out seventy tons of CO_2. An SUV will spit out a hundred tons!

People are fond of saying that it's not the car that's bad, it's the fuel. That's largely true, but driven in large numbers automobiles can contribute to the waste stream in unexpected ways. As rubber tires wear down, rubber dust ultimately finds itself in our waterways. Ditto the metal in brake pads. To make themselves hospitable to cars, cities are forced to shell out millions for roads, parking lots, garages, and so on, when that money might be better spent elsewhere.

Today city planners are mindful of this, but it often takes superhuman effort to wean a city off its cars. That's because many people have used only cars to get around their whole lives. In some places, mass transit was never an option. Even when it is, they're too attached to their cozy little ride to give it up.

Seattle has come up with a novel way to help people make the switch, and to collect some excellent research to boot. The Way to Go, Seattle program, promoted through various news outlets, invited Seattleites to volunteer for a study on car use. For the first week of the study, people were instructed to drive their car or cars as they normally do, keeping tabs on where they drove, how far they drove, how they felt after their drives, and the cost of operating the vehicle. Then, for the next five weeks, they were instructed not to touch their car, or to use one less car, and use mass transit instead. (The program is also known as One Less Car since two-car families are so ubiquitous.)

Jemae Hoffman, mobility manager of Seattle's Department of Transportation, dreamed up the project. It's her job to come up with ways to make it easier to walk, bike, take transit, and move freight through the growing city. She herself was curious to see what would happen at the end of those five weeks.

"People made hugely different choices when they discovered they were saving $70 a week," says Hoffman. The small group of test families drove forty-two thousand fewer miles and reported feeling less stressed. "That's fifteen swimming pools worth of global warming gases not put into the air and a lot less neighborhood traffic And safer places for our kids to play." Participants reduced their car miles by 22 percent and increased transit-use mileage by 125 percent,

Seattle's "One Less Car" program is the brainchild of Jemae Hoffman, mobility manager of the city's Department of Transportation.

walking mileage by 38 percent, and biking mileage by 30 percent.

The program does have its critics, who say One Less Car preaches to the converted. That is, the only people who would challenge their behavior and give up their car voluntarily are those who are already committed to environmental issues. If Seattle is going to clean up its act, they say, it must do what it takes to stop encouraging people to drive everywhere they want to go. That means investing more in mass transit than in roads and parking facilities.

Hoffman counters by saying that the city *is* headed in that direction. There is no one solution, she says. We need to create communities where people have more frequent and reliable transit service and have facilities for biking and walking. That's the only way to become less reliant on the automobile.

If anything, the One Less Car study was a perfect illustration of the "feedback loop": show people concrete results of behavior change, and they'll opt to make that change permanent or, at the very least, a regular habit. "This is a challenge to stop and think, the same way we think about recycling an aluminum can," says Hoffman. "Every time you walk down your driveway, you think about whether or not you really need the car for that trip and start to change. If you can live in a place where you don't have to own a car or if you can save four to six thousand dollars a year, bells go off in your head. You also realize that you're less stressed, getting more exercise, and getting

Getting Around Better in Cars

You'd like to make a difference in your family's CO_2 emissions, but cars are an absolute necessity where you live? Take heart, there are other choices. The next time you're in the market for a car, consider one of the new hybrid-electric vehicles. No, you do not have to plug it in! Hybrids seamlessly marry a conventional gas engine with rechargeable electric battery technology. The result is high gas mileage and a smooth transition between platforms. Talk about milking the feedback loop! The best hybrids have a built-in monitor on the dashboard that shows you whether you're driving in the most energy-efficient "zone." With a little practice, most drivers are able to train themselves to stay within the zone at all times. At this writing, eight different models are in production by Ford, Chevrolet, Lexus, Honda, and Toyota. The best-selling model—and the darling of car maniacs and designers—is the Toyota Prius, a $20,000 five-seater that can get as much as 60 miles per gallon in the city. But if a small car is not for you, take heart. You can now choose from at least three hybrid SUVs: the Ford Escape (mileage: 36 city/51 highway); the Lexus RX 400h (30/26); and the Toyota Highlander (32/27). Unlike regular gas-driven autos, hybrids tend to get better mileage in cities because frequent braking pumps up the battery! Hybrids do cost more than other cars of their size and class. Historically the higher markup means you don't necessarily save that much at the pump, unless you keep the car for a long time. But that advice may be outdated now that fuel is inching closer to $3 a gallon. It appears to us that hybrids are truly a bipartisan solution. Potential buyers ought to investigate tax breaks offered to hybrid owners by the IRS and state and local tax offices.

to know your neighbors, and you have more of a sense of community."

It worked in the case of David and Bobbi Martin, a couple with two sons who took the challenge for six weeks and ended up giving up their second car. They haven't needed it since February 2002. They found that Seattle's bus system was perfectly adequate for getting them where they needed to go. David, for example, works only about five miles from home. A bus could get him there lickety-split; he just didn't need to have that extra car, and to be shelling out that extra money each year on insurance, fuel, and maintenance.

The couple says that they hardly miss the extra car. "It's no big deal," says David. "It's a matter of getting used to it more than anything else. We found that it really wasn't a hardship. It was just a matter of changing the way you think about things, and planning a little bit more." The couple found that if they communicated more about who needed the car more, who was shuttling the kids around that day, they could easily map out their daily driving strategy. "Whoever is dropping off the kids somewhere, that person usually gets the car and the other person takes the bus," he says. "Either one of us can take the bus pretty much as easily."

"Well, I will say that I don't think it works for everyone," says Bobbi Martin. "We're in a situation where it works for our family. We live and work within the city of Seattle. If we were working on the East Side or had to make a longer commute, it would be difficult. The effort is worth it. We find that we spend more time together as a family as a result of this. It's really been beneficial for all of us, and we are contributing to the environment that we live in, in a positive way, and we're happy to do that."

The realization that you can get by without a car is not the only benefit, says Hoffman. "One woman said to me that before she used to always drive to Costco. Now she's walking more to her neighborhood stores, and as a result she's seeing her

David and Bobbi Martin and their two sons participated in the "One Less Car" challenge in 2002 and turned a six-week stint into a permanent situation after discovering that the lack of a second car actually improved their lifestyle.

neighbors, she's seeing the flowers in the garden, getting to know the local people who work at the neighborhood stores. That's giving her more of a sense of community and making getting there part of the fun. She's been really enjoying it."

"I'd like to think of it as a responsible thing to do for the city," says David of his family's choice. "It's also a responsible thing for us to do for one another, and it teaches our kids good values. You don't drive a car just because you can. There are alternative ways to get around the city, and it can be better for you; you can be burning less gas and spending less money."

FRENCH FRIES IN THE TANK?

Imagine running your car engine with the icky sludge dumped out of the fryer of the nearest fast-food restaurant. That's exactly what many Americans are now doing. They're staunch believers in the alternative fuel biodiesel, which can be made from any plant-based oil, such as soy, canola, sunflower, rapeseed, or peanut. To work as a fuel these oils have to be chemically modified to remove the naturally occurring glycerols—the chief ingredient in soap—from them. (Recycled cooking oil requires additional filtering to remove excess food bits.)

The resulting liquid, which is safer than petroleum-based diesel or even gasoline to transport, handle, and breathe, can be poured directly into any vehicle—car, truck, tractor, or boat—with a diesel engine. (The car requires no retrofit whatsoever!) A tank filled with biodiesel runs 78 percent cleaner than a petroleum-filled engine and produces no CO_2! The vehicle gets similar or better mileage and has a longer engine life because plant oils have greater lubricity than petroleum based fuels. That is, they do a better job of lubricating and scrubbing the interiors of engines than ordinary "dino-fuel." Biodiesel mixes well with other fuels, so you can easily switch back to petrodiesel if you can't find your fuel of choice on a long car trip.

Biodiesel is already popular in Europe, since any nation that can grow soybeans or sunflowers can make its own fuel. The technology is slowly catching on in the United States as forward-thinking companies unveil new biodiesel pumps and grassroots organizations form cooperatives to brew and sell the stuff.

According to the Web site Biodiesel.org, which features a clickable map showing all such retail outlets in the United States, Seattle alone is home to eight different biodiesel retail locations. The Washington State senate is considering a bill to help farmers grow enough "fuel crops" to produce 20 million gallons of biofuel by the year 2020. Since this technology has the potential to radically reduce American dependence on foreign oil and halt global warming, the bill also calls for generous tax breaks intended to bring the cost in line with that of ordinary gasoline. (As we go to press, biodiesel costs about $2.96 a gallon—slightly more than ordinary gas.)

One drawback: biodiesel limits your car choices. Currently, the only passenger diesel vehicles sold in the United States are trucks and Volkswagens. Some diehards solve the problem by buying older diesel cars, such as used Mercedeses.

On a recent visit to Seattle, we spent time with a number of biodiesel entrepreneurs, from those who brewed the stuff for their own use in their garages to large companies that are nailing down a serious business model for this little-known commodity. The day we stopped by Seattle Biodiesel, a railroad car filled with twenty-six thousand gallons of soybean oil had just pulled into the facility, which can hold up to eight such railcars. Right now, Seattle Biodiesel uses the processed vegetable oil to crank out 5 million gallon of biodiesel a year. At the moment, the closest source for all that vegetable oil is South Dakota. The railcars come in, dump their loads in tanks, and head back east to the Great Plains. The owners of Seattle Biodiesel, John Plaza and Martin Tobias, dream of lining up enough vegetable oil producers closer to home.

Tobias's conversion to the new fuel came after he'd spent scads of cash supercharging his SUV to make it go faster. A few talks with Plaza and he was hooked. He sold his gas guzzler, switched to a couple of Volkswagens, and pumped some money into Plaza's fledgling company. As Tobias says, his investment was more than a smart business move. It was a major reassessment of a lifetime in business.

"I've been investing in software companies for about five years myself," he says. "I started my own software company, and I really believe in the American spirit, the American ability to innovate our way out of any problem. Biodiesel is one way that we can do it. There's absolutely no reason why we should be so dependent on foreign oil when we can grow all the fuel that we need here. We can grow it, we can do it more efficiently, and there's no reason why we shouldn't. The industry just needs a bit of help from some professional businesspeople with some capital. I looked at my own investing history and I said, 'Do we really need another Internet security software company, or do we need to innovate and solve our problem of dependency on foreign oil?' I think we need to apply more capital to that problem, and then as Americans we can solve it. Biodiesel gives us the ability to solve a huge issue *today*, not twenty years from now, not thirty years from now. We don't have to invent a new technology, we don't have to change the infrastructure, we don't have to change our vehicles, we don't have to change our behavior. We just have to change our source of energy."

His partner, Plaza, says their work is just one link in the chain toward a sustainable Seattle. "By starting this company we can change our city from burning petroleum and only petroleum. We can start to see a change in behavior. Seattle has the largest population of personal biodiesel users in the nation. We have over 1,500 individuals driving diesel

John Plaza and Martin Tobias own and operate Seattle Biodiesel, a company that converts processed vegetable oil into biodiesel. Photo by Erik Stuhaug

cars for which they did no modifications. That's a huge change that we've seen in just the past two to three years. That's people empowering their community to effect change. What better hope can we have than to contribute to that movement? Two years ago when I started Seattle Biodiesel, I'd wear my shirt and there'd be people wouldn't even have an idea about biodiesel. Now, when I walk down the street everybody knows about biodiesel, they all want to talk about it."

When was the last time you hung out at your gas station, chatting with your fellow gasoline buyers about your choice to switch to Super Unleaded? It never happens. But biodiesel converts are a different breed, and the places that supply their fuel have become a little like well-loved coffeehouses or organic co-ops where people gather to see

friends and swap the latest news on their ever-growing circle. They congregate in places like Dr. Dan's Alternative Fuelwerks, on Fiftieth Street, or Pacific Pride, under the West Seattle Bridge. In his Seattle garage, activist Lyle Rudensey brews his own fuel, and he spreads the word by maintaining a website of biodiesel news, visiting school classrooms, and running an organization called the Breathable Bus Coalition, which tries to convince school districts to switch their buses over to biodiesel. Such a switch would not only reduce toxic emissions but also lessen the harmful impact of those emissions on children and bus drivers, because, as Rudensey points out, studies have shown that children and drivers are exposed to up

Biodiesel produces no CO_2 and runs 78 percent cleaner than traditional fuel. Photo by Erik Stuhaug

to seventy times as much cancer-causing, asthma-inducing diesel emissions inside the bus as off the bus.

The emissions issue is an important one for families with young children. Seattle resident Tom Kilroy switched his family to biodiesel a few years ago, after he was appalled by the low mileage of the new cars he was thinking of buying. When he heard about biodiesel, he couldn't sell his old cars fast enough. He and his eight-year-old son Dillon made a trip to San Diego to pick up their new Volkswagen, carefully planning their trip back to visit all the biodiesel filling stations from California to Washington.

"While we were fueling in Garberville in the redwood forest," he recalls, "a big eighteen-wheeler pulled up and Dillon told the driver about biofuels. The trucker was clearly impressed and put in about thirty gallons of pure biodiesel. He thanked Dillon for his enthusiasm and info. Quite the little spokesperson for the national biodiesel board! We now have three vehicles that run on biodiesel: two Volkswagens and a Toyota diesel pickup truck. We also use biodiesel as home heating oil for our furnace. Home heating oil is a huge untapped market!"

The switch thrilled Tom's wife, Sandy, who works for King County as a watershed coordinator in salmon restoration efforts. "Biodegradable, nontoxic fuels such as biodiesel fit into her goals of reducing water and air pollution," says Tom.

IN SEARCH OF SEATTLE'S DOWNTOWN BEACH

"Seattle not only ignored its waterfront, it built an early American freeway, called the Alaskan Way Viaduct, like the Great Wall of China around it. The wall still stands, its traffic noise making conversation well-nigh impossible at times, and it serves as a concrete screen to keep office workers from gazing out across the Sound when they should be typing or posting bills."

—ARCHIE SATTERFIELD, *The Seattle Guidebook*, 1994

Sometimes it takes nature to rediscover nature. In February 2001, an earthquake rippled through Seattle and damaged State Route 99, otherwise known as the Alaskan Way Viaduct, a massive double-decker highway that runs along Seattle's waterfront. Though damaged beyond repair, the viaduct is still operational, carrying about one hundred thousand cars a day. Eventually, it must be torn down and rebuilt. Whether the city should rebuild or take a bolder tack is one of the hot debates facing Seattleites today.

No one denies that the viaduct is ugly, or that it obliterates the view of Elliott Bay for much of the city, or that it seems woefully out of place in a city whose inhabitants crave connections with nature. In other port cities in America, the waterfront is the main attraction. In contrast, fifty-five years ago Seattle turned its back on the sound, and

Seattle's waterfront is one of the city's strongest assets, and its restoration is an ongoing topic among citizens and city officials. Photo by Sean Scott, ShutterStock

now it is stuck with a cacophonous roadway that severs the water from the rest of town. Not long after the earthquake, a nonprofit group called the Allied Arts of Seattle sponsored a charrette—the same free-flowing-ideas workshop we mentioned in our Los Angeles chapter—to come up with ideas for how to redesign State Route 99. All the groups assumed the roadway would be rebuilt, except one: the team led by landscape architect Julie Parrett and urban designer and planner Cary Moon. In their vision, Seattle simply chose *not* to rebuild State Route 99 and focused its resources instead on making the waterfront a livable,

wonderful beach destination. They envisioned bike paths and comfortable lawns where downtown workers could lunch outside. They saw kayakers paddling the bay and salmon swimming freely along the water's edge—their preferred path—thanks to a better coastal design.

"This is a place where we're actually able to reconnect by putting a beach here just south of the aquarium," says Parrett, "and adding some infill development with green building strategies where we have green roofs. We're doing good things with stormwater, allowing it to get clean before it washes into the bay. One of the major problems is car exhaust runoff and stormwater contamination going directly into the bay and contaminating the water. So we're trying to use some of our sustainable strategies to do good measures to help that process."

"It's an amazing opportunity to build a functional shore ecology that works for the salmon and works for the civic life of Seattle," says Moon, an engineer who grew up in Michigan and has lived all over the United States. She and Parrett, along with poet-activist Grant Cogswell—the same fellow who sparked the monorail initiative—have formed the People's Waterfront Coalition (PWC), a group of citizens united to prevent the rebuilding of this freeway on Seattle's downtown waterfront.

"I was on the city's design commission at the time they were thinking about what to do," recalls Moon. "All the smart people were saying, 'Do we really need to rebuild this thing?' And the state said, 'That topic is not on the table.'"

The state of Washington, which basically "owns" the roadway, is rightfully concerned with the movement of goods and traffic through its most important city. The state department of transportation has come up with five options, all for replacing this highway's capacity in its current location. The best of those—supported by the mayor and concerned citizen groups such as People for Puget Sound, Sierra Club, 1000 Friends

of Washington, and Transportation Choices Coalition—would send all that traffic underground, in a sixteen-block tunnel. The construction of such a project would take ten years and cost $4.5 billion. "I appreciate Cary's position, but for us, getting the highway off the surface is the real priority," says Kathy Fletcher, executive director of People for Puget Sound, an environmental group, "so we can then push for restored habitat and wildlife."

"It really doesn't make sense for it to happen," asserts Cogswell, "because it doesn't allow us to reconnect with the water. The process we're involved in right now is convincing people that we need to connect to the waterfront and that the options that are given by the state aren't enough. We're pressing for an option that will let traffic and transit through and still open up what could be one of the most incredible spaces in the country."

The tunnel option has its supporters among developers, downtown businesses, and the city administration. In talks and op-ed pieces in the local newspapers, the mayor has touted the tunnel because he believes it will allow Seattle to get back in touch with the waterfront. All the traffic will be diverted underground. "We trying to build a city in Seattle that isn't just for today," says the mayor, "but one that will be sustainable into the future."

It's clear that both sides want a beach and crave access to nature. They just differ on how to do it.

An improved coastal design would transform Seattle's beach, shown now (above) and in an artist's rendering (below).
Photo courtesy of People's Waterfront Coalition

Moon and her friends say the tunnel won't make the traffic just go away. They spend much of their energy visiting community groups, trying to get this message across. All tunnels have a beginning and an end, they point out, and both of these would be downtown. Second, most people think a tunnel will free up real estate in the city's heart; not so, counters PWC, because you cannot build on the "lid" of this tunnel. Last, they worry that the cost could spiral out of control, as it often has in tunnel projects in other cities.

Regardless of what outsiders think of this debate, you cannot help but learn something from the most important component of the PWC's plan: if they don't build the tunnel, where will all those cars go? That's the interesting part, because it gets to the heart of sustainable cities.

At the moment, the road carries vehicles making eighty thousand to one hundred thousand trips daily. That seems like a huge number, but it really isn't. In fact, argue Moon and the others, much of that traffic could easily be absorbed by existing roads in the area. For decades Americans have built roads to alleviate gridlock, only to find that the gridlock returns a few years later. Why? What goes wrong? Finally, as a nation, it's dawning on us: sometimes more roads encourage traffic. The PWC calculates that Seattle will be back to gridlock level in nine to thirteen years after it builds the tunnel.

What does work, they say, is rethinking the issue. Better-designed traffic patterns work better. Better still is to invest more in mass transit and make it easier for people to get where they need to go without taking their cars. All sides would agree, though, that if a city is dense enough, that is, if it has a rich collection of shops, restaurants, services, and business packed into every block, people will overwhelmingly choose to walk or hop on mass transit rather than rev up their cars. The trick is building that richness into every city block, and helping those who live outside the city reach downtown in the most sustainable fashion possible. That means trains and buses.

Landscape architect Julie Parrett (left) and urban designer and planner Cary Moon (center) with activist Grant Cogswell (right) have formed the People's Waterfront Coalition, a group committed to preventing the rebuilding of State Route 99 along Seattle's waterfront.

The PWC says that when you factor in all the other options for where the traffic could go, you realize that not building the tunnel is a viable option. Seattle has no shortage of roads. In fact, argues the group, Seattle has more highway surface per person than many big cities in America, and more than the four other cities in the United States with larger ports.

Because highway construction has become so expensive, and because cities are looking into smarter ways to move their citizens around, reducing highway capacity has actually becoming something of a trend in the nation. A 1998 study found that cities that reduced roads also reduced traffic by an average of 25 and up to 60 percent. After

San Francisco dismantled its elevated waterfront highway, the Embarcadero Freeway, which was damaged during the 1989 Loma Prieta earthquake, the city liked the results so much that it took down another one.

Seattle's challenge is one facing many American cities. Post–World War II America grew up with the notion that cars and individual travel were the ideal. We may be on the verge of realizing that that ideal is unsupportable. "Yes," says Moon, who lives downtown within earshot of the viaduct, "the traffic in Seattle is bad, but mostly because we sprawled. From 1980 to 1990 we tripled the rate at which we used up land outside the city. The miles driven for the average person increased three times in that period. We're driving three times as much."

One day, wandering down by the water in the shadow of the viaduct, Moon points out the tourists and city folks hanging out there. "Look how many people are here," she says. "People want to touch the water, they want throw rocks in it, they want to be on the edge where water meets land. Our proposal can be paid for by the same kind of sources that are going to fund the transportation project. To do the park development and the stormwater strategies that we're talking about is cheaper than a heavy underground infrastructure. So it's a simpler solution. It's a lower-tech solution, it's more progressive,

A rendering of the proposed tunnel design that would place State Route 99 underground and out of sight, with parkway and open space where the double-decker freeway used to be. Courtesy of Mithun

and it's more sustainable, and it lets Seattle connect to the water."

It's worth saying, of course, that the PWC's no-replacement plan sounds incredibly naïve to many in Seattle. A brief traffic study, commissioned by City Hall and released in 2004, argued against the PWC's plan. "Not replacing the viaduct would result in severe congestion on downtown streets, I-5, and Alaskan Way from early morning until late evening, even with optimistic assumptions about shifting traffic to other routes, increasing transit ridership, and managing travel demand," read the report. The San Francisco argument doesn't hold much water with officials, who contend that Seattle's viaduct is far busier than the two-and-a-half-mile spur dismantled in the Golden Gate City.

Because of Seattle's laudable history of citizen activism, the PWC is confident that their approach will triumph if they take the time to get the word out. In summer 2005, the group got a boost from two disparate sources. Jan Gehl, a Danish architect who is an internationally acclaimed expert on public spaces, visited the city for four days of lectures and talks on urban planning issues. He was widely quoted as advising city officials and local leaders not to replace the viaduct. "You'll gain nothing for a lot of money," he was reported as saying during a speech. Later that summer, when Seattle was still smarting over

A rendering of the proposed tunnel design. Detractors of the tunnel plan raise concerns about the potential traffic congestion at entry and exit points to the tunnel and the consequences for downtown Seattle in that scenario. Courtesy of Mithun

the monorail budget, the Seattle *Post-Intelligencer* questioned the wisdom of replacing the viaduct with a tunnel. "An underground roadway that would allow the city to reunite with its waterfront would make Seattle a more beautiful and livable city, if its residents were willing to pay for it. We doubt that they are." This view was expressed in the same editorial in which the newspaper urged citizens to give up their monorail dreams. Editors urged the city to repair the existing viaduct and get on with life.

Listening to all these arguments, it's tough to know whom to support, but we wonder what would happen if the city dismantled the highway—and then just waited. Waited to see whether traffic rerouted itself, as the PWC believes it will. Waited to see whether the phenomenon that occurred in other cities happened in Seattle. Tunnels aren't built in a day. Before building that hole in the ground, the city could have a chance to conduct a powerful experiment. It could live without a viaduct, just as it did after the earthquake. Back then, the city got by for weeks without the viaduct. People adapt in a crisis; why wouldn't they adapt permanently? The tunnel can always be an option. We propose this because we think that the wisdom of New Urbanism and the spirit of sustainability deserve a chance. Tomorrow Seattle will not be the city it is today. Who knows? Light rail may work wonders.

And so may the will of the people. "I was one of the two people who wrote the monorail initiative," says Cogswell, "and we went out with just a ragtag team of two people at the beginning and gathered the signatures to put it on the ballot. The whole campaign cost us $2,500 and we won!"

Moon, Parrett, and Cogswell—who are all in their thirties and early forties—are among the youngest activists we interviewed for this project. Like the young politicians who are shaping Los Angeles's future, they are heralding an era of young people who intuitively see in cities what their parents and grandparents didn't.

When she's out giving talks, Moon notices that she gets the warmest reaction from people her age or younger. The hard part is showing them that their passion can effect change. But Cogswell has been there and done that. He knows in his heart that perfectly ordinary people can indeed transform our cities.

"I think a lot of people don't get into politics because they feel helpless, and that is absolutely understandable," he says. "It's so painful to stay engaged and feel powerless at the same time."

Other citizens, of course, thrive in that arena and have learned to make contributions to their cities from within the system. Steve Nicholas, director of Seattle's Office of Sustainability and Environment, has spent a lifetime in public service. He, too, is concerned about inspiring young people to be active partners in Seattle's future. "I think getting the word out to the young people of our community is extremely important," he says. "One, it's their future, and they're the decision makers and the policy makers and the elected officials and the CEOs of tomorrow. But also, they have enormous influence over what happens in their families, what happens in their households, what happens in their neighborhoods."

Speaking up has staying power. It sticks with people long after the goal has been accomplished or they've simply moved on. "The monorail was an illustration to me that you can come out of nowhere," adds Cogswell, "come out of that powerlessness with the right kind of idea and make it happen." Maybe that isn't the case every time. Granted, the monorail didn't happen, but Cogswell certainly developed a template for direct democracy that deserves to be emulated. "It's worked for me once, and I think it's going to work again," he says. "And so that's why I'm here. I think this is the most important thing you could be doing."

THE FISH SEATTLE LOVES

For nearly six months, a sixty-gallon fish tank stood in the lobby of the Stevens Elementary School in downtown Seattle, filled to the brim with tiny baby salmon, called fry. The fish are part of an innovative program designed to help schoolkids get a hands-on look at the processes of nature and understand the importance of protecting Seattle's waterways.

The program, offered by Seattle Public Utilities and the Washington State Depart-

ment of Fish and Wildlife, has operated since 1991, ever since a retired school-teacher got the idea of hatching baby salmon in his bathtub and sharing the hatch with local schools. The program has evolved considerably since then. (The bathtubs are out.) Each year in January, three hundred schools throughout Washington State—one hundred and thirty in Seattle alone—receive a batch of fertilized salmon eggs to deposit in a tank, which is provided by the program's sponsors. The students raise the fish for a few months, while their teachers strive to incorporate ecology and salmon issues into their lesson plans.

"The idea is to help kids who never had an opportunity to enjoy nature to get that experience," says Carlton Stinson, who runs the program for Seattle Public Utilities.

"It's a great way to get kids thinking about important questions," says Dave McMillin, a fourth-grade teacher at Stevens. "Like, 'Why are we having to replace salmon in the first place?' 'What conditions are best for salmon?' 'What's a watershed, and why should we be careful what we put in our watershed?' Kids are still passionate about animals at this age. They enjoy watching the salmon grow and are pretty jazzed about it."

In the past, teachers at Stevens have used the salmon project to teach units on Native Americans, Washington State history, art, writing, and science, not to mention literature and legends. Once, recall administrators, a ceramic artist visited the school to talk about salmon-inspired art.

The tank fish grow up in freshwater cooled to between 46 and 48°F. When the fish reach a certain age, the plan calls for students to release them in local waterways. Normally they're released in early spring, but in 2005, the students at Stevens didn't get around to this chore until early June. Some weeks before the end of the school year, McMillin rounded up his students, handed them each a plastic water bottle filled with tiny fish, and ushered them onto a schoolbus bound for Lake Washington.

The school is located right on the edge of what used to be considered the inner city of Seattle. Twenty years ago, some citizens would not even wander into the area, but now the school straddles the opposing forces between city and suburbia. The school is about half minority students, some with language challenges, since they've recently immigrated with their families to the United States.

The kids lowered their bottles to the water and gentled poured out the fish. In the daylight, you could make out the shapes of the tiny fish darting for freedom. Across the lake live some of the region's wealthiest people, among them Microsoft founder Bill Gates.

Dave McMillin and two of his students return salmon fingerlings to Lake Washington, beginning the salmon life cycle anew.

A few days earlier, as the salmon project was drawing to a close, McMillin asked his students to write about their experiences. Their responses strike a chord with anyone who dreams of an even better Seattle, where the salmon live free and unthreatened. They are the voices of Seattle's newest, and youngest, ecologists.

"I have learned that salmon are in danger because of pollution, hydroelectric dams, and fish ladders. I don't think houses should be built near streams, because they affect the salmon greatly."

—ABBY Z., AGE 10

"I have learned that salmon are in danger because of hydroelectric dams. I also learned that only one out of one hundred fish make it to spawn. I feel bad for the salmon. Salmon help us in many ways and are in danger because of the things we do."

—LAURA B., AGE 10

"I have learned that the salmon population has declined greatly over the past thirty years. I feel that we all should try to protect salmon because they are so important to people that live in the Puget Sound area."

—LANE A., AGE 9

"I have learned that we really have to take care of our rivers and not pollute. I think we should walk and bike more because cars use a lot of gasoline, and we should try not littering and or doing things that pollute."

—CAMILLE G., AGE 10

A project like this is the kind that resonates with a child, and the child within, forever. When these children grow up, they will remember the time they made a difference in a small way, and it may inspire them to work for a better Seattle all over again. Their city is a vibrant one, working hard to solve its problems, and will continue to prosper because it heeds the voices of its citizens, young and old.

EPILOGUE

"Tug on anything at all and you'll find
it connected to everything else in the
universe."

—JOHN MUIR

The work of urban renewal can often seem overwhelming. A new downtown park can engender feasibility studies, traffic analysis reports, drainage system studies, years of community meetings, and the like long before the first patch of sod is ever pressed to the earth or the first laughs of children ring out over the playground. But cities are enriched and become magical every day with far simpler projects. One or two people are all it takes to change and enrich the fabric of city life.

If you doubt this, notice how each storefront, each window display, each shop sign on a city street looks different from every other. At holiday time the cheerful facades of apartment buildings enchant us because all those windows were decorated by different people with their own ideas of taste and design. The plots in a community garden likewise are a leafy patchwork of vegetable and floral diversity. This richness is achieved rarely by committee action, but instead by one or two people listening to their own hearts. Even the large coalitions we encountered in the course of our project drew their initial energy from one or two people deciding to take action.

Many of the people you met in this book embarked on their careers as neighborhood activists by doing something as simple as picking up litter. Doris Gwaltney did this in her neighborhood every week at the same time, so her neighbors would interpret her action as a serious commitment and respect her efforts by not littering. Later, Doris led efforts to restore the neighborhood park she'd loved as a child. Ed Elliss got sick of watching the vacant lot across from his stoop deteriorate; his metamorphosis occurred the day he stalked across the street and pulled his first weed. Today, a park stands there in memory of his son. New to this country and unsure of her language skills, Iris Brown labored in the background of her community, cleaning up lots. In time her words and energy blossomed, and she led the charge in the reclamation of more than fifty abandoned lots. Today six are award-winning gardens, and Iris is hailed internationally as a pioneering urban activist.

Make no mistake: One person can make a difference. You, sitting in your chair reading this book, are already taking the first step toward action. You're educating yourself. You can take what you've learned, scout out candidates for public office who recognize the importance of sustainability, and support them. If you can make a greater commitment, consider doing something in your community to further the cause of sustainability. You need only walk outside your door, look around, and see what needs doing.

You may like the structure that comes from working in a group, or you may want to make new friends while doing something you love. If so, seek out grassroots organizations that tackle a small piece of the sustainability puzzle. Deb Shore, editor of *Chicago Wilderness* magazine, volunteered weekends to help restore native prairie lands when she first relocated to Chicago. Darrell Clarke forged a friendship with people in his neighborhood as they fought for more than eighteen years to bring light rail to their part of Los Angeles. Still others merged their small organizations with larger coalitions, so-called groups of groups. Such alliances are capable of tackling multiple issues, or different facets of the same issues. Coalitions give individuals and organizations something to rally around. They provide an identity, a sense of place, longevity, and continuity. Being part of a larger organization means you won't have to do everything yourself, and you can rely on the skills and talents of others.

Don't worry if change doesn't happen quickly. The kinds of problems cities face were a long time coming, and it will take time to sort them out. The important thing is to work steadily on your piece of the problem and share what you learn with others. If your neighbor stares at you quizzically as you dig a trench in your backyard, tell him proudly, "I'm building a rain garden!" If he leans over the fence to ask for details, don't be shy about telling him all you've learned about the subject. The next time he wonders why his shrubs look faint, he just may build his own. Example is a powerful force.

The activists we met on this project possessed calm, patience, and resilience. Deep down, they know that they will prevail. They know that others will come around eventually to seeing their way. Each new convert is a small victory, because change hastens as your community grows.

Think how quickly your workplace went from having no Internet access to dial-up to high-speed access. In the blink of an eye— five years, tops—our businesses and workplaces have been completely revolutionized by the Web. Businesses were quick to perceive the advantages of having people pay bills, submit claims, and perform a host of other tasks electronically. The revolution happened fast because everyone could see how he or she would benefit. Everyone wins. Everyone benefits. *When we all learn a better way of doing things, we act fast.*

In Los Angeles, public officials who had been resistant to activists' proposals for water conservation were blown away when they saw how every backyard in the county could be turned into a water catchment system. Public policy changed overnight. "My hope lies in people being able to turn on a dime," says Andy Lipkis, the Los Angeles activist, and he is absolutely right. Two decades ago, you'd be hard pressed to find mulching lawnmowers for sale in the suburbs. Everyone

15 Easy Ways to Get the Word Out

1. Every chance you get, bill yourself as a supporter of sustainability.
2. Call a speak-out line. Many local newspapers have call-in phone lines where you can leave a message or state an opinion on a designated answering machine. The messages are later printed in an edition of the newspaper.
3. Write a letter to the editor.
4. Write and submit an essay to the op-ed page of your local paper on the issue of sustainability, using factual information from any number of available sources.
5. Be a caller or guest on talk radio.
6. Take a photo of an event promoting sustainability and submit it to the local newspaper, properly identified.
7. Get involved with your local cable station. Consider working to get your own public access show or being a guest on someone else's show.
8. Put the local press on your e-mail lists or mailing list to receive updates, notices, and the like.
9. Make a practice of sending out announcements to the local press.
10. Make yourself an expert on, and media resource for, sustainability issues, or recruit someone else to do so.
11. Call a reporter and introduce yourself. Ask whether he or she would meet you for coffee, and use the opportunity to give an overview of local sustainability issues and activities you or others are involved in, and their importance to our communities.
12. Visit local newspaper editorial boards. Prepare your message and take it to the editors. Make sure you know your stuff—these folks can be tough-minded!
13. Go places reporters go. Reporters cover community events such as service club luncheons, charity fund-raisers, candidate debates, and so forth.
14. Stockpile illustrative stories about sustainability to share with the media as appropriate.
15. Post an item about the sustainability issues that most concern you to an on-line form or Web site devoted to sustainability topics.

bagged their lawn clippings and hauled them to the dump. Now local communities are urging people to mulch their clippings instead, and bagless mowers are de rigueur at the "big box" home centers. Composting was once regarded as something only hippies and die-hard farmers did. Now many city halls across the nation are giving away compost bins to their citizens in an effort to stanch the flow of green waste pilling up in landfills.

The seeds of sustainability are blowing across the continent, but there's always more to be done, and you don't have to be a city dweller to do it. The next time a field is plowed under to build a strip mall, someone should ask why. When banks and dry cleaners and supermarkets are built with tons of parking but little room for trees and swales, someone needs to speak up. Someone has to be the first on the block to replace his or her driveway with porous materials. Someone has to show city kids that the color green isn't found only on money or in a box of crayons. Someone must paint a mural on the dull brick wall greeting strangers to town. Someone has to stand up in a town hall meeting and say,

"Let's build a park instead." Someone has to drive one less car. Someone needs to paddle down the newly cleaned rivers, salute the returning birds and beavers, and show everyone else what fun it is to leave the world a brighter, cleaner place than we found it.

This book is just a start. Today, tomorrow, and all the days after, why not become a steward of your own neighborhood and help yourself and the ones you love find, rescue, and cherish those Edens close to home?

ACKNOWLEDGMENTS

In May of 2004, we approached Chelsea Green Publisher Margo Baldwin with the idea of a companion book to accompany our PBS project *Edens Lost & Found*. Chelsea Green is known throughout the world for its books on the environment. Harry traveled to Chelsea Green's headquarters in White River Junction, Vermont, to meet with Margo and to discuss the full scope of the project. This kind of collaboration would be a first for Chelsea Green. Margo became intrigued by the possibilities of reaching a larger PBS audience and agreed to publish the PBS companion book. We concluded that the mini-series would be strengthened by a serious but accessible companion book. Eighteen months later, we are convinced we have made the right decision. The book stands alone as an invaluable resource for those interested in urban restoration and renewal.

Edens Lost & Found would not have been possible without the support of a dedicated core team, including Producer-Writer-Editor Beverly Baroff. Beverly's insight and creative expertise have been invaluable throughout the project. Associate Producer Robin Rosenfeld supervised the research phase and was instrumental in coordinating the first year's multi-city production trips. When Robin left to study landscape architecture, Associate Producer Rebecca Hartzell helped us for six months, followed by Brenda Lee Gauthier and Harold Linde, both of whose associate producer responsibilities included coordinating the community and national outreach campaigns. Throughout the project, Line Producer Vicki Mills has managed the business and financial aspects of our company. Special thanks goes to Associate Producer Therese Avedillo for transcribing hours of tape into coherent transcripts for inclusion in the book.

This is the second special project that we are producing with Oregon Public Broadcasting acting as our presenting station. We continue to enjoy working with Dave Davis, OPB's executive in charge of production, and his Portland-based team. We also want to acknowledge the extraordinary work of PBS over the years; we are honored to be a part of this invaluable national resource. We look forward to working again with Colby Kelly and Karen Salerno as outreach coordinators for the project much the same way they did for *And Thou Shalt Honor*.

We want to especially thank Joe D'Agnese for his unstinting enthusiasm and expertise in helping us write the book. Joe's talents provide a style and vision that make us all proud. Our book editor Mary Bahr has seamlessly guided the process through to completion and deserves much of the credit for making the book look as good as it does. Always with good humor, Chelsea Green's Editor-in-Chief John Barstow continues to offer constructive ideas and suggestions along the way.

Chicago Wilderness, Openlands, TreePeople, Learn and Serve America, and the Pennsylvania Horticultural Society are but a few of the many local organizations that have made both the book and the series possible. Special thanks to Jerry Adelmann, Blaine Bonham, Helen Doria, Dick Jackson, Colby Kelly, Andy Lipkis, Steve Moddemeyer, Steve Nicholas, Joan Reilly, Karen Salerno, Debra Shore, Scott Simon, Peter Whybrow, Jennifer Wolch, and the scores of participants without whose cooperation and support the project would not have been possible. The cities of Chicago, Philadelphia, and Seattle became second homes for us during the production phase. We hope the project conveys the warm welcome they gave the project and hope our efforts reflect their greatness.

None of this would have been possible without the generous support of our underwriters. The funding organizations are listed on page 275. Special thanks to those who helped us get started, including Paul Brown of CDM, Kathy Im of MacArthur, Jim Newcomb of Boeing, Peggy Chamness of ISTEP, Gerry Wang of the William Penn Foundation, Rich Martinez of Scotts Miracle-Gro, and Belinda Faustinos of San Gabriel & Los Angeles Rivers & Mountains Conservancy.

Without the support of our families *Edens Lost & Found* would not have been possible. We give special thanks to Holly, Winona, and Diana for putting up with us throughout the production. We traveled more than we wanted to but always looked forward to coming home. We look forward to our continued walks with Andy Lipkis around our wonderful neighborhoods of Venice, California, with, of course, Valentine and Scarlet in tow.

HARRY WILAND AND DALE BELL
Santa Monica, California
February 2006

This list of organizations and resources is not meant to be comprehensive, but it is a good first start toward getting involved in your own community. *Edens Lost & Found Action Guides* for Chicago, Philadelphia, Los Angeles, and Seattle include additional groups and practical suggestions. They can be found at www.edenslostandfound.org, where you can also sign up to receive the *Edens Lost & Found Newsletter*. For those who don't live in these areas, you may want to look at the action guide for the city with challenges that resemble those of your community to generate ideas and find support.

Edens Lost & Found
Media & Policy Center Foundation
Wiland-Bell Productions, LLC
2125 Arizona Avenue, 2nd Floor
Santa Monica, CA 90404
(310) 828-2966
www.edenslostandfound.org
www.mediapolicycenter.org
www.wilandbellprod.com

NATIONAL RESOURCES

Agriculture

EPA's Biopesticides Web site
www.epa.gov/pesticides/biopesticides

EPA's Green Landscaping Web site
www.epa.gov/greenacres

USDA's Backyard Conservation Web Site
www.nrcs.usda.gov/feature/backyard

USDA's PLANTS Database
www.plants.usda.gov

Community Service

Corporation for National & Commmunity Service
(Senior Corps, AmeriCorps, Learn & Serve America)
1201 New York Avenue NW
Washington, DC 20525
(202) 606-5000
www.nationalservice.org

Energy

American Solar Energy Society
2400 Central Avenue, Suite A
Boulder, CO 80301
(303) 443-3130
www.ases.org

U.S. Department of Energy
1000 Independence Avenue SW
Washington, DC 20585
(800) DIAL-DOE
www.eere.energy.gov
www.doe.gov

U.S. EPA ENERGY STAR Program
Climate Protection Partnerships Division
ENERGY STAR Programs Hotline & Distribution
   (MS-6202J)
1200 Pennsylvania Avenue NW
Washington, DC 20460
(888)-STAR-YES
www.energystar.gov

Environmental Protection and Activism

Greenpeace
702 H Street NW, Suite 300
Washington, DC 20001
(202) 462-1177
www.greenpeaceusa.org

National Audubon Society
700 Broadway
New York, NY 10003
(212) 979-3000
www.audubon.org

National Resources Defense Council
40 W 20th Street
New York, NY 10011
(212) 727-2700
www.nrdc.org

The Rocky Mountain Institute
1739 Snowmass Creek Road
Snowmass, CO 81654-9199
(970) 927-3851
www.rmi.org

Sierra Club
85 Second Street, 2nd Floor
San Francisco, CA 94105
(415) 977-5500

Sierra Club Legislative Office
408 C Street, NE
Washington, DC 20002
(202) 547-1141
www.sierraclub.org

U.S. Environmental Protection Agency
Office of Sustainability
Office of Science Policy
1300 Pennsylvania Avenue NW, MC 8104R
Washington, DC 20460
(202) 564-6752
www.epa.gov/sustainability
www.epa.gov

World Wildlife Fund in the United States (WWF)
1250 24th Street NW
Washington, DC 20037
(202) 293-4800
www.worldwildlife.org

Green Building

Greenroofs.com
3449 Lakewind Way
Alpharetta, GA 30005
(675) 580.1965
www.greenroofs.com

Green Spaces and Urban Forestry

Center for Invasive Plant Management
733 Leon Johnson Hall
Montana State University
Bozeman, MT 59717-3120
(406) 994-5557
www.weedcenter.org

City Parks Alliance
733 E 15th Street NW, Suite 700
Washington, DC 20005
(202) 783-6604
www.cityparksalliance.org

Forest Stewardship Council US
1155 30th Street NW, Suite 300
Washington, DC 20007
(202) 342-0413
www.fscus.org

International Society of Arboriculture
PO Box 3129
Champaign, IL 61826
(217) 355-9411
www.treesaregood.com

Urban and Community Forestry Program
USDA, Forest Service
STOP Code 1151
1400 Independence Avenue
Washington, DC 20250
(202) 205-8333
www.fs.fed.us/ucf

Wildbirds.com
www.wildbirds.com

Land Conservation

The Nature Conservancy
4245 N Fairfax Drive, Suite 100
Arlington, VA 22203-1606
(703) 841-5300
www.nature.org

The Trust for Public Land
116 New Montgomery Street, 4th Floor
San Francisco, CA 94105
(415) 495-4014 or (800) 714-LAND
www.tpl.org

CHICAGO-AREA RESOURCES

Community Service

Center for Neighborhood Technology
2125 W North Avenue
Chicago, IL 60647
(773) 278-4800
www.cnt.org

Fuller Park Community Development
331 W 45th Street
Chicago, IL 60609
(773) 624-8686

Green Building

Chicago Guide to Rooftop Gardening
Chicago Department of Environment
www.cityofchicago.org/environment

Green Spaces and Urban Forestry

Bold Chicago
111095 S St. Lawrence
Chicago, IL 60628
(773) 728-7150

Chicago Office of Tourism
    Visitor Information Centers
Chicago Cultural Center
78 E Washington Street
Chicago, IL 60602
(312) 744-2400
egov.cityofchicago.org

Chicago Wilderness
5225 Old Orchard Road, Suite 37
Skokie, IL 60077
(847) 965-9275
www.chicagowilderness.org

Friends of the Chicago River
407 S Dearborn, Suite 1580
Chicago, IL 60605
(312) 939-0490
www.chicagoriver.org

Millennium Park
Chicago, IL 60602
(312) 742-1168
www.millenniumpark.org

Openlands Project
25 E Washington Street, Suite 1650
Chicago, Illinois 60602
(312) 427-4256
www.openlands.org

Southeast Environmental Task Force
13300 S Baltimore Avenue
Chicago, IL 60633
(773) 646-0436
www.setaskforce.org

PHILADELPHIA-AREA RESOURCES

Agriculture

Institute for Innovations in Local Farming
Somerton Tanks Farm
2220 Kater Street
Philadelphia, PA 19146
www.somertontanksfarm.org

Pennsylvania Association for Sustainable Agriculture
114 W Main Street
PO Box 419
Millheim, PA 16854
(814) 349-9856
www.pasafarming.org

Pennsylvania Certified Organic
406 S Pennsylvania Avenue
Centre Hall, PA 16828
(814) 364-1344
www.paorganic.org

Community Service

New Kensington Community Development Corporation
2515 Frankford Avenue
Philadelphia, PA 19125
(215) 427-0350
www.nkcdc.org

Norris Square Neighborhood Project
2141 North Howard Street
Philadelphia, PA 19122
(215) 634-2227
www.nsnp.com

Philadelphia Association of Community Development Corporations
1315 Walnut Street
Suite 1600
Philadelphia, PA 19107
(215) 732-5829
www.pacdc.org

Environmental Protection and Activism

Academy of Natural Sciences
1900 Ben Franklin Parkway
Philadelphia, PA 19103
(215) 299-1000
www.acnatsci.org

American Rivers
Mid-Atlantic Field Office
105 N Front Street, Suite 220
Harrisburg, PA 17101
(717) 232-8355
www.amrivers.org

Environmental Leadership Program
1609 Connecticut Avenue NW, #400
Washington, DC 20009
Phone: 202.332.3320
(202) 332-3327
www.elpnet.org
ELP: Delaware Valley Regional Network
(215) 292-3040

Pennsylvania Department of Environmental Protection
Rachel Carson State Office Building, 16th Floor
PO Box 2063
400 Main Street
Harrisburg, PA 17105-2063
(717) 783-2300
www.dep.state.pa.us

Pennsylvania Environmental Council
Southeast Regional Office
123 Chestnut Street, Suite 401
Philadelphia, PA 19106
(215) 592-7020
www.pecpa.org

Pennsylvania League of Conservation Voters
300 N 2nd Street, Suite 707
Harrisburg, PA 17101
(717) 234-2651
www.palcv.org

**Philadelphia Neighborhood Transformation
    Initiative**
1401 JFK Boulevard
Philadelphia, PA 19102-1583
(215) 686-2154
www.phila.gov/nti

Green Spaces and Urban Forestry

City Parks Association
Regional Parks Instititute
6868 Scotforth Road
Philadelphia, PA 19119
(215) 849-6178
www.cityparksphila.org

Fairmount Park
One Parkway, 10th Floor
1515 Arch Street
Philadelphia, PA 19102
(215) 683-0200
www.fairmountpark.org

Fairmount Water Works Interpretive Center
640 Waterworks Drive
Philadelphia, PA 19103
(215) 685-4908
www.fairmountwaterworks.com

**Morris Arboretum Urban Forestry and
    Arboriculture Program**
100 Northwestern Avenue
Philadelphia, PA 19118
(215) 247-5777
www.business-services.upenn.edu/arboretum/uf

Northeast Pennsylvania Urban Forestry Program
1300 Old Plank Road
Mayfield, PA 18433
(570) 282-5025
businessservices.upenn.edu/arboretum/uf/nepa.html

**Pennsylvania Department of Conservation
    and Natural Resources**
Rachel Carson State Office Building
PO Box 8767
400 Main Street
Harrisburg, PA 17105-8767
(717) 787-2869
www.dcnr.state.pa.us

Pennsylvania Horticultural Society
100 N 20th Street
Philadelphia, PA 19103
(215) 988-8800
www.pennsylvaniahorticulturalsociety.org

Pennsylvania Native Plant Society
1001 E College Avenue
State College, PA 16801
www.pawildflower.org

**Pennsylvania Organization for
    Watersheds & Rivers**
610 N 3rd Street
Harrisburg, PA 17107
(717) 234-7910
www.pawatersheds.org

**Pennsylvania Urban and Community
    Forestry Council**
56 East Main Street
Mechanicsburg, PA 17055
(717) 766-5371
www.dcnr.state.pa.us/forestry/pucfc

Philadelphia Parks Alliance
PO Box 12677
Philadelphia, PA 19129-0077
(215) 879-8159
www.philaparks.org

Philadelphia Water Department
Aramark Tower, 5th Floor
1101 Market Street
Philadelphia, PA 19107-2994
(215) 685-6300
www.phila.gov/water

The Rodale Institute
611 Siegfriedale Road
Kutztown, PA 19530-9320
(610) 683-1400
www.rodaleinstitute.org

Sustainable Business Network of
**   Greater Philadelphia**
White Dog Cafe Foundation
3428 Sansom Street, 2nd Floor
Philadelphia, PA 19104
(215) 386-5211 ext. 104
www.sbnphiladelphia.org

TreeVitalize
c/o Pennsylvania Horticultural Society
100 N 20th Street, 5th Floor
Philadelphia, PA 19103
(215) 988-8874
www.treevitalize.net

Land Conservation

Green Space Alliance
c/o Pennsylvania Environmental Council
Southeast Regional Office
123 Chestnut Street, Suite 401
Philadelphia, PA 19106
(215) 592-7020
www.pecpa.org

Neighborhood Gardens Association
**   A Philadelphia Land Trust**
100 N 20th Street, Suite 309
Philadelphia, PA 19103
(215) 988-8797
www.ngalandtrust.org

Pennsylvania Land Trust Association
105 Locust Street
Harrisburg, PA 17101
(717) 230-8560
conserveland.org

LOS ANGELES-AREA RESOURCES

Environmental Protection and Activism

American Rivers
Fairfax Field Office
6 School Street, Suite 200
Fairfax, CA 94930-1650
(415) 482-8150
www.amrivers.org

California League of Conservation Voters
10780 Santa Monica Boulevard, Suite 210
Los Angeles, CA 90025
(310) 441-4162
www.ecovote.org

California Public Interest Research Corp.
11965 Venice Boulevard, Suite 408
Los Angeles, CA 90066
(310) 397-3404
www.calpirg.org

Concerned Citizens of South Central Los Angeles
4707 S Central Avenue
Los Angeles, CA 90011
(213) 846-2500
www.ccscla.org

Environmental Defense Fund
Los Angeles Regional Office
3250 Wilshire Boulevard, Suite 1400
Los Angeles, CA 90010
(213) 386-5501
www.environmentaldefense.org

Friends of LA River
570 W Avenue 26, #250
Los Angeles, CA 90065
(323) 223-0528
www.folar.org

Los Angeles City Bureau of Sanitation, Watershed
    Protection Division
2714 Media Center Drive
Los Angeles, CA 90065
(323) 342-1576
www.ladpw.org

Los Angeles County Department of Public Works,
    Environmental Defense
900 S Fremont Avenue
Alhambra, CA 91803
(626) 458-3579
www.ladpw.org

National Wildlife Federation
Western Natural Resource Center
3500 5th Avenue, Suite 101
San Diego, CA 92103
(619) 296-8353
(619) 296-8355
www.nwf.org

Southern California Council on Environment &
    Development
626 Santa Monica Boulevard, #253
Santa Monica, CA 90401-2538
(310) 281-8534
www.scced.org

TreePeople
12601 Mulholland Drive
Beverly Hills, CA 90210
(818) 753-4600
www.treepeople.org

University of California at Los Angeles
    Environmental Coalition
UCLA Campus, Kerckhoff Hall, Room 160
Los Angeles, CA 90024
(310) 206-4438

University of Southern California Center for
    Sustainable Cities
Kaprielian Hall 416
University of Southern California
3620 S Vermont Avenue
Los Angeles, CA 90089-0255
(213) 821-1325
www.usc.edu/dept/geography/ESPE

Green Spaces and Urban Forestry

California Native Plant Society
6223 Lubago Avenue
Los Angeles, CA 91367
(818) 881-3706
www.cnps.org

National Urban & Community Forestry
    Advisory Council
USDA Forest Service
20628 Diane Drive
Sonora, CA 95370
(209) 536-9201
www.fs.fed.us

Land Conservation

Los Angeles and San Gabriel Rivers Watershed
    Conservancy
111 N Hope Street, Suite 627
Los Angeles, CA 90012
(213) 367-4111
www.lasgrwc.org

San Gabriel and Lower Los Angeles
    Rivers and Mountains Conservancy
900 S Fremont Avenue
Annex Bldg, 2nd Floor
Alhambra, CA 91802-1460
(626) 458-4315
www.rmc.ca.gov

SEATTLE-AREA RESOURCES

Community Service

City of Seattle
www.seattle.gov

City of Seattle Boards & Commissions
(206) 615-0958
www.seattle.gov/html/citizen/boardsportal.htm.htm

City of Seattle, Department of Neighborhoods
Arctic Building
700 3rd Avenue, Suite 400
Seattle, WA 98104-1848
(206) 684-0464
www.seattle.gov/neighborhoods

City of Seattle, Office of Sustainability and Environment
700 Fifth Avenue, Suite 2748
PO Box 94729
Seattle, WA 98124
(206) 615-0817
www.seattle.gov/environment

City of Seattle, Office of the Mayor
PO Box 94749
Seattle, WA 98124-4749
(206) 684-4000
www.seattle.gov/mayor

Seattle Public Utilities
700 Fifth Avenue, Suite 4900
PO Box 34018
Seattle, Washington 98124-4018
(206) 684-3000
www.seattle.gov/util/services

Seattle Parks and Recreation
100 Dexter Avenue N
Seattle, WA 98109
(206) 684-4075
www.seattle.gov/parks

Lists of Seattle-area nonprofits:
www.seattleataglance.com/list_nonprofits.htm
www.iloveseattle.org/ils/groups
   -main/environment.html

Energy

Northwest Biodiesel Network
www.nwbiodiesel.org

Seattle Biodiesel
www.seattlebiodiesel.com

Seattle City Light
700 5th Avenue, Suite 3300
Seattle, WA 98104-5031
(206) 684-3000
www.seattle.gov/light

Environmental Protection and Activism

EarthCorps
6310 NE 74th Street, Suite 201E
Seattle, WA 98115
(206) 322-9296
www.earthcorps.org

Flexcar
307 Third Avenue S, Suite 220
Seattle, WA 98104
(206) 332-0330
www.flexcar.com

People's Waterfront Coalition
PO Box 2332
Seattle, WA 98111
(206) 624-1061

Puget Sound Clean Air Agency
110 Union Street, Suite 500
Seattle, WA 98101
(206) 343-8800
www.pscleanair.org

Puget Sound Clean Cities Coalition
618 Second Avenue, Suite 1200
Seattle, WA 98104
(206) 684-0935
pugetsoundcleancities.org

Puget Sound Online
PO Box 40900
Olympia, WA 98504-0900
(360) 725-5444
www.psat.wa.gov

Washington Toxics Coalition
4649 Sunnyside Avenue N, Suite 540
Seattle, WA 98103
(206) 632-1545
www.watoxics.org

Green Building

Built Green
Master Builders Association of King & Snohomish
    Counties
335 116th Avenue SE
Bellevue, WA 98004
(425) 451-7920
www.builtgreen.net

Martha Rose Construction
7356 15th Avenue NW, Unit C
Seattle, WA 98117
(206) 784-0147
www.martharoseconstruction.com

Mithun
Pier 56
1201 Alaskan Way, Suite 200
Seattle, WA 98101-2913
(206) 623-3344
www.mithun.com

Northwest EcoBuilding Guild
PO Box 58530
Seattle, WA 98138
(503) 666-8746
www.ecobuilding.org

Green Spaces and Urban Forestry

Seattle Parks Foundation
860 Terry Avenue North, #231
Seattle, WA 98109
(206) 332-9900
www.seattleparksfoundation.org/jobs_volunteers.htm

Washington Native Plant Society
6310 Northeast 74th Street, Suite 215E
Seattle, WA 98115
(206) 527-3210
www.wnps.org

Woodland Park Zoo
601 North 59th Street
Seattle, WA 98103
(206) 684-4800
zoo.org

FUNDING ORGANIZATIONS

Edens Lost & Found gratefully acknowledges the support of the following corporations and organizations:

CDM

JOHN D. AND CATHERINE T. MACARTHUR FOUNDATION

BOEING

WILLIAM PENN FOUNDATION

SCOTTS COMPANY

SAN GABRIEL AND LOS ANGELES RIVERS AND MOUNTAINS CONSERVANCY

ISTEP (ILLINOIS SUSTAINABLE EDUCATION PROJECT)

CITY OF SEATTLE'S OFFICE OF SUSTAINABILITY/ENVIRONMENT

FJC

APTA (AMERICAN PUBLIC TRANSPORTATION ASSOCIATION)

THE PENNSYLVANIA DEPARTMENT OF CONSERVATION AND NATURAL RESOURCES

PHILADELPHIA WATER DEPARTMENT

CITY OF LOS ANGELES, DEPARTMENT OF PUBLIC WORKS, BUREAU OF SANITATION, WATERSHED PROTECTION DIVISION

COUNTY OF LOS ANGELES, DEPARTMENT OF PUBLIC WORKS

RICHARD DRIEHAUS FOUNDATION

CHICAGO COMMUNITY TRUST

LASALLE BANK

EPA REGION #5

INDEX

Page numbers in italic type refer to photographs or illustrations.

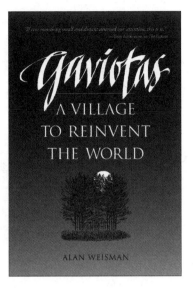
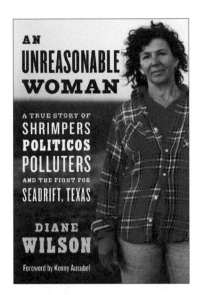

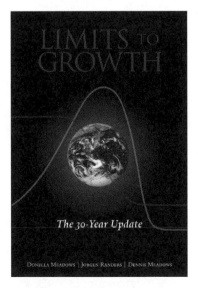

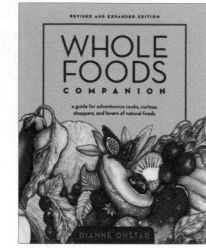